Civil Procedure in Israel

Civil Procedure in Israel

Stephen Goldstein†
Ido Baum
Nili Karako-Eyal
Yuval Merin

This book was originally published as a monograph in the International Encyclopaedia of Laws/Civil Procedure.

General Editor: Roger Blanpain
Associate General Editor: Michele Colucci
Volume Editor: Piet Taelman

Wolters Kluwer
Law & Business

Published by:
Kluwer Law International
PO Box 316
2400 AH Alphen aan den Rijn
The Netherlands
Website: www.kluwerlaw.com

Sold and distributed in North, Central and South America by:
Aspen Publishers, Inc.
7201 McKinney Circle
Frederick, MD 21704
United States of America
Email: customer.service@aspenpublishers.com

Sold and distributed in all other countries by:
Turpin Distribution Services Ltd.
Stratton Business Park
Pegasus Drive, Biggleswade
Bedfordshire SG18 8TQ
United Kingdom
Email: kluwerlaw@turpin-distribution.com

Printed on acid-free paper.

ISBN 978-90-411-5163-6

This title is available on www.kluwerlawonline.com

Printed and Bound by CPI Group (UK) Ltd, Croydon, CR0 4YY.

The Authors

The late Stephen Goldstein was the emeritus Edward S. Silver Professor of Civil Procedure at the Faculty of Law of the Hebrew University of Jerusalem. Prior to his retirement in 2004, he served as the active Edward S. Silver Professor of Civil Procedure since he joined the Hebrew University Law Faculty in 1976. During part of this period, he also served as Dean of the Faculty (1987–1990) and as Director of the Harry and Michael Sacker Institute for Legislative Research and Comparative Law (1984–1987). Prior to his moving to Israel in 1976, he served as Professor of Law at the University of Pennsylvania Law School (USA) from 1966–1976.

Prof. Goldstein has also been a Visiting Professor at a number of other law faculties, including the University of California at Berkeley; Cambridge University, Tulane Law School, the University of Hong Kong, Oxford University, Chuo University, Japan, and Cornell University, USA.

He has also served as a Judge on the Israeli Uniform Contracts Tribunal.

He was active in a large number of professional associations including the American Law Institute, the International Association of Procedural Law and the International Academy of Comparative Law.

Prof. Goldstein authored numerous works on Israeli and comparative civil procedure and was one of Israel's leading scholars on civil procedure.

Ido Baum is a Senior Lecturer at the Haim Striks School of Law in the College of Management-Academic Studies (COMAS) in Israel, where he also holds the position of Director of the Integrated Study Programmes. He teaches and researches in the fields of Procedural Law, Law and Economics, Media Law, Payment Law and Securities Law.

In 2007, Dr Baum obtained his doctoral degree from the Graduate College Law & Economics at Hamburg University, Germany, *summa cum laude*. He wrote his dissertation on 'Economic Analysis of Professional Testimonial Privileges' and it was subsequently published by Gabler Publishing. Dr Baum was a visiting researcher at Boalt Hall School of law at UC Berkeley during the spring term 2006 and at the University of Tilburg Law and Economics Center (Tilec) during the spring term 2012.

Dr Baum obtained his bachelor and master degrees in law from Tel Aviv University, Israel, and a European master in law and economics (EMLE), *cum laude*, for which he was also awarded the best dissertation prize for his thesis on 'The Influence of Concentration of Ownership in the Media Business on Information Delivered to Consumer'.

Before joining the Haim Striks School of Law in Israel, Dr Baum worked as an attorney for the Claims Resolution Tribunal on Dormant World War II Era Swiss Bank Accounts in Zurich, Switzerland. Prior to embarking on an academic career, he served as the spokesperson of the Israeli Ministry of Justice and as the legal assistant of the Israeli Attorney General for civil, fiscal and administrative affairs.

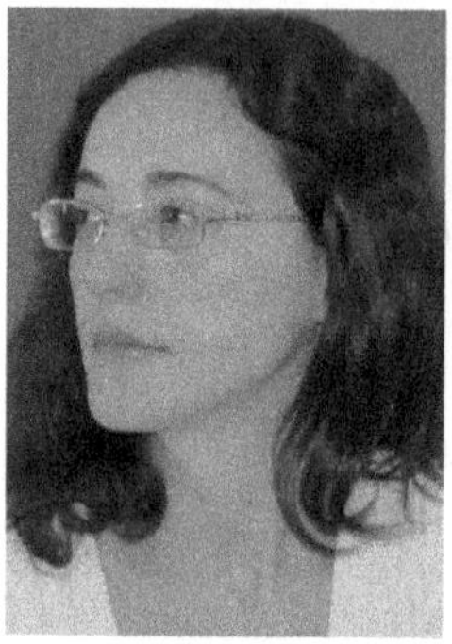

Nili Karako-Eyal is a Senior Lecturer at the Haim Striks School of Law, The College of Management-Academic Studies, Israel. Dr Karako-Eyal teaches courses in Civil Procedure, Tort Law and Medical Negligence. She is the director of a patient rights clinic, which provides free legal assistance for patients and their families. She provided legal opinions to public organizations and bodies, such as the Institute of Certified Public Accountants in Israel, the Ministry of Health and the Israeli Society for Autistic Children. In addition, she frequently lectures at professional trainings for lawyers.

Her research spans such issues as professional negligence, informed consent, the right to autonomy, patients' rights, gender, disability and damages. She was the editor of the legal journal at her law school.

Dr Karako-Eyal received her LL.B. (with Honours) from Tel Aviv University and her J.S.D. from The Hebrew University of Jerusalem School of Law. She wrote her dissertation on 'The Patient's Autonomy Principle and the Informed Consent Doctrine as Applied in the Patient's Rights Law, 1996' and it was subsequently published as a book. She received the 2012 Award of the Israeli Health Ministry Award for outstanding research.

Yuval Merin is a Senior Lecturer at the Haim Striks School of Law, the College of Management-Academic Studies in Israel, where he also holds the position of Head of the Teaching Committee. He teaches and researches in the fields of Evidence Law, Civil Procedure, and Sexuality and Gender law.

Dr Merin received his LL.B. from the Hebrew University of Jerusalem in 1993 and his LL.M and J.S.D. from New York University School of Law (NYU) in 2000. His doctoral dissertation concerned the legal status of same sex relationships from a comparative perspective, and his book on the topic, 'Equality For Same-Sex Couples: The Legal Recognition of Gay Partnerships in Europe and the United States', was published by the University of Chicago Press in 2002.

Dr Merin was a visiting scholar at UCLA School of Law during the Spring term of 2004, and served as the Deputy Dean of the Haim Striks School of Law from the Fall term of 2004 until 2008.

Table of Contents

Preface

First edition

The authors express their appreciation to Ms. Miriam Laufer for her invaluable help in the final editing of this manuscript and in preparing the index, and to Ms. Morissa Amittai for her unstinting devotion and outstanding work in typing the many drafts of this work.

Jerusalem
February, 1994

First revised edition

This revised edition has been prepared solely by Professor Goldstein, who expresses his appreciation to Attorneys Talia Fisher and Eran Tausig, for their help in preparing it.

Jerusalem
July, 2001

Second revised edition

This revised edition has been prepared by Ido Baum, Nili Karako-Eyal and Yuval Merin after the passing away of Stephen Goldstein.

Baum revised and updated the General Introduction and Parts I, II and VI.

Karako-Eyal revised and updated Parts III through V (with the exception of the paragraphs regarding res judicata).

Merin revised and updated Parts VII through X as well as paragraphs 169–179 in part IV, concerning the topic of res judicata.

Tel Aviv
April, 2013

General Introduction

§1. General Background

I. The Political System

1. Since its founding in 1948, the Israeli political system has consisted of a democratic parliamentary regime based on the principle of separation of powers. It is democratic in that it rests on the will of the people, who elect their representatives to the Knesset (the Israeli parliament).

It is a republic headed by a President elected by the Knesset for a seven-year term. His functions are primarily ceremonial and symbolic.

The Israeli system operates as a typical parliamentary system. That is, following elections to the Knesset, the President consults with the various political parties represented in the Knesset and determines which party is most likely to be able to form a government, i.e., to obtain the support of a majority of the 120 members of the Knesset. He then asks the leader of that party to try and form a government. If he is successful, he then presents his government for a vote of confidence in the Knesset. Following that, the government serves until the next Knesset election (approximately four years) unless it falls before that time by a vote of no-confidence. Such a no-confidence motion requires the affirmative vote of the majority of Knesset members.

Early elections for a new Knesset, without the fall of the government, may be achieved by a law disbanding the Knesset, which has been passed in all three readings by an affirmative vote of a majority of all Knesset members. Finally, if the prime minister is convinced that, due to the nature of the Knesset, the government is unable to govern he can request the President to order the disbanding of the Knesset and the holding of new elections. And, indeed, that happened several times including as recently as 2012.

2. The Knesset, itself, consists of 120 members elected for a term of four years by secret ballot in direct, equal and proportional elections, with the entire State being considered as one electoral district. Each electoral list receives the number of Knesset members in proportion to the votes cast for it, subject to the condition that the list receives at least 2% of the total votes cast. Every citizen of 18 years of age or older has the right to vote; every citizen aged 21 years or older may be elected as a member of the Knesset. The minimum age for election of Prime Minister is 30.

The Knesset is, of course, the Legislative authority. In the next section of this chapter, we will discuss in detail the nature of legislation in Israel.

3. The Government, which is the executive authority, has always been a coalition Government, since no Israeli party has ever achieved an absolute majority in the Knesset. The Government acts and functions by virtue of authority granted to it by the Basic Law on the Government. The number of ministers and governmental ministries varies.

4. The Judiciary in Israel consists of a central system of courts, alongside with other courts function. The regular court system is three-tiered; Magistrate Courts, District Courts, and the Supreme Court. The Supreme Court also sits as the High Court of Justice. Within the central system of courts, there is a specialization whereby some judges are allocated to deal with particular fields of law such as administrative law. Specialized tribunals for competition law and for standard form contracts are based in the District Court of Jerusalem. In the District Court of Tel Aviv, there is a department for corporate law matters, which was established in 2010. Family and succession law are adjudicated by specialized Family Courts which are part of the central system of courts. Parallel with the regular judicial systems are the separate systems of the Labour Courts and the Religious Courts of the various religious communities living in Israel.

II. The Legal System

A. *Historical Background*

5. The Israeli legal system is based on a complex matrix of sources which include both those derived from the English common law and the civil law system of continental Europe, as well as Jewish, Moslem and other national-religious systems of law.

Until the end of the First World War, Palestine, including the territory that is now the State of Israel, formed an integral part of the Ottoman Empire. Turkish rule was followed by British rule, first military, and from 1922 as the Mandatory authority. On 14 May 1948, the date of the British evacuation of Palestine, the State of Israel was established.

Each succeeding governmental authority in this sequence originally retained the pre-existing legal structure, while gradually changing it or adding to it in accordance with its own legal traditions.

6. Thus, Israeli law, today, is derived from the following distinct sources:

(1) The Ottoman law that predated the British Mandate. Positive law from this period exists now only as remnants, almost all of it having been replaced by Israeli legislation. However, the structure of the law of personal status of the Ottoman period remains the basis of Israeli personal status law, regulated by the different national-religious laws of the various groups that make up the population.

(2) The Mandatory courts drew in great measure from the ordinances enacted by the British Administration during the Mandate and the English common law.

This Mandatory period law still retains major significance in the Israeli legal structure.

(3) The laws enacted by the Knesset, since 1948, judicial decisions that have been handed down by Israeli courts, as well as regulations, rules, orders, and directives of Israeli governmental ministries.

Furthermore, when adopting legislation, the Knesset has found inspiration and guidance from many sources, including Anglo-American law, the law of continental Europe, as well as traditional Jewish law. So too have the Israeli courts in developing judicial principles of law.

B. Constitutional Norms and Basic Laws

7. Israel is one of the few States that lacks a formal constitution in the sense of one written, unified document. This situation was not the original intention of the founders of the State of Israel. Indeed, the Declaration of Independence of 14 May 1948 expressly stated that the permanent and elected governmental organs of the State would be established under a constitution to be determined by an elected constituent assembly. However, even before the election of a constituent assembly, there began a vigorous public debate in Israel as to whether the time was ripe for the young State to adopt such a formal, written constitution.

The constituent assembly was, indeed, duly elected despite this debate. However, it never really operated as a constituent assembly but was, instead, transformed into the first Knesset. And this Knesset accepted a compromise as to the proposed constitution, which is commonly known as the Harari Resolution.

According to the Harari resolution, a constitution would not be written and adopted immediately, nor would the task of creating a constitution be postponed completely to some later date. Rather a Constitution would be adopted piecemeal in a series of 'basic laws' by the Knesset, i.e., the regular parliament. Following the completion of these individual basic laws, they would be unified in one document that would then constitute the Constitution of the State. As of this writing, the following Basic Laws have been adopted: The Knesset, the President, The Government, The Army, Economy, State Lands, Jerusalem, Adjudication, the State Comptroller, Freedom of Occupation, and Human Dignity and Liberty.

These last two, i.e., Freedom of Occupation and Human Dignity and Liberty were adopted only in March 1992. Prior to that time, the basic laws had little relevance to the protection of human rights, but were concerned almost exclusively with the organization of the State's governmental organs.

The Supreme Court has held that these Basic Laws have a constitutional status and that, therefore, ordinary laws which are in violation of such Basic Laws are invalid and may be so held by the courts. And, indeed, the Supreme Court has invalidated provisions of ten ordinary laws as being in violation of the 1992 Basic Laws concerning human rights.

8. It must also be emphasized that since the foundation of the State, the Israeli courts in general and the Supreme Court, sitting as the High Court of Justice, in particular, have been concerned actively with the protection of individual liberties, despite the lack of basic laws or other legislative norms that specifically authorized them to do so.

This has been accomplished primarily by the adoption and implementation in the Israeli judicial system of the fundamental principle that the individual is free to do as he pleases, except insofar as the Legislature has deprived him of, or restricted, his freedom.

The operative effect of this doctrine is that the court should not interpret vague or ambiguous Knesset legislation as restraining individual liberty, but rather should construe such legislation as not doing so. If the legislature wants to restrict individual liberty, it should do so in clear language. Furthermore, general delegations of power from the Knesset to the government ministries to enact regulations, should not be interpreted as delegating the power to enact restrictions on individual liberty. In other words, ministry regulations that restrict individual liberty should be invalidated in the courts unless they are supported by explicit Knesset empowering legislation.

Thus, while operating within a basic system of parliamentary authority, Israeli courts have exercised the power of protecting human rights and civil liberties, in a manner not too dissimilar from courts in States that operate pursuant to a written constitution.

§2. Delimitation of the Subject Matter

9. The term 'civil procedure' as used in Israel may be defined by examining each of its component words. 'Procedure', or procedural law, is distinguished from substantive law. Substantive law is that part of the legal norms that determines and defines rights and obligations. Procedural law, however, is that part of such norms that determines the means of enforcing such rights and imposing such obligations.

10. The term 'civil' is contrasted with 'criminal'. In Israel, due to the heritage of English law, the systems of civil and criminal procedure are relatively similar, as compared, for example, to States of Continental Europe. However, even in Israel there are differences between the two systems of procedure, and thus Israeli law recognizes two separate legal disciplines:

(1) civil procedure; and
(2) criminal procedure.

11. The term 'civil' may also be contrasted with 'administrative'. As of 2001, Israel has a system of Administrative Tribunals created within the District Courts in the central system of the courts. Due to the fact that the Administrative Tribunals are located within the central court system, the judges sitting in these tribunals are judges of the central judicial system and in some cases judges may deal with both civil and administrative cases. When administrative matters are adjudicated by the judges in their capacity as judges of the administrative tribunals, special rules of administrative procedure apply. The general rules of civil procedure may not be applied in administrative cases unless a matter has not been regulated by the special rules of administrative procedure and the judge holds that applying the rules of civil procedure is required for the due administration of the law after giving the parties the opportunity to object. Historically most administrative matters have been adjudicated in a special court, i.e., the Supreme Court sitting as the High Court of Justice. In this court special rules do apply, particularly concerning the use of affidavits in lieu of oral testimony. The Administrative Tribunals in the District Courts now adjudicate some of the matters previously determined by the High Court of Justice.

12. There are separate systems of Courts that have different rules of procedure. There are the Labour Courts, and the Religious Courts. The procedure of the Labour Courts is essentially the same as that applicable in the general courts, with only some rather minor modifications due to the special nature of these courts. The procedure in the Religious Courts is a combination of the general procedural norms applicable in Israel and the unique norms of the particular religious system. The latter, of course, are only valid if they do not conflict with fundamental procedural norms aimed at protecting the basic rights of litigants.

Finally, we should note that there are special procedural rules, which apply in the Family Courts and the Small Claims Courts. The Small Claims Court and the Family Court are special divisions of the Magistrate Court, the lower level of the ordinary courts. The rules in these specialized divisions, *inter alia*, relax the rigid provisions of procedure and evidence for these types of matters.

§3. Sources of Civil Procedure Law

13. During the period of the Mandate, the British introduced into mandatory Palestine, rules of civil procedure that were taken almost verbatim from the then English Rules of the High Court. These were the Rules of Civil Procedure 1938, as to the Supreme Court and the District Courts, and the Rules of Civil Procedure in the Magistrates' Courts, 1940, providing similar rules but with slight differences for the latter courts. The above two Mandatory rules of civil procedure were enacted by a judicial council with the approval of the High Commissioner.

On the establishment of the State of Israel, the authority to enact rules of civil procedure was entrusted to the Minister of Justice. This authority of the Minister of Justice was stated in section 46 of the Courts Law in 1957 (now section 108 of the Law of the Courts [Consolidated Version] of 1984), as authorizing the Minister of Justice 'to regulate, in rules of procedure, the procedure and custom before the courts … '. In exercising this authority, the Minister of Justice is assisted by an Advisory Committee on Civil Procedure. Although there is no statutory authority for the Minister being assisted by such an Advisory Committee, this has long been the practice.

Based on this authority, the Minister of Justice made various changes and additions to the Mandatory rules. However, fifteen years elapsed after the establishment of the State before the Mandatory rules were replaced by Israeli rules, i.e., by the Rules of Civil Procedure, 1963.

These new Israeli rules, however, did not purport to make any fundamental changes in the English based procedure effective in Israel. Their purposes were more limited. The first was to consolidate into one set of rules the previous different rules for District Courts and Magistrates' Courts respectively, as well as other specific rules pertaining to civil procedure, thereby also narrowing the differences between the practice before the District Courts and the Magistrates Courts. The second purpose was to adopt rules in the Hebrew language, as opposed to the Mandatory rules, the official language of which was English.

In 1984, the 1963 Rules were replaced with new rules, i.e., the Rules of Civil Procedure, 1984. Again, however, no fundamental changes were made in the Rules. Rather they further implemented the consolidation aims of the 1963 Rules, such that under the 1984 Rules there is virtually no difference between the Magistrate Courts and the District Courts as to their procedure. Hereinafter, we will refer to the existing Rules of Civil Procedure, i.e., the 1984 Rules, as the Rules of Civil Procedure or RCP.

14. The Courts Law, 1957 sets forth other provisions as to civil procedure, including the subject matter jurisdiction of the various courts, the panels of the judges sitting in court, transferring trials from one place to another, the right of appeal as to final judgments as opposed to an appeal by leave of court for other decisions, and a basic principle of Israeli civil procedure – a public trial.

The Courts Law, 1957 was re-enacted in the Courts Law [Consolidated Version], 1984, which also consolidated a number of other acts.

15. A further legislative act concerning civil procedure is the Basic Law: Adjudication, also enacted in 1984. This Basic Law includes a number of important principles of civil procedure, as follows:

(1) No court or judicial tribunal shall be created to act in a specific event, that is, no ad hoc courts may be created to adjudicate on matters that have already occurred.
(2) The judge is subject to the law and only to the law.
(3) The court shall sit in public, unless determined otherwise in law or the court orders otherwise in accordance with the law.
(4) A judgment of a court sitting at first instance may be appealed as of right, with the exception of a judgment of the Supreme Court sitting as the High Court of Justice.

16. It should be noted, however, that despite the aim to consolidate all the rules of procedure relating to civil matters, even after the enactment of the RCP in 1984, there remain a number of rules outside this framework. These are the Rules of the

High Court of Justice 1984, the Rules of Further Hearing 1984, and rules relating to procedure in the Labour Courts and the Small Claims Courts.

It should be noted further that while the Rules of Civil Procedure are, therefore, an independent product of the Israeli legal system, they continue to be based primarily on the English rules. Thus, it is not surprising that in interpreting these Rules, the Israeli courts continued to be influenced by – though not bound by and at a diminishing rate – English precedents that interpret parallel provisions of the English Rules.

§4. General Features of the Administration of Justice in Civil Matters

I. Characteristics of the Procedure

17. Israel follows the generally accepted principle that the basic role of adjudication is the resolution of controversies and the enforcement of rights recognized by the law. While there is relatively widespread use in Israel of actions for declaratory judgment, the principle is quite clear that even such actions must relate to actual and concrete issues and not to hypothetical or academic questions.

The primary goal of judicial proceedings is to determine the issues of fact so as to reach the truth and then to apply correct legal principles to this factual truth. The basic goal of the procedural system is to facilitate this process. This is true, for example, of the rules of civil procedure and of the principles of evidence. Yet the ascertainment of truth, while the primary goal, is not the exclusive one. Thus, for example, in order to attain goals of certainty and the prevention of multiple litigation, rules concerning the finality of litigation, res judicata, may bar a plaintiff from proving what might be a just claim. Similarly, in excluding evidence, not because of its lack of probative value but in order to protect such values as the preservation of confidential relationships (e.g., attorney-client, physician-patient, etc.), the Israeli system of adjudication has chosen to further these objects at the expense of ascertaining the truth. It should be mentioned herein that the generally accepted principle of Israeli law is that the granting of evidentiary privileges is a legislative matter. The courts have been very careful in recognizing privileges in addition to those that have been recognized by the legislature and they have done so in very few cases (e.g., confidential journalistic sources).

18. Israeli procedure is essentially based on the concept of the adversary system, leaving the conduct of the trial primarily in the hands of the parties. However, the system includes modifications of inquisitorial nature, which draw it away from the systems that exist in England or the United States.

In Israel, while the basic system is adversary, the judge is allowed quite an active role both in the pre-trial and the trial process itself. Many provisions of the Israeli RCP allow the judge to act on his own initiative without the need of a request by a party. These provisions include dismissing the action as to parties who were not properly joined and adding necessary parties who were not joined, ordering separate trials where claims or parties have been joined, dismissing a complaint for failure to state a cause of action, ordering the consolidation of separate complaints involving the same or similar questions that are pending before the same court, and dismissing complaints for failure of prosecution.

A most important procedural device for judicial management of the trial is that of the pre-trial conference which precedes the trial of the case. At this pre-trial conference, the judge may decide on almost all issues concerned with the pleadings, the discovery process and with preliminary relief. Most importantly, the pre-trial conference rules expressly empower the judge to determine what are the issues that are really in dispute between the parties; to order that a witness proposed by a party first present his evidence by affidavit or that a fact in issue be proven by affidavit (as distinguished from oral testimony which, as we will discuss, is the traditional method of proof in Israeli law); 'to determine the stages of the trial process and the order by which factual and legal issues will be determined, as well as the matters which will be determined separately'; and 'to issue any [other] procedural order which will simplify or ease the trial process'.

At the trial itself, the judge may exert a considerable restraining influence on the questioning of witnesses by the attorneys. Moreover, the RCP expressly authorize the judge himself to put questions to a witness at any stage of their examination. The court is also expressly empowered by the RCP to appoint expert witnesses at its own initiative. In addition, despite the lack of express authority in the RCP, the courts have held that the judge has inherent authority to receive evidence and call ordinary witnesses, at his initiative, that neither party has called.

All the above powers must, however, be exercised with restraint, as the system remains that of a modified adversary process. Thus, for example, the weight of authority suggests that a judge's power to call witnesses at his own initiative should be exercised only to clarify matters, which have already been raised at the trial, and not to open new evidentiary issues.

19. In general, the role of the judge with regard to the termination of the proceedings is similar to that of other aspects of the proceedings, i.e., a modified adversary system. In general, the consensual termination of proceedings is at party initiative and without court supervision. Thus, if the parties agree to terminate proceedings they can generally do so without the need of court authorization. The only two exceptions to this general rule concern actions that have been brought by or on behalf of persons lacking legal competence, i.e., minors, mentally incompetent people, etc., and representative actions (see Part VIII).

If the parties wish their agreement to be embodied in a formal judgment, as distinguished merely from the plaintiff withdrawing his action, they may request the court to issue a consent judgment. The court is not required to issue such a consent judgment automatically, but has discretion in the matter. However, except for the cases mentioned above as to actions brought by or on behalf of incompetents and class actions, such discretion does not include determining the 'correctness' or 'fairness' of the compromise. Rather it is limited to determining the questions of whether the parties really have agreed on the consent judgment and ensuring that the requested judgment is capable of enforcement and does not exceed the jurisdictional limits of the court involved.

Note that a plaintiff need not receive either the consent of the other party or leave of court to withdraw his complaint voluntarily although if he does so he may be liable for costs as well as being barred by res judicata from refiling the complaint at a later time. However, if the plaintiff wishes to avoid the bar of res judicata, he must receive judicial permission to withdraw his complaint.

A 1992 amendment to the Court's Law [Consolidated Version], 1984 authorizes the court, where the parties agree, to render a compromise judgment of an issue in dispute, or part thereof. The amendment further states that this authority shall not detract from the general authority of the courts to suggest compromise settlements to the parties.

Prior to this amendment, the only mention in legislation or the RCP of the role of the courts in promoting settlements concerned the very specific case of the pre-trial hearing of an appeal. However, many judges have long been quite active in promoting settlements both during the pre-trial conference and the trial process. In this respect the 1992 amendment, provides recognition for what has long been common practice.

20. This 1992 amendment also authorizes a court, with the agreement of the parties, to transfer a matter to arbitration. (See Part X.) It also establishes a new form of proceedings: mediation.

Mediation is defined as a proceeding in which a mediator meets the parties in order to reach an agreement to settle the controversy. The mediator does not have authority to decide on the issue. The amendment states that a court may, with the agreement of the parties, transfer an issue to mediation proceedings. The parties, with the courts approval appoint the mediator: where the parties cannot reach an agreement as to who the mediator will be, he may be appointed from a list presented to the court by the parties or where no such list exists, at the court's discretion. During the mediation proceedings, the mediator may meet with the parties together or separately, as well as with any other person connected to the controversy. With their agreement, he may meet with the parties without their counsel.

The discussions of the mediation proceedings are privileged such that they cannot be used against a party if the judicial action is resumed.

A court that refers a matter to mediation, will stay the judicial proceedings for a stated period of time, which can then be lengthened, with the agreement of the parties. However, at any time during the mediation proceedings, at the request of the mediator or a party, the court may order the reinstatement of the judicial process. In all events, it must do so if the parties have not reached agreement by the end of the period set for the mediation.

If the parties have reached agreement, the mediator will so notify the court, which may then give their agreement the force of a judgment.

In the eight years since the adoption of these mediation provisions, they have become very popular. Many people have been trained as mediators, mediation centres have been established and judges routinely refer litigants to mediation.

20.1. A further development with respect to the reception of mediation as a means of alternative dispute resolution occurred in 2008 with an amendment that added Rules 99A-99K to the RCP. According to the amendment the Administrator of the Courts is authorized to publish a list of courts within which an obligatory meeting of the parties must take place after all the pleadings have been submitted and before a judge or a registrar may hear the case. A court may however exempt the parties from this obligatory meeting and proceed immediately to trial.

Rule 99A defines the meeting as a 'Meeting for information, acquaintance and coordination for the purpose of examining the possibility of resolving the dispute by means of mediation in accordance with the provisions of this paragraph' (the 'Mediation Meeting'). The Rules stipulate that an invitation to the meeting will be issued to the parties within seven days after the last pleading has been submitted and a date will be set therein for the meeting, which shall take place no later than forty-five days from the issuance of the invitation. The Mediation Meeting is chaired by a mediator selected from a list of experienced mediators published by the National Center for Mediation within the Ministry of Justice. Whereas in most proceedings, parties are not obliged to appear themselves and it is sufficient that they are represented by an attorney, Rule 99G requires that the parties themselves appear in the Mediation Meeting, although they may be represented by an attorney in this meeting. In that sense, the Mediation Meeting is similar to the pre-trial conference. See *infra* paragraph 161. The court may impose the costs of the mediator and the opposing parties on a party that failed to attend the Mediation Meeting as required.

The essence of the Mediation Meeting is to inform the parties as to the possibility of resolving their dispute by means of mediation and as to the nature of the mediation process. The Rules were conceived in order to encourage the choice of mediation by parties and the unique compulsory attendance imposed on the parties themselves is the result of the understanding by the drafters of the amendment that it would often be adverse to the interests of the attorneys to convince their clients to resort to mediation. While attending the Mediation Meeting is compulsory, the parties are not obliged to resolve their dispute by mediation. Rule 99I requires the parties to notify the court within ten days of the Mediation Meeting whether they have decided to refer their dispute to mediation or not. If the parties elect not to resolve their dispute by mediation, the case will continue to trial.

The Mediation Meeting procedure has so far been applied restrictively. According to Rule 99J the Mediation Meeting applies to claims valued at upwards of NIS 75,000 with the exception of claims based on the Accident Victims Compensating Law, 1975. However, the Administrator of the Courts has initiated the procedure only in eleven Magistrate Courts. To date, the data published by the Court Administration indicates that approximately two thirds of the disputes which parties were compelled to attend a Mediation Meeting elected to attempt to resolve the dispute via mediation. Furthermore, the data indicates that half of the disputes, which proceed to mediation, are resolved thereby.

It should be noted that if a mediation procedure fails, documents and admissions exchanged or uttered within the process of mediation remain privileged and the parties may not use them afterwards in court. Having said that, many attorneys remain wary of the mediation process as it involves the potential exposure of information and litigation strategy to the opposing party, which may turn out to be adverse to their client's case in the event that the mediation fails.

Given the significant burden of cases on the Israeli court system and the growing trend of alternative dispute resolution, we anticipate a further expansion of the Mediation Meeting procedure to additional courts.

21. The Rules of Civil Procedure number some 532 provisions, thus attempting to provide parties to a dispute with a certain and predictable process on which they can rely. However, these important interests of certainty and predictability may, at times, conflict with a desire for flexibility and discretion that will allow a court to achieve 'justice' in the individual case.

The essential conflict between the different interests and values involved may be clearly demonstrated in the rules pertaining to sanctions on procedural irregularities and provisions of the RCP for opposition. These will be discussed in paragraphs 123–125.

22. In concluding this description of the general characteristics of the Israeli civil process, we should note again its basic derivation from English procedure. However, we should also note herein the basic differences between English and Israeli process. First, in a number of particulars, such as the incorporation of the American inspired pre-trial conference discussed above, Israeli procedure has de jure deviated from English practice. This is true also of other specifics of Israeli practice, such as the expedited judgment proceedings which we will discuss at length in Part IV, *infra.*

More important, however, are the de facto differences between Israeli and English practice. We have already mentioned the more interventionist role of the judge in Israel than in England. Even more important is that, in general, Israel does not follow the English practice of holding a concentrated, continuous trial. As is well known, English procedure is based on a relatively clear demarcation between the pre-trial proceedings and that of the evidentiary stage, which is denominated the 'trial'. This trial is held in a concentrated, continuous fashion, i.e., it continues, uninterrupted during normal working hours, for the required hours, days or weeks needed to hear all the evidence in one concentrated period of time. Judgment is then entered very shortly after, if not immediately upon, termination of the concentrated trial.

Such a continuous, concentrated trial in English procedure was essentially dictated by the use of juries when the English practice crystallized.

In contrast, juries have never been used in Israel, neither before nor after the establishment of the State. Thus, the necessity of a concentrated, continuous trial required by the use of juries never existed in Israel.

It is true that Rule 152(a) of the RCP, which is taken directly from English procedure, does require a concentrated, continuous trial unless there are special reasons for not doing so in a particular case. Yet this Rule is, in practice, generally ignored, and trials are in most cases neither concentrated nor continuous, but rather consist of a series of short sessions, which may take place over a period of months or even years. In this regard, an Israeli 'trial' resembles more the procedure of continental Europe than that of England.

23. Yet, unlike the practice of continental Europe, Israeli trial practice has been based on that of England in terms of the emphasis on oral testimony, cross-examination and rigid rules of evidence.

Even this aspect of Israeli trial practice now may be beginning to undergo changes in the direction of continental European practice. In 1988 the Advisory Committee on the Rules of Civil Procedure circulated a draft of proposed amendments to the Rules of Civil Procedure, 1984, the essence of which was the requirement that the pleadings be supported by detailed affidavits as to the relevant facts, which affidavits, *inter alia*, might then be used at trial in lieu of the direct examination of the affiant.

These proposals provoked a great deal of opposition, primarily from the Bar Association, and, as of this writing, the Minister of Justice has not promulgated the proposals that would require that pleadings generally be supported by affidavits as to the facts.

However, part of the Advisory Committee's proposed amendments were accepted by the Minister of Justice and promulgated by him in August 1991. These include a general prohibition on pleading contradictory factual allegations against the same party, as well as strengthening the authority of the judge, at the pre-trial conference or at trial, to order that a potential witness first submit an affidavit or that a given fact be proved by affidavits. Such affidavits would then serve as the direct testimony of the affiant unless the court, for special reasons, decides otherwise. In keeping with the English emphasis on cross-examination, the affiant would still be subject to oral cross-examination (although the cross-examining party may waive this right at will) even if his affidavit was used in lieu of his direct oral examination.

Also of interest in this regard is the fact that a number of special rules of civil procedure adopted since 1991, base their proceedings on affidavits, which the parties are required to file. Most important in this regard are the Rules of Civil Procedure that apply in all matters adjudicated in the Family Courts.

To a significant extent, these provisions inaugurated a fundamental change in Israeli procedure as in a large part of the regular civil proceedings the initial testimony of witnesses is now substituted by an affidavit.

II. Fundamental Guarantees

24. In terms of Israel's constitutional structure, it must be emphasized that Israel, like England, has no written Constitution.

Unlike England, however, Israel has adopted a number of basic laws, which may be viewed as having a quasi-constitutional status. The Basic Law: Adjudication, adopted in 1984 is most important for the subject of this chapter as will be discussed below.

However, the influence of constitutional principles on Israeli civil procedure is not limited to this basic law.

The Basic Law: Human Dignity and Freedom adopted in 1992, has also relevance to Civil Procedure. Moreover, many constitutional principles, in the broad meaning of this term, i.e., fundamental, structural principles, are embedded in regular Israeli legislative provisions, both of primary and of secondary legislation.

25. Additionally, even in the absence of positive legislative provisions, Israeli courts, and in particular, the Supreme Court, sitting as the High Court of Justice, while operating within a system of parliamentary supremacy, exercise powers of protecting individual rights and liberties, including concepts of natural justice in the adjudicative process. A cornerstone of the Israeli legal structure is that fundamental human rights may not be abridged or curtailed except by express parliamentary legislation.

The operative effect of this doctrine is that the courts do not interpret broadly vague or ambiguous parliamentary legislation so as to restrain fundamental rights, but rather they interpret such legislation narrowly so as not to do so. If the legislature desires to restrict fundamental freedoms, it must do so in clear language. Furthermore, general delegations of power from the legislature to government ministries are interpreted as not delegating powers to limit or curtail fundamental freedoms. In other words, ministerial actions or regulations that restrict fundamental rights are invalidated by the courts, unless they are supported by explicit, empowering, primary legislation. Moreover, ministerial actions are subject to judicial review as to their reasonableness and will also be invalidated if based on irrelevant, or discriminatory considerations.

Below some of the fundamental constitutional principles guaranteed by the Israeli legal system will be discussed.

A. *Judicial Jurisdiction determined by Law*

26. Adjudication in Israel, as in every modern state, is distributed among a number of courts and tribunals, each having its defined scope of jurisdiction. In addition to the three regular courts – the Magistrates' Courts, the District Courts, and the Supreme Court – there exist Religious Courts and other judicial tribunals, for example the specialized Labour Courts. The existence, structure and jurisdiction of all of these courts are grounded firmly in specific statutes, with the exception of the Bahai and Christian Religious Courts. Even these latter courts are, however, based on internal traditions and principles of the different denominations.

Thus, there is no place in the Israeli legal structure for the creation of ad hoc courts to adjudicate upon matters that have already occurred.

This situation is embedded in positive Israeli law by the opening paragraph of the Basic Law: Adjudication which, after providing for the extension of the judicial power to the existing courts, including religious and other judicial tribunals, as well as new courts that may be established by the legislature, expressly provides: 'No court or judicial tribunal shall be created to act in a specific event.'

B. *The Judge as Subject to the Law and Only to the Law*

27. A basic principle of Israeli Law is stated in the second paragraph of the Basic Law: Adjudication, as follows: 'one in whom there is vested judicial authority shall, in judicial matters, be subject to no authority other than that of the law'.

This statement contains two elements:

(1) that one in whom judicial authority is vested is not to be influenced by outside forces and factors. i.e., he is independent of them; and
(2) that he is controlled by the law. i.e., his independence is subject to his duty to act according to law.

These principles form the cornerstone of Israeli adjudication and present no problems of implementation as to professional judges of the regular, judicial system, consisting of the Magistrates' Courts, District Courts and Supreme Court. And, indeed, the above quoted provision has applied to such judges since its enactment as part of the Judges Law, 1953.

28. However, when in 1984, the provision was transferred from the Judges Law to the Basic Law: Adjudication, its application was broadened significantly. By its express terms, this provision now applies not only to judges of the regular court system, but also to those of special tribunals, such as the Religious Courts.

The application of these principles to judges of Religious Courts is far from simple. As has been mentioned above, the appointment of judges to the Jewish, Islamic and Druze court systems is regulated by specific Israeli statutes. The appointment to the various Christian denominations and to the Bahai Courts is not, however, regulated by statue and is viewed as an internal matter of these religious groups. As to Jewish, Islamic and Druze courts, appointments are made by the President of the State on the advice of the relevant committee – a different one for each group – that consists of a number of the judges as well as other recognized religious officials in the group. In each group, a person to be appointed as a religious judge must be a qualified authority in the religious law of his sect.

The religious judge is required to comply with a dual loyalty. He must follow the above principles and give his total obedience to the positive secular Israeli law. He must also, however, judge in accordance with the religious legal system, which system deems itself autonomous and does not necessarily admit the superiority of the secular State law.

The situation is ameliorated, however, by the general unity of forum and law as to the Religious Courts. That is, under Israeli positive law when Religious Courts have jurisdiction in a matter, generally the applicable substantive law is that of the religious system of which the Religious Court is a part.

Moreover, while the Religious Courts are self-contained units with their own internal structure of trial and appellate courts, being a component of the Israeli governmental system they are subject, as are other components of the system, to supervision by the Israeli Supreme Court, sitting as the High Court of Justice.

The High Court of Justice is authorized to intervene in determinations of the religious courts in the case of a violation of clear statutory provisions, or if the procedures have been found to be in violation of the principles of natural justice. It should be noted, however, that there have been relatively few interventions of this kind. First, such violations by the religious courts are rare. Second, the High Court of Justice is reluctant to intervene and has made it clear that its power does not mean that it is, in effect, an appellate court reviewing decisions of the religious courts.

29. Another problematic area concerning paragraph 2 of the Basic Law: Adjudication concerns lay representatives of employees and employers on the Labour Courts. These representatives have a limited tenure of office and thus do not have the same degree of independence as is assured to judges by permanency of tenure. Moreover, the partisan nature of the representatives of the public is emphasized by the balanced composition of the panel required for individual cases. In the regional court, the panel consists generally of a judge, who presides, and two representatives of the public, one from among the representatives of the employees and one from among the representatives of the employers. The national court generally sits in panels of seven, composed of three judges and four representatives of the public, two employees' representatives and two employers' representatives.

In such balanced panels, it is most difficult for the representatives not to be partisan and to be subject to the law and only the law.

C. Access to the Courts

1. The Legal Right of Access to the Courts

30. There are no restrictions on the legal right of access to the courts. All persons, whether or not they are citizens or even residents of the State, are entitled to file actions in the Israeli courts. According to the Rules of Civil Procedure, persons who lack legal competence, such as minors and those who have been declared incompetent, may also sue, either by means of a 'close friend' or by means of a guardian.

A 2012 amendment to the RCP required a plaintiff who is not an Israeli resident to specify his passport number and country of issue of the passport. The amendment has been strongly criticized on the ground that it may prevent persons who do not hold an Israeli citizenship or a valid passport from filing a claim in Israeli courts and consequently will deny their right of access to the courts. In response to the criticism, a later amendment to the RCP explicitly states that if the plaintiff does not have an Israeli identification number he should indicate this in his claim as well as the reasons for the lack thereof. In this case, the Chief Secretary of the court may approve the application of the complaint. See *infra* paragraph 129.

2. The Right to Representation by Counsel

31. With only one exception, in civil proceedings all parties have an unqualified right to be represented by counsel of their choice, provided that such counsel is a qualified and registered attorney under Israeli law.

The one exception to this rule concerns Small Claims Courts, where the representation of a party is only by permission of the court and for special reasons that shall be recorded.

This provision was adopted at the instance of consumer advocates who believed that preventing the appearance of attorneys in the Small Claims Court would aid in reducing the costs of litigation in these courts, would tend to prevent them from becoming vehicles used by commercial creditors against consumers and would encourage the informality and simplicity desired in such courts.

It is questionable whether such an analysis is true and whether the prevention or limitation of legal representation will not in fact burden the consumer who does not always know the extent and basis of his rights and does not have at his disposal the experience or even legal advice (outside the courtroom) available to a commercial creditor.

D. Public Proceedings

32. In the Israeli view, the provisions for the conduct of trials in public are a major guarantee that the rights of the parties to fair proceedings will be respected.

The basic norm in this regard is set forth in paragraph 3 of the Basic Law: Adjudication:

> A court will sit in public, unless it is determined otherwise by [statutory] Law, or the court has ordered otherwise in accordance with [statutory] Law.

This provision of the Basic Law: Adjudication is consistent with the long-standing provision of the Courts Law, 1957 (now found in the Consolidated Version, 1984), of which paragraph 68(a) sets forth the basic principle: 'A court shall sit in public'. The primary exceptions to this basic principle are provided for cases where public trials would unduly infringe other important social values. Thus, a court may deal with the whole or any particular part of a matter *in camera* if it deems it necessary to do so in order to safeguard State security, to protect morality, or to protect the well-being of a minor. It may also sit *in camera* when dealing with interim relief, provisional orders, and in matters concerning personal status.

The basic requirement that trials be heard in public also finds expression in the negative view taken by the Israeli Supreme Court against conversations held in judges' chambers during the course of a trial, even when all sides are present.

In a criminal case, but in language equally applicable to civil proceedings, the then President of the Supreme Court, Justice Landau, stated: 'There is no place for "casual conversation" between a judge and representatives of the parties on a matter related to a criminal trial being held before the judge. Rather he should "preserve his distance" and say what he has to say in public in the court room, if it is worth saying at all.'[1]

E. The Right to be Heard

33. Israeli law strongly emphasizes the right of a party to be heard in the proceedings. The Israeli Supreme Court has accepted the proposition that one of the most important fundamental principles of natural justice is that one should not judge a person until after he has been heard. A most important expression of this principle

1. *The State of Israel v. The Angel Baking Co.*, 34 (4) P.D. 277, 278 (1980).

in civil litigation has been in the provisions both in the Rules and in case law allowing the setting aside of default judgments. These demonstrate a very strong adherence to the proposition that, if at all possible. One should not judge a person until he has been heard.

Another expression of this right to be heard is found in the restrictions on ex parte judicial actions.

In general, the Israeli Rules of Civil Procedure restrict the availability of ex parte orders to those situations in which there is no other alternative. The basic principle is that orders are to be made in the presence of all parties.

The strong adherence of Israeli law to the principle of *audiatur et altera pars* also has been reflected in an historical reluctance to extend the res judicata aspects of judgment to non-parties (*ultra partes*). Thus. the courts have held that one who will be bound by the judgment has a right to intervene in the pending court proceedings. Even more significantly, the reluctance to bind absent class members in the event a class action fails has been a major factor in the historic reluctance of the Israeli law to adopt American-style class actions.

F. The Right to Reasoned Decisions

34. Israeli law emphasizes strongly the obligation of the judge to give fully reasoned decisions, both at the trial and appellate levels.

Rule 192 of the RCP requires that a first instance judgment in a case in which a defence has been served include a summary of the issue, the court's findings in respect of the material facts, the questions to be decided, the operative decision and the *reasons* therefore.

Thus, for example, in a 1990 decision in a criminal case, but which is equally applicable to civil proceedings, the Supreme Court overturned a lower court decision on the grounds that the court had not complied with its obligation to give full and particular reasons for its decision. Indeed, the court had, in general, explained its reasons for its decision, including its preference for one version of the disputed facts over the other. However, in the view of the Supreme Court it had not been sufficiently specific in its factual findings and in the attribution of these findings to particular evidence.

In the words of the court:

> There is no possibility to learn from the [Court's] summary [of the facts] … which testimony it felt to be credible and which not, and what version of the events it adopted. The first instance court only wrote the bottom line, without attributing its findings to specific testimony or to a credible section [of the protocol].
>
> In so doing the first instance court did not fulfil its obligation. A decision in the first instance must include findings of fact accompanied by references to particular pieces of evidence believed by the court, from which these findings are derived.[2]

2. *Totri v. The State of Israel*, 44 (2) P.D. 573 (1989).

In this case, the Supreme Court justified this demand for particularized factual findings as an essential requisite for proper appellate review of trial court findings.

The insistence on reasoned decisions, however, may also be viewed as satisfying the right of the parties, particularly the losing party, to know the reasons for the decision. Such a right follows, indeed, from the party's right to be heard. The right to be heard, under this view, includes the right to have the decision maker address the matters argued by the party and expressly accept or reject them.

The obligation to write reasoned opinions may also be seen as one owed to the public. Reasoned opinions allow the public better to evaluate the work of the courts and, thus, may be seen as a supplement to the right of public hearings.

Last but not least, it is generally viewed that the requirement to write reasoned opinions will improve the quality of the opinion itself. Under this view, a judge who is compelled to articulate fully his reasons for his decisions will be compelled also to think through more fully the decision itself.

There are, of course, costs to the writing of reasoned decisions, which include the extensive time devoted by Israeli judges to decision writing. There has been a recent attempt to deal with this aspect of the problem as to appellate decisions, as follows.

35. As with decisions of first instance courts, the basic rule is that appellate decisions must be reasoned. Thus, the long-standing rule as to appellate decisions, now found in Rule 460(a) of the RCP provides that an appellate decision must include:

(1) the questions to be decided;
(2) the decision itself; and
(3) the reasons for the decision.

However, in 1986 this Rule was amended to provide, that despite these requirements an appellate court that decides to reject an appeal may include in its decision only the bare announcement of the rejection of the appeal, i.e., without giving its reasons, provided that it has decided that there is no basis for rejecting the factual determinations of the lower court, that these factual determinations support that court's legal conclusion and there has been no legal mistake as to law.

In such an event, pursuant to Rule 460(c), for purposes of a further appeal, the contents of the first instance decision are to be viewed as contained in the appellate decision involved.

It has been argued that this arrangement violates the fundamental principle of Israeli procedure requiring reasoned decisions. In a decision in 1990, the Supreme Court rejected this argument.[3] The court emphasized that, indeed, Israeli procedure does require reasoned decisions. However, in the opinion of the court, the amended procedure as to appellate decisions rejecting appeals does comply with the demand for reasoned decisions. This is so, since by adopting the reasoning of the first instance court, the appellate court makes it its own. In making the reasoning of the lower court its own, the appellate court must carefully examine the factual findings and legal reasoning of the first instance court.

3. *Pe'air v. Beit Frishman Co and Others*, 44 (4) P.D. 693 (1989).

Thus, the court concludes that 'There is no basis for the claim that the parties or a higher appellate court will be left without knowledge of the reasons for the decision; as to a [higher] appellate court the matter is even further specified in 460(c) quoted above.'[4]

In our view, the court too easily disposed of the argument that the amended rule infringes upon the requirement of reasoned decisions.

It is true that the procedure does tell the parties that the appeal was rejected because the appellate court agreed with the first instance court as to its findings of fact and conclusions of law. However, that is not a reasoned response to the appellant's arguments on appeal. On appeal the appellant argued, and based this argument on reasoning, that the lower court was wrong.

By the appellate court telling the appellant only that it agrees with the first instance court, the appellate court tells him only that it has rejected his arguments; not why it has done so. The 'why', of course, is the essence of a reasoned decision.

Moreover, the court did not address at all the important function that this requirement of reasoned decisions performs in promoting better decisions. This function is not at all served by the amended process.

Thus, the amended process does infringe on the demand for reasoned decisions. Yet that does not necessarily mean that the amended procedure is invalid or even undesirable. As to its validity, it is clear that under positive Israeli law the amended Rule is a valid exercise of the rule making power of the Minister of Justice. As to its desirability, the issue is the need to balance the requirement of reasoned decisions with the desire to expedite the work of the appellate courts by relieving them of the burden of writing opinions in cases of routine rejection of appeals. While this issue is not free from doubt, our view is that the amended rule is justified by the need to expedite the appellate process.

G. The Right of Appeal

36. Paragraph 17 of the Basic Law: Adjudication provides: 'A final judgment of a Court of First Instance is subject to appeal as of right, except for a judgment of the Supreme Court.'

This provision, adopted in the Basic Law of 1984, as a basic norm is a new development in Israeli law. Prior to its adoption the Israeli courts had held that there is no inherent right to appeal judicial decisions and, thus, the only rights of appeal recognized were those granted by specific statutes. However, the Israeli Supreme Court had recognized the importance of the right of appeal, for example, in holding that the fact that a winning party may not appeal a decision serves as a primary reason for not precluding such a party (by the doctrine of collateral estoppel or issue preclusion) in later litigation as to issues determined against him in the litigation in which he was victorious. Moreover, with only the relatively minor exceptions, to be discussed below, the Israeli statutory system has always provided one appeal of right as to all judgments.

---

4. *Ibid.*, at 3.

37. The first exception to the right of appeal as to final judgments is reflected in the final phrase of paragraph 17 of the Basic Law: Adjudication when it excepts 'a judgment of the Supreme Court'. This exception concerns actions, primarily against governmental authorities, that are filed in the first instance in the Supreme Court sitting as the High Court of Justice. By virtue of the fact that the Court of First Instance is the highest court in the State, there is no appeal at all, either by right or with leave, from such a decision. There is, however, even in such situations the possibility that the case will be heard again by an enlarged panel of the Supreme Court, if it was heard in the first instance by a panel of only three judges. Such a rehearing by an enlarged panel may be granted at the initiative of the Court itself or by petition of one of the parties. The granting of such a petition is in the discretion of the President of the Supreme Court or other justices designated for this purpose.

38. The second exception in Israeli law to the principle of appeal by right from final court judgments concerns Small Claims Courts, which were set up by the Small Claims (Jurisdiction) Law 1976, which provisions have since been incorporated into the Courts Law (Consolidated Version) 1984. In accordance with the desire to provide an expeditious and inexpensive procedure for small claims – the present monetary limit being NIS 33,200 (approximately USD 8,500) this law provides that from Small Claims Courts there is no appeal as of right; rather the only form of appeal is by leave of the appellate court.

The status of this exception from the principle of appeal as of right as to final judgments is, however, in doubt since the passage of the Basic law: Adjudication. Unlike the case of the Supreme Court sitting as a Court of First Instance, paragraph 17 of the Basic Law does not except from its provisions judgments of Small Claims Courts. Thus, there is a clear and unequivocal conflict between the specific statutory provisions as to Small Claims Courts and the general provisions of the Basic Law: Adjudication.

Further analysis of the legal situation as to this conflict would go far beyond the confines of this monograph and would involve us in difficult problems of public law.

39. In terms of the more general principles applicable to appeal, Israeli law recognizes a distinction between a 'final judgment' and all 'other decisions'.

A final judgment of a Magistrates' Court is appealable as of right to a District Court, and a final judgment of a District Court sitting as a Court of First Instance is appealable as of right to the Supreme Court. It should be noted, however, that there is only one appeal as of right as to each final judgment. Thus, when a case is litigated in the first instance in a Magistrates' Court, the judgment is appealable as of right to a District Court. However, the District Court's appellate decision in such a case (as distinguished from a District Court's judgment when it sits as a Court of First Instance) is appealable to the Supreme Court only if leave to appeal is allowed, either from the District Court or from the Supreme Court.

'Other decisions' are appealable at the time of their rendering only if leave to appeal is granted by the appellate court. The courts have held that a final judgment for purposes of this rule is one that 'closes the file' at the first instance, regardless of whether it does or does not preclude further litigation on the matter at issue.

It should be emphasized that these 'other decisions', i.e., primarily interlocutory orders, are appealable not by right but only by leave of the appellate court, *at the time of their entry*. This is so, since the Rules of Civil Procedure expressly provide that if not appealed at the time of entry, either because leave to appeal was not requested or because such leave was requested and denied, such other decisions are appealable as of right at the time of final judgment as part of the appeal on that judgment, assuming, of course, that they are still relevant to the result. Thus, it may be stated that, in essence, the Israeli rules provide for appeal of right as to all these decisions relating only to the time of the appeal as of right, not to its existence.

In an effort to restrict the right of appeal by leave at the time of rendering 'other decisions', the Minister of Justice issued a decree in 2009 which states that leave to appeal shall not be given in types of cases listed in the decree. The types of decision listed in the decree are characterized by their technical nature, e.g., decisions on dates for filing of pleadings, the length of pleadings, hearing dates, etc.

Part I. Judicial Organization

Chapter 1. The Courts and Their Members

§1. Courts

I. Structure of the Court System

40. Judicial bodies in Israel can be divided into several independent groups, each with its own legal proceedings, its own Court of Appeal and generally its own judges.

(1) *The general courts* currently include the Magistrates' Courts, the District Courts and the Supreme Court. This group possesses residual judicial authority, and every case that does not fall in the realm of the other groups belongs to the general courts.[5] Most civil and criminal cases are heard in this framework.
The Magistrates' Court serves as the Court of First Instance for certain issues, and the District Court as the Court of First Instance for other issues. The District Court is the Court of Appeal for decisions of the Magistrates' Court: the Supreme Court is the Court of Appeal for the District Court, whether the latter acts as a Court of First Instance or as Court of Appeal.
The division of jurisdiction among the general courts themselves, and between them and other courts of laws, has been influenced by Ottoman and Mandatory law, as well as that of the independent State of Israel.
(2) *The Religious Courts* include regional Rabbinical Courts and the Rabbinical High Court of Appeal, authorized to try cases involving Jews, as well as Muslim, Christian, Bahai and Druze courts, at first instance and as courts of appeal. These courts deal with matters of personal status, and are based on the Ottoman millet system.
(3) *The Labour Courts* include Regional Labour Courts, serving as first instance in certain issues, and the National Labour Court, serving as first instance in the remainder of cases, and as courts of appeal for the decisions of the regional courts. The Labour Courts are authorized to hear cases involving employer/employee relations, disputes between workers unions and employers associations, etc. The Labour Courts are authorized to deal with certain criminal labour cases. The imprint of the Israeli legislature is clearly evident in this group.

5. The terminology usually distinguishes between a judicial body belonging to this group called a court (*beit mishpat*), and a judicial body of a different group called a *beit din*.

(4) *The High Court of Justice* was created during the Mandatory period. The intention was to create an institution authorized to issue prerogative orders, which are decrees used in England primarily to protect individuals from unlawful harm on the part of the authorities. In England, the court authorized to issue such decrees is the High Court of Justice, which is usually a regular first instance court. In Mandatory Palestine, for political reasons, this authority was given to the Supreme Court, which has retained it until this day.

The jurisdiction of the High Court of Justice today includes judicial review of administrative and judicial authorities, including that of the religious and labour courts.

As noted above in paragraph 11, part of the High Court of Justice's administrative law jurisdiction is now subject to the jurisdiction of special administrative divisions of the District Courts. As of 2012, a proposed bill has been drafted with the purpose of erecting special administrative divisions in the Magistrates Courts, which will be granted jurisdiction primarily in disputes regarding the activities of local government.

For further discussion of the division of jurisdiction among the judicial bodies discussed above, see Part II on Jurisdiction.

II. Administration of the Courts

41. The Minister of Justice is responsible for the administration of the general court system. He appoints, with the agreement of the President of the Supreme Court, the Director of the Courts and that Director is accountable to him. The Director of the Courts need not necessarily be a judge. The Minister of Justice may enact Rules of Court and is responsible, through the Court Administration, an office subject to the Minister of Justice, for the preparation of the budget of the general court system. The Office of the Court Administration is also responsible for the administration of the courts on a day-to-day basis. The Courts Law (Consolidated Version) 1984 provides for the appointment of a President and Vice Presidents for each court. The President is responsible for the assignment of cases to the judges and for fixing the dates of trials. Presidents and Vice Presidents are appointed by the Minister of Justice. As per an amendment to the Law of the Courts [Consolidated Version] 1984 from 2007 the Presidents and Vice Presidents are appointed for a single term of seven years, which may not be prolonged. The Amendment included a limitation barring the appointment of a President or Vice President with less than three years of service before retirement. However, in 2012 the Knesset passed another amendment to lift the restriction in the case of the Presidents and Vice Presidents of the Supreme Court and of the National Labour Court. The latter amendment was enacted as a result of a political battle over the appointment of the incoming President of the Supreme Court.

Judicial salaries are determined by the Finance Committee of the Knesset.

III. 'Ministère Public'

42. In Israel, there is no *ministère public* as such who is considered a member of the court system. On the other hand, many of the functions performed by the *ministère public* in other systems are performed in Israel by the Attorney General, whose position and functions are discussed below in paragraphs 60–61.

§2. MEMBERS OF THE JUDICIARY

I. Nature and Appointment

43. Despite the strong historic connection between the Israeli and English adjudicative systems, neither the use of lay juries nor of lay magistrates has ever been introduced into Israel.

The basic principle of Israeli law is that adjudication is in the hands of professional judges.

44. The Basic Law: Adjudication, provides for appointments to all three of the general courts, the Magistrates' Courts, the District Courts and the Supreme Court, by the President of the State, upon the advice of a special appointment committee consisting of the following nine persons:

(1) three justices of the Supreme Court, including the President of the Supreme Court;
(2) two governmental ministers, one of whom must be the Minister of Justice, who serves as chairman of the committee;
(3) two members of the Knesset;
(4) two practicing attorneys selected by the Israeli Chamber of Advocates.

No one may be appointed as judge of a Magistrates' Court or a District Court unless he is a member of the Bar, or is qualified to be so admitted and has practiced law, engaged in equivalent legal work in government service, or taught law for specified, minimum periods of time.

The only minor exception to the need to be a qualified attorney in order to be appointed to the bench is that regarding the Supreme Court, as distinguished from the lower courts, 'an eminent jurist' who is not a qualified attorney may be appointed. This exception was created in order to allow the appointment to the Supreme Court of learned jurists in religious law in light of the important role that religious law plays in the Israeli legal system. And, indeed, an eminent rabbi was appointed to the first Israeli Supreme Court. Since then this exception has not been utilized.

45. The appointments of judges to the Jewish, Islamic and Druze court systems is regulated by specific Israeli statutes. The appointment to the various Christian denominations and to the Bahai courts is not, however, regulated by statue and is viewed as an internal matter of these religious groups. As to Jewish, Islamic and Druze courts, appointments are made by the President of the State, on the advice of the relevant committee – a different one for each group – that consists of a number of judges as well as other recognized religious officials in the group, along with public representatives. In each group a person to be appointed as a religious judge must be a qualified authority in the religious law of his sect. Thus, the appointment process is similar to that of the appointment of judges to the regular courts, as described above. Despite the fact that they are not necessarily qualified to be attorneys under Israeli law, they are, without doubt, professional 'jurists' in the law of their respective sects. The same would also seem to be true as to the denominations concerning which there are no governing statutory provisions. Thus, again, the appointment of non-attorneys to these courts is not a manifestation of a desire to de-professionalize adjudication in Israel, but of the result of the broad meaning of 'professionalism' in the Israeli context.

46. The one outstanding exception to the general Israeli rule of legal professionalism is that of the appointment of 'representatives of the public' to the Labour Courts, as discussed in paragraph 29.

II. End of Functions

47. Judges are appointed until mandatory retirement at age 70. However, the judicial appointments committee, discussed above is authorized to terminate a judge's appointment prior to his reaching age 70, upon the recommendation of either the Minister of Justice or the President of the Supreme Court and with the affirmative vote of at least seven of its nine members. When such a recommendation is made to the judicial appointments committee, prior to its decision it may appoint, from its members, a subcommittee to investigate the matter and report its findings and recommendations. Both the full committee and such subcommittees if appointed, must allow the judge involved an opportunity to be heard.

If the committee does determine to terminate the appointment of a judge, it also determines the pension he should receive.

Pursuant to a 2006 amendment to the Courts' Law, retired judges may be appointed as 'associate judges' in a court not higher than that in which they have served, for a period up to four years or age 75, whichever is earlier. Such an associate judge is a judge in all respects except that he may serve part-time. This amendment serves to wrestle the ongoing case backlog problem in the lower courts.

III. Discipline

48. In addition, judges are subject to disciplinary proceedings, which may be initiated by the Minister of Justice, acting either on his own initiative or on the basis of a complaint presented to him. The initiation of such disciplinary proceedings are set forth in the Courts Law as:

(1) improper behaviour in the discharge of official duties;
(2) conduct unbecoming a judge;
(3) conviction of a criminal offence involving moral turpitude; and
(4) a finding by the judicial appointments committee that the judge's appointment was unlawfully obtained.

Upon the filing of such a disciplinary complaint by the Minister of Justice, the President of the Supreme Court appoints a disciplinary panel of either five judges (of whom three must be judges or retired judges of the Supreme Court), or of three judges (of whom two are judges or retired judges of the Supreme Court). In practice, the President of the Supreme Court usually appoints himself to the panel and chairs the proceedings.

The disciplinary panel may impose any of the following five penalties:

(1) a comment on the action of the judge involved;
(2) a warning;
(3) a rebuke;
(4) transfer to another judicial position;
(5) termination of the judicial appointment, either with or without pension rights.

IV. Registrars

49. A registrar is a court official who has extensive administrative responsibilities. He, however, also has important judicial duties, with the general trend of the Rules of Civil Procedure being to expand those judicial duties. In general, today a registrar has authority to hear and determine almost all matters except the oral trial on the merits of the case.

Thus, for example, a registrar may preside, and indeed in practice generally does, over expedited judgment proceedings and may give judgments on these proceedings, even if, it would seem, it is necessary for him to hear evidence in order to do so.

50. In contrast to judges who are appointed by the President of the State on the recommendation of a select committee as discussed above registrars are appointed in a less formal process. A registrar may be appointed to the Supreme Court, the District Court and the Magistrates' Court.

These appointments are made by the President of the Supreme Court, with the approval of the Minister of Justice, without the need for any decision of a select committee.

However, the law requires that all those appointed registrars either already be Magistrates' Court judges or possess the minimal professional requirements necessary for appointment as a judge of the Magistrate's Court. In practice, all registrars of the District Court are appointed from sitting judges of the Magistrates' Courts and continue to have the status of judges of the Magistrates' Courts while serving as registrars of the District Court.

51. All decisions of a registrar are subject to appeal as of right before a judge. These appeals are, however, relatively infrequent as the registrars generally perform well the task assigned to them. Indeed, because of their specialization in preliminary matters, including those involved in determining requests for leave to defend in expedited judgment proceedings, it is generally believed that they determine these matters better than judges who are not called upon to do so on a regular basis.

Chapter 2. The Bar

§1. Organization and Structure

52. The Bar in Israel is organized through the Chamber of Advocates, (hereinafter 'The Chamber') in which all recognized active lawyers must be registered members.

The Chamber of Advocates Law, 1961 provides that the Chamber is to supervise the standards and integrity of the legal profession. It is responsible, *inter alia*, for admission to the profession as well as disciplinary matters concerning lawyers.

The Chamber is a corporation and, as such has the capacity to enter into contracts, be possessed of legal rights and obligations, perform legal acts, etc. As a public body, it is subject to the oversight of the State Comptroller.

In general, the Chamber both represents the members of the legal profession in relation to the State and its organs and the general public, and engages in internal activities within the profession for the benefit of its members.

Thus, for example, as discussed in paragraph 44, it has specific statutory authority to appoint two members of the judicial appointments committee. In addition, it is authorized to present its views on draft statutes concerning the courts, and their procedures, to provide legal aid for persons of limited means, to appoint arbitrators or act itself as arbitrator, etc.

In terms of the internal aspects of the profession, the Chamber acts for the professional interests of its members, through such activities as the establishment of insurance funds, pension funds and other institutions of mutual aid for its members, the promotion and participation in legal research projects, the publication of professional literature, and the organization of continuing education.

53. The Chamber comprises six organs: the National Conference, the National Council, the Central Committee, the District Committees, the National Disciplinary Tribunal and the District Disciplinary Tribunals.

The National Conference meets at irregular intervals, once a year or even once every two years. It is comprised of hundreds of delegates elected in the Chamber's general elections. Matters of particular importance to the legal profession are brought before it, for example in recent years a draft for the reform of the court system prepared by the Minister of Justice.

The National Council meets as a rule once a month and reviews suggestions for amendments and changes to the Chamber of Advocates Law 1961, and Rules pursuant to this law. It is comprised of forty-three members: the head of the Chamber, twenty members elected in the Chamber elections, sixteen representatives from the local councils and six members appointed directly by the Minister of Justice. The council elects members of the Central Committee and representatives to various statutory bodies, for example to the committee for the selection of judges.

The Central Committee is the executive organ of the Chamber. It comprises fifteen elected members; meets, as a rule, once a week; and deals with matters of professional public day-to-day importance. Many subcommittees have been established under its auspices, for example a committee responsible for law clerks, a committee of legal ethics, a committee for matters of legislation.

The District Committees are responsible both for professional and ethical matters and also cultural and social events organized by the Chamber. There are today five District Committees, that is, a committee for each of the districts in which a District Court has jurisdiction (the committee for the Tel Aviv and Central Court Districts is unified).

The Disciplinary Tribunals consist of District Tribunals and a National Tribunal acting as an appeal level for the District Disciplinary Tribunals. They are authorized to try matters referred to them by the legal ethics committee of the Chamber. We will discuss the disciplinary process in greater detail *infra*.

§2. Exercise of the Legal Profession

I. Conditions for Admission

54. Under Israeli law, anyone wishing to become a member of the legal profession must serve a clerkship following the completion of his legal education. The length of this clerkship is determined by statute. However, it has been changed quite frequently. From two years, it was reduced to one and a half years and, it is now one year. There currently exists a proposal endorsed both by the Ministry of Justice and the Chamber to lengthen it once more to a year and a half, yet the proposal has been on hold for several years. Whatever its total length, there generally are requirements of a minimum time that must be served in the office of a private advocate as distinguished from government service.

The current proposal for change in the clerkship also includes required training courses that traditionally have not been part of the Israel clerkship requirements.

At the conclusion of the clerkship, there are both written and oral examinations on Israeli law prepared and administered by the Chamber of Advocates. In order to be admitted to the Bar, a person must pass these examinations.

The Chamber of Advocates has also initiated courses in order to prepare applicants to the Bar for these examinations. While these courses are not required, the majority of clerks take them in order to prepare better for the examinations.

Passing the Bar admission is required for receiving a license to practice law. Once receiving this license, a lawyer may practice in all aspects of the profession. There is no division between barristers and solicitors in Israel. Nor is there any differentiation in training or technical qualifications between those who practise as private lawyers or those who work in the public sector, including judges.

II. Rights and Duties

55. The Chamber of Advocates Law defines the acts, which may be performed by an advocate in the scope of his profession, and prohibits any other person from performing such acts for remuneration. Only a qualified and registered advocate may represent persons who do not represent themselves before any court, tribunal, arbitrator or before a number of other institutions, for example the Execution Office and the Land Registry. Similarly, only a registered advocate may draft legal documents for another person including representing him in negotiations leading to the drafting of such documents, and may give legal advice and legal opinions.

There are a few minor exceptions to the above rule concerning the exclusive representation of parties in court only by a registered advocate. The first exception concerns the religious courts. Under Israeli law, any registered lawyer is also qualified to practice before the religious courts. However, other authorized persons may also represent parties before these courts. It should be noted, however, that while these 'pleaders', as they are called, who may represent parties before the religious courts, are not necessarily registered advocates, they are professionals in terms of the religious law and court system involved. They must attend certain courses of higher religious learning and pass professional examinations in the relevant religious law.

Two other exceptions to the above rule are found in the special provisions concerning the Labour Courts and the Small Claims Courts.

Section 34 of the Labour Courts Law, 1969 provides that 'a party may be represented before a [Labour] Court by a person designated for that purpose by an employees' or employers' organization of which that party is a member', provided that the party has specifically authorized such representation.

Similarly, section 63 of the Court Law [Consolidated Version], 1984 provides that in the Small Claims Courts 'a party may, with leave of court, be represented by an organization designated for this purpose by the Minister of Justice ... '. Pursuant to this provision, the Israeli Consumers Council has been designated by the Minister as an organization to represent parties in the Small Claims Courts.

However, the significance of such a right of 'representation' by organizations (labour union, management associations or consumer organizations) should not be exaggerated.

In any event, these organizations could provide legal counsel, i.e., a licensed lawyer, to a party without these specific statutory 'representation' rights. Moreover, they could also give informal advice as, indeed, is done both by labour unions and by the Consumers Council without these specific statutory provisions.

This probably accounts for the fact that these representation provisions are not extensively used. Statistics for the regional Labour Courts as to individual employee claims indicate that representation of the plaintiff employee by a union representative occurs in a very small per cent of the claims.

Even more striking is the fact that, as distinguished from the very useful services provided by the Israeli Consumer Council providing help to individual parties in filing claims by having people experienced in this regard, including law students, available at the small claims courts to provide advice, we know of no instance in which the Israeli Consumer Council has 'represented' a party in the Small Claims Court pursuant to section 63 of the Courts Law.

56. We should emphasize that we have been discussing herein the exclusive *representation* rights of lawyers under Israeli law. Of course, a person need not be represented at all and may act on his own.

Indeed, a basic principle of Israeli law is that a competent adult may always represent himself in adjudicative proceedings, i.e., he need not be represented by counsel.

To this basic principle, there are no exceptions. Of course, if the person involved is not a competent adult, but a minor or a legally incompetent individual, he must be represented by another, such as a general guardian or guardian *ad litem*, a next friend, etc. More significant, however, is the fact that despite this unqualified absolute legal right of a competent adult to represent himself in all adjudicative proceedings, as a practical matter it is most difficult for laymen to conduct their own cases in court. Thus, in practice almost all parties to litigation are represented by attorneys.

The only two major exceptions to this practice are that of Small Claims Courts and individual employee claims brought in the Labour Courts. These courts operate informally and by simplified procedures, so that it is expected that a layman should be able to represent himself, without the aid of a lawyer.

Indeed, as discussed *supra* in paragraph 31, as to Small Claims Courts the Israeli law goes even further and actually restricts the basic right of parties to be represented by lawyers even if they so desire. In these courts, a party may only be represented by an attorney (or by an organization as described above) by leave of court and for particular reasons to be noted. As such, it represents the only exception in Israeli law to the basic right of parties in a civil proceeding to be represented by counsel of their choice, provided, of course, that such counsel is a qualified and registered attorney.

57. Rules regarding professional ethics are laid down in the Chamber of Advocates Law, 1961 and in the Regulations enacted in accordance with that Law. The Law and Regulations provide that an advocate must preserve the honour of his profession and refrain from doing any act liable to affect it adversely. In the performance of his duties, the advocate must act faithfully for the good of his client and must assist the court in achieving justice. For example, an advocate may not reveal any fact brought to his knowledge by his client except where required in legal proceedings or investigations, and may not tape-record any discussion with his client or with another lawyer without their knowledge. An advocate may not represent a party in legal proceedings if he is to be a witness for that party in the proceedings. Whilst an advocate may meet with witnesses about to give evidence for his own client's claim, he may not meet with witnesses about to give evidence for the opposing party, except with the prior approval of that party or his advocate.

The Regulations lay down rules ensuring good relations not only between an advocate and the opposing party but also amongst the advocates themselves. Where the opposing party is represented by an advocate, an advocate must always approach the opposing party's advocate and not the opposing party itself. An advocate may not deal with a matter which he knows is in the care of another lawyer without the other lawyer's written consent, and the other lawyer may not refuse to give such consent unless the client is in his debt and has not fulfilled the conditions laid down in the Regulations.

An advocate may not advertise himself as practicing as a lawyer. He may not, by himself or by means of another person, solicit any person to give him professional work.

An advocate must indicate his profession by means of the title 'advocate' or by a corresponding title in another language, and not by any other title. He may not practice in his profession in partnership with a person who is not an advocate, nor share his income with any such person in consideration for services or assistance to his business from that person. An advocate may not employ in his office, without permission from the Chamber, a person whose membership in the Chamber is currently suspended or a person who has been expelled from the Chamber.

There are a number of occupations which advocates are prohibited from practicing or restricted from doing so. Notable amongst these is the occupation of accountancy. Currently, a person may obtain both professional titles but is prohibited from offering both professional services to the same client.

58. Attorney's fees are not set by law. Rather they are a matter of agreement between attorney and client. Until recently there existed a minimum fee schedule set by the Chamber of Advocates pursuant to legislative authority. However, this has now been abolished.

III. Discipline

59. The acts or omissions constituting disciplinary offences are defined in the Chamber of Advocates Law, 1961 and the Law further lays down that an advocate is answerable before the Disciplinary Tribunals of the Chamber for a disciplinary offence even if it was committed abroad. The penalties the Disciplinary Tribunal may impose on a person convicted of a disciplinary offence are:

(1) a warning;
(2) a reprimand;
(3) a fine (not exceeding a stated sum);
(4) suspension for a period not exceeding ten years;
(5) expulsion from the Chamber.

Where a punishment of suspension or expulsion has been imposed, the decision, including the name of the convicted advocate, must be published.

A Disciplinary Tribunal may also, upon the application of an accuser, impose upon the advocate one of the penalties listed above if he has been convicted by a final judgment in an ordinary court (or in an army court) of a criminal offence involving moral turpitude.

The National Disciplinary Tribunal acts as an appellate level from the District Disciplinary Tribunals. Both the accused and the accuser may appeal to the National Tribunal, and so may the Attorney General, even if he was not an accuser. The parties may lodge a further appeal against a conviction by the National Tribunal to the Supreme Court.

Chapter 3. The Attorney General

60. The Attorney General of Israel is a unique institution. He is appointed to his position by the Government on the recommendation of the Minister of Justice. While technically a part of the Ministry of Justice, the Attorney General, in performing the functions entrusted to him, is independent of the Minister of Justice. The latter, the Minister of Justice, is a political figure and member of the Government. While in recent years the practice has developed of the Attorney General attending meetings of the Government, he is not a member of the Government and is not a political figure.

Attorneys General have generally been chosen from the highest ranks of the legal profession – and following their tenure as Attorney General have in some cases been appointed to the Israeli Supreme Court. (Two recent Presidents of the Supreme Court, Meir Shamgar and Aharon Barak were former Attorneys General). Thus, the Attorney General has traditionally been a personality of great stature, a fact that has contributed to his independence.

61. A full description of the unique role of the Attorney General in the Israeli legal system is beyond the role of this chapter. However, in brief, the Attorney General has the following four primary roles:

(1) He is the legal advisor to the Government. This may be viewed as his most important role. Indeed, while the accepted English title of his position is 'Attorney General', the Hebrew title is properly translated at 'Legal Advisor to the Government'. This role is most important in the field of public law and the tradition has developed such that the Attorney General often performs more the role of final arbitrator rather than that of mere advisor concerning important public legal issues. In this role, the Attorney General has been said to express the 'Rule of Law' in Israel.
(2) The Attorney General's office is, within the Ministry of Justice, responsible for the drafting of all legislation.
(3) The Attorney General is the head of the criminal prosecuting authority.
(4) The Attorney General also plays a very significant role in non-criminal litigation. In this regard, he, or his representative, is authorized to represent the State in all proceedings, including those in the High Court of Justice, to which the State, or its subsidiary organs such as municipalities or governmental corporation, is a party.

In addition, section 1 of the Procedure (Appearance of the Attorney General) Ordinance authorizes the Attorney General or his representative to appear and to be heard in proceedings to which the State is not a party if this is necessary in order to protect the public interest. In construing the section, the courts have held that the Attorney General is not a party when he appears in such circumstances.

Thus, his appearance in a case does not present him with a right to appeal. However, it has been held that he is entitled to present evidence and when he intends to do so he should file papers similar to pleadings so as to allow the parties to prepare properly.[6]

There is no requirement in Israel that a representative of the Attorney General be in attendance at civil trials in which the State is not a party. Thus, the use of the Ordinance is generally a result of the initiative of a party in notifying the Attorney General's office or of an invitation by the court.

There are, however, a few situations in which notice of civil matters must be provided to the Attorney General. Thus, notice of almost every petition matters of probate must be given to the Attorney General through the office of the Administrator General. In addition, section 20 of the Standard Contracts Law 1982 requires the court to notify the Attorney General – and thus provide him with an opportunity to appear pursuant to the Ordinance – if in a civil action between a supplier and customer it is argued that a restrictive clause is invalid.

6. *The Russian Ecclesiastical Mission in Jerusalem v. The Attorney General*, 31 (3) P.D. 317 (1977). For a critical analysis of this decision, see S. Ginossar, *The Role of the Attorney General in Civil Litigation*, 14 Isr. L. Rev. 237 (1979).

Part II. Jurisdiction

Chapter 1. Domestic Jurisdiction

§1. Subject Matter Jurisdiction

I. Basic Principles

62. As we have already mentioned, Israel contains a number of judicial systems. In this section, we will discuss the allocation of jurisdiction both among those systems and within each of them.

A. The General Court System

63. At the trial level, the general court system consists of the Magistrates' Courts and the District Courts, with the Supreme Court having appellate jurisdiction.

The jurisdiction of the general courts is residual as to the other court systems, and the jurisdiction of the District Court as a first instance court is residual as to the jurisdiction of the Magistrates' Court. The remedy sought is the primary basis for the division of jurisdiction between the Magistrates' Court and the District Court at first instance.

64. The basic civil jurisdiction of the Magistrates' Courts concerning monetary claims is based on the amount in controversy; or those that can be evaluated in monetary terms. Jurisdiction as to non-monetary claims relating to real property is based on the type of remedy sought.

As to monetary claims or those that can be evaluated in monetary terms, as of this writing the Magistrates' Courts have exclusive jurisdiction up to NIS 2,500,000 (c. USD 650,000). This limit has been raised continually over the past years in excess of the inflation rate, with the avowed purpose of shifting more cases from the District Courts to the Magistrates' Courts.

It should be emphasized that the above sum relates to the value of the subject matter and does not necessarily refer to an amount of money. Thus, the statement of claim must include the value of the subject matter of the action, so far as it is determinable. In a claim for damages for personal injury, however, the above does not apply. The statement of claim in such a case that does not specify the amount claimed – where the claim is filed in the Magistrates' Court, it is regarded as limited to an amount not exceeding the amount over which the Magistrates' Court has jurisdiction; where the claim is filed in the District Court, it is regarded as a claim for an amount exceeding the said amount.

Due to the high inflation experienced in Israel in the past years, unpaid sums may be increased over time by the addition of cost of living adjustments or interest, either by contractual agreement or by judicial decision. For purposes of determining the jurisdictional limits, the determining date is that of the filing of the action. All such additional sums that have accrued to that date are part of the monetary sum for jurisdictional purposes; those that accrue after that date are not. Reimbursement of costs of the litigation, which are normally paid to the prevailing party, are not part of the value of the subject matter for purposes of jurisdiction.

65. Both the Small Claims Courts and the Family Courts are divisions of the Magistrates' Courts. As of this writing, the Small Claims Courts have jurisdiction for monetary claims up to NIS 33,200, as well as claims for the exchange or repair of an item, or the cancellation of a transaction, when the value of the item, repair or transaction does not exceed the above sum. Only individuals, not corporations, may file claims in the Small Claims Court. Furthermore, the Small Claims Court may refer the case to the regular Magistrates' Court if the claim was filed by a plaintiff who has filed more than five claims that year in the Small Claims Court.

The Small Claims Courts have no exclusive jurisdiction; all of the above-stated jurisdiction is concurrent. Thus, a plaintiff has a free choice between filing a claim, which is within the jurisdiction of the Small Claims Court in such a court or in a regular Magistrates' Court. Moreover, even after a claim has been filed in a Small Claims Court, the judge has discretion to transfer it to the regular Magistrates' Court.

In contrast, the Family Courts, which are staffed by Magistrates' Court judges especially appointed to the Family Courts, have exclusive jurisdiction over all family disputes that are determined in the general court system, regardless of the matter in controversy. Such disputes include traditional family law matters such as custody and adoption of children, and support for wives and children, as well as matters of inheritance and estates. They also include other types of disputes, such as ordinary tort and contract actions, where the parties are family members, i.e., spouses, parents, including parents-in-law, children, siblings, including spouses of siblings and grandchildren. In addition, while these courts do not have criminal jurisdiction as such, they do have jurisdiction to enforce the civil law aspects, such as the issuance of restraining orders, of family violence.

As stated above, the judges in these courts are chosen and trained especially to deal with sensitive matters involving the family. They are also aided by staffs of social workers. These courts are relatively new, having been established by statute only in 1995, yet they have been well received both by the legal profession and the public and seem to be quite successful.

66. The District Courts have residual jurisdiction, both as to the Magistrates' Courts and as to courts and tribunals not included in the group of general courts. Regarding the Magistrates' Courts, the District Court is authorized to deal with any case beyond the jurisdiction of the Magistrates' Court, i.e., claims in which the amount requested or its equivalent exceeds NIS 2,500,000 on the day the claim is filed. As to claims dealing with land, the District Court deals mainly with long-term leases or ownership.

Any cases not involving land and incapable of being assigned a monetary value are also within the exclusive jurisdiction of the District Courts vis-à-vis the Magistrates' Courts.

There are also numerous specific statutes which provide for exclusive jurisdiction of the District Courts. These include such matters as actions to affirm or set aside arbitration decrees, Corporate Law and Securities Law matters, bankruptcy and dissolution of corporations and partnerships.

As noted above in paragraph 11, starting in 2001, special divisions of the District Courts, designated Administrative Courts, adjudicate some of the less important administrative law matters which were previously adjudicated in the High Court of Justice, as described in paragraph 74, *infra*.

B. Religious Courts

67. The religious court system includes the regional Rabbinical Courts and the High Rabbinic Court of Appeal, authorized to deal with cases involving Jews; also Muslim, Christian and Druze courts, as first instance and courts of appeal. The system deals with matters of personal status, following the Ottoman legal system, which adopted the system of personal law regarding personal status. The Israeli legislature adopted and expanded the existing arrangement.

68. The Rabbinic Courts are the religious courts for Jews, who represent about 82% of the population of Israel. They have exclusive jurisdiction as to matters of marriage and divorce and matters pendent to divorce proceedings, where both members of the couple are Jewish, both are citizens or permanent residents of Israel, and both – or at least the defendant – are physically in the country.

Matters of marriage include declarations as to the legal validity of a marriage, determining a person's eligibility to marry and determining the consequences of a marriage when the consequences are closely related to religious law. Matters of divorce include determining the validity of a divorce, actions for divorce, as well as actions involving the enforcement of divorce agreements.

Matters pendent to divorce proceedings include matters which are inherently pendent to divorce proceedings, such as the rights of each of the parties in common property, or matters which are in fact appended to the divorce proceedings at the initiative of one of the parties and as to which a determination is necessary in order to resolve the conflict between the parties, for example, maintenance claims and determining the custody of children.

When a husband sues for divorce and seeks to append a related matter such as the determination of maintenance for his wife and children, it is required that both the divorce action and the appending of the related matter be done honestly and in good faith and that the Rabbinic Court actually issue the divorce judgment. However, when a wife sues for divorce and seeks to append similar related actions, the law does not impose on her the same type of restrictions in this regard as are imposed on the husband. The primary reason for this difference is the basic option given to the wife to file an independent action for maintenance either in the regular District Courts or in the Rabbinic Courts.

As this last point indicates, the Rabbinic Courts also have concurrent jurisdiction with the District Courts concerning maintenance, custody, adoption and inheritance. Unless the matter is appended to a divorce claim as described above, a wife has the option of bringing a maintenance action either in the District Court or the Rabbinic Courts, assuming, of course, that both parties are Jewish. As to custody, adoption and inheritance matters, the Rabbinic Courts only have jurisdiction if all the parties consent thereto. In the absence of such consent, the exclusive jurisdiction in these matters is, as discussed above, in the District Courts.

69. The Shariya courts serve Muslims who are Israeli citizens or whose country of origin impose Muslim law on matters of personal status. The jurisdiction of these courts is more extensive than the other religious courts, as a result of the Ottoman origins of the system of personal law. The Shariya courts have exclusive jurisdiction over *all* matters of personal status – defined as including debts of orphans' property, custody, annulment of and ineligibility for marriage, absent persons, marriage and divorce, dowry, maintenance, parenthood and raising children. Regarding matters of adoption and inheritance that have been explicitly dealt with by the Israeli legislature, the Shariya court can exercise jurisdiction only upon written agreement of the parties.

70. Druze Courts were created by the Israeli legislature. They have exclusive jurisdiction in matters of marriage and divorce of the Druze in Israel, both citizens and non-citizen residents. With the agreement of all parties, they also may adjudicate matters of alimony, maintenance, custody, legitimacy of minors, adoption and inheritance.

71. Finally, nine Christian communities have courts in Israel: Greek Catholic, Malakhite, Maronite, Syrian Orthodox, Greek-Orthodox, Catholic, Gregorian-Armenian, Catholic-Armenian, Syrian Catholic and Casadit Uniatit. The Bahai community also has a court in Israel.

These courts have exclusive jurisdiction over Israeli citizens who are members of the respective communities in matters of marriage, divorce and alimony. With agreement of all parties, they also may adjudicate matters of maintenance, legitimacy of minors, custody, adoption and inheritance.

C. The Labour Courts

72. The regional Labour Courts have exclusive jurisdiction in the following matters:

(1) individual disputes between an employee and employer arising from the employment relationship;

(2) disputes between the parties to a special collective labour agreement, i.e., one covering only one enterprise or employer, as to any matter arising from such agreement;
(3) disputes between retirement funds and their members or the employers of their members;
(4) certain disputes concerning the National Insurance Institute, as well as the enforcement of certain, specific labour and social welfare laws.

73. The national Labour Court has exclusive, original jurisdiction as to disputes between parties to a general collective agreement, i.e., one that is nationwide in scope or that covers a significant portion of the country, or several enterprises or employers in the same industry, as to any matter arising from such agreement; and disputes among labour unions or employer associations. It also has appellate jurisdiction over the regional Labour Courts.

D. The High Court of Justice

74. As discussed in the last chapter, the Israeli Supreme Court, i.e., the highest court in the general court system which usually sits in that system as an appellate court, also sits as a Court of First Instance and, in this capacity, is designated the High Court of Justice.

The High Court of Justice has jurisdiction to award a remedy in matters beyond the jurisdiction of other courts and as to which it, the High Court of Justice, sees a need to intervene in the interests of justice. The High Court of Justice is, essentially, an administrative court, authorized to review administrative and judicial authorities.

A full analysis of the jurisdiction and authority of the High Court of Justice would go well beyond the purposes of this monograph. However, we will describe the working of the Court, in brief, according to the following three subjects:

(1) institutions subject to the review of the High Court of Justice;
(2) matters treated by the Court; and
(3) remedies awarded by it.

The institutions subject to the review of the High Court of Justice are the State's administrative authorities and judicial tribunals. The administrative authorities are State authorities, local authorities and their officials, and other institutions fulfilling a public function as defined by law. The judicial tribunals reviewed are courts of law and institutions and persons fulfilling judicial or quasi-judicial functions, as defined by law.

The matters treated by the High Court of Justice are stated by statute to be those matters that are not within the jurisdiction of any other judicial tribunal. However, it has been necessary to qualify this generalization, since as we have discussed above, the District Courts also have statutorily based residual jurisdiction.

Thus, the case law has qualified the general grant of jurisdiction to the High Court of Justice by the following criteria. First, in general, issues of public law are in the domain of the High Court of Justice, while private law is for the general courts. Equally, when the true grounds of the dispute are administrative, the dispute is for the High Court of Justice, whereas if the grounds stem from private law, the regular courts should determine the matter. Finally, since the High Court of Justice does not employ usual Israeli procedure, which is based primarily on oral evidence, but rather relies on written affidavits as to factual matters, the Court will decline jurisdiction where the matter is not suitable for such proceedings.

As discussed above in paragraph 66, as of 21 January 2001 some of the administrative law jurisdiction of the High Court of Justice have been transferred to the new Administrative Law Divisions of the District Courts, in which they are adjudicated pursuant to the Rules of Procedure of the Administrative Tribunals, 2000.

The remedies that the High Court of Justice is authorized to award are also stated in most general terms as those required in the interest of justice. However, without thereby limiting this general power, a number of specific remedies are also explicitly set forth in the designated powers of the High Court of Justice. These include ordering the release of persons unlawfully arrested or detained; ordering administrative authorities to act or to refrain from acting as the law requires; ordering certain types of judicial tribunals, such as the Labour Courts to adjudicate or refrain from adjudicating specific matters and cancelling 'unlawful' decisions of such tribunals. In this last situation the term 'unlawful' has been given a more restrictive interpretation than it has in regard to administrative tribunals. Thus, for example, a mistaken decision of the Labour Court, either mistaken as to law or as to fact, is not *ipso facto* 'unlawful'. Rather it must be a substantial mistake of law which justice requires rectification. This last point emphasizes that the review of the High Court of Justice over special judicial systems, such as the Labour Courts, is not that of appellate review, but rather of a more limited nature which may, perhaps, be compared to cassation, as distinguished from appeal.

This is also true indeed even more so, as to the religious courts. Here again, the High Court of Justice is specifically authorized to order a religious court to determine a matter within its jurisdiction, as well as to cancel a determination made without jurisdiction. It should be noted that the expression 'without jurisdiction' is clearly narrower that of 'unlawful'.

Of course, lack of jurisdiction may be extended to include such things as 'clear errors of law' and, indeed, in some cases the High Court of Justice has done so. Yet, in general, as we have stated above, the difference in terminology does reflect a lesser tendency of the High Court of Justice to intervene in decisions of the religious courts than in those of the Labour Courts.

In both cases, however, it intervenes less than in matters concerning administrative bodies.

II. Main Claims and Ancillary Claims

75. Every procedural system in which subject matter jurisdiction is allocated among different courts based on the type of claim involved must attempt to deal with the situation in which multiple claims and counterclaims may arise out of the same transaction or occurrence.

In such situations, procedural efficiency would seem to require that such claims at least be allowed, if not required, to be litigated together in one judicial proceeding. This would seem to be true not only as to multiple claims between the same two litigants but also as to multi-party transactions or occurrences.

Moreover, even where multiple claims between the same parties do not arise out of the same transaction or occurrence there may be social advantage in allowing the parties involved to resolve finally all their mutual disputes in one judicial proceeding.

Moreover, as to defendants, the ability to file a counterclaim, even one completely unrelated to the plaintiff's claim, may be most important for two reasons. First, it may provide a basis for international jurisdiction over the plaintiff that might otherwise be lacking. Second, it may allow the setoff of judgments, thereby allowing the defendant to avoid a situation in which he must first pay the plaintiff's judgment against him and then seek to collect his own judgment from the plaintiff.

Yet the desires for procedural and dispute resolution efficiency may be frustrated by the rules of subject matter jurisdiction which, prima facie, at least may require that such claims be tried in separate courts.

This problem is even more aggravated in Israeli procedure due to the rules of subject matter jurisdiction described above concerning the general courts whereby jurisdiction is frequently allocated between the Magistrates' Courts and the District Courts not based on the general claim involved, but rather on the specific remedy sought. Thus, these rules would seem to require that even when multiple remedies arise from the same claim, the disparate remedies would have to be sought in different courts.

Thus, for example, an alleged breach of a complex land transaction may involve litigation seeking possession of the land in dispute (a remedy in the jurisdiction of the Magistrates' Courts), a declaration as to the ownership of the land (a remedy in the jurisdiction of the District Court), and damages for breach of the contract (a remedy that could be either in the Magistrates' Courts or the District Courts depending on the amount in controversy).

76. Both Israeli case law and legislation have attempted to deal with these problems. In terms of multiple remedies arising from the same claim, the major development has been in case law.

Thus, if all remedies are non-monetary, the rule developed by the courts is that jurisdiction is determined by the 'primary' remedy, with the court thus seized with jurisdiction being thereby empowered also to deal with the 'ancillary' remedy.

This doctrine of primary-ancillary remedies greatly helps to overcome the need to split a multiple remedy claim between different courts that the jurisdictional rules would otherwise require. However, it does not present a complete solution to the problem.

First, it is often most difficult to determine which remedy is primary and which ancillary. Moreover, the implication of the Israeli case law in this area is that this determination may be effected heavily by the way the complaint is drafted. As we will discuss later in this chapter, such a situation is contrary to the basic principle that subject matter jurisdiction is a matter of legislative policy as to which the litigants have no right of determination.

Furthermore, for reasons more historic than logical, the principle of 'primary-ancillary' remedies is not applied when one of the remedies is monetary and the other non-monetary. In such a situation, the rule is that the court in which the complaint is filed must have independent subject matter jurisdiction as to both the monetary and the non-monetary remedies.

This situation forces litigants not infrequently, to split complaints for relief which should be brought as one since they arise out of the same transaction or occurrence. Thus, for example, in a case of continuing trespass or private nuisance, where the damages thus far incurred are in excess of the jurisdictional ceiling of the Magistrates' Court, the plaintiff must split his action and bring his complaint to cease the trespass or private nuisance in the Magistrates' Court while filing his suit for damages in the District Court.

77. As to multiple claims, as distinguished from multiple remedies arising from one claim, historically the basic rule as to non-monetary claims has been that the court must be independently seized of jurisdiction as to each claim even if they are filed by the same plaintiff and arise out of the same transaction or occurrence.

Recent case law has, however, cast some doubt on this historic position, at least as concerns venue.[7] Where all the claims are monetary, the rules have always allowed their joinder in one court. The Rules of Civil Procedure provide that where claims are joined by the plaintiff in one complaint, the sum of all the claims so joined determines the amount in controversy. Thus, the District Court may have jurisdiction to determine all the joined claims, whilst not one of the claims, standing alone, would be within its jurisdictional minimum, and despite the fact that there may be no connection at all between the claims except for the fact that the parties are the same.

78. The Rules of Civil Procedure do not address the question of subject matter jurisdiction as to multiple parties when all the claims involved are monetary. However, case law has determined that the same rule that applies to claims joined by a single plaintiff against a single defendant should apply also to claims joined through the joinder of plaintiffs and defendants. That is, the total amount determines the jurisdiction. It should be noted, however, that as distinguished from the joinder of claims by a single plaintiff against a single defendant, the Rules of Civil Procedure as to the joinder of parties do require a connection among the parties joined.

79. The Magistrates' Courts may entertain a counterclaim that would otherwise be within the jurisdiction of the District Courts *provided* that the original claim and the counterclaim arise out of the same transaction or occurrence.

The District Courts, in contrast, are not so limited, and may determine as counterclaims any claims that would otherwise be within the jurisdiction of the Magistrates' Courts, even if there is no connection except for the identity of the parties, between the original claim and the counterclaim.

Finally, as to the Small Claims Courts, there is yet a third solution to this problem. In these courts the defendant may not claim in a counterclaim any sum in

7. *Levi v. Poleg*, 49 (2) P.D. 731 (1995).

excess of the maximum amount of the Small Claims Court jurisdiction, even if his claim for a greater amount arises from the same transaction or occurrence as that of the plaintiff's original claim.

What then can a defendant do if he has a counterclaim in excess of the jurisdictional amount of the Small Claims Court? Here we should note that, in general, under Israeli procedure any claimant may sue on only part of a monetary claim in order to reduce it to the relevant jurisdictional amount. For example, a plaintiff who has a monetary claim for NIS 2,600,000 may choose to sue only for NIS 2,500,000 in order to bring his claim within the jurisdictional limits of the Magistrates' Courts. Similarly, a plaintiff who has a claim in excess of the jurisdictional limit of the Small Claims Court may choose to sue only up to jurisdictional limit in a Small Claims Court.

In these examples, the plaintiff may achieve his goal of suing in a Magistrates' Court or a Small Claims Court. However, in so doing he thereby waives his right to sue on the remainder of his claim.

The rule as to counterclaims in Small Claims Courts provides for an exception to this general rule. That is, a defendant who chooses to file a counterclaim in a Small Claims Court may do so up to the jurisdictional limit of that court *without* thereby waiving his right to sue on the remainder of his claim in the appropriate court.

Thus, we have here three different solutions, adopted by the same legislator, to the problem of balancing the legislator's desire to protect the division of exclusive subject matter jurisdiction, which he has determined, with the need to allow counterclaims for purposes of judicial efficiency and fairness to the defendants.

These three solutions reflect a different balance as to each type of court, which difference is a product of the legislator's desire, or lack thereof, to protect the exclusive jurisdiction involved.

Thus, in the division of jurisdiction between the Magistrates' Courts and the District Courts, the legislator does not put much value, if any, on the protection of the exclusive jurisdiction of the Magistrates' Courts. Therefore, any claim in the exclusive jurisdiction of the Magistrates' Courts may be filed in a District Court even if there is no connection whatsoever between the counterclaim and the primary claim, except for the identity of the parties. This lack of legislative concern with the protection of Magistrates' Courts jurisdiction from encroachment by the District Court is also reflected in the rules discussed above as to the joinder of monetary claims and parties.

However, the legislator is interested in protecting the exclusive jurisdiction of the District Courts. Thus, a claim that would ordinarily be within the exclusive jurisdiction of the District Courts can be filed as a counterclaim in a Magistrates' Court only where there is clear judicial efficiency attained by so doing, that being in a case where the primary claim and the counterclaim arise from the same transaction or occurrence. Otherwise, the exclusive jurisdiction of the District Court prevails over the interests of the defendant in filing a counterclaim in the Magistrates' Court.

Finally, in this regard, because of the special nature of the proceedings in the Small Claims Courts, the legislator does not want these courts to dispose of any matters in excess of their small jurisdictional amount. Thus, they may not entertain counterclaims in excess of this amount even if the claim and the counterclaim arise out of the same transaction or occurrence. However, the legislator did not want to prevent a defendant entirely from enjoying the benefits of being able to file a counterclaim where his claim is in excess of the jurisdictional amount of the Small Claims Court. Thus, the Law allows him to counterclaim up to the maximum amount of the Small Claims Court jurisdiction, while not, thereby relinquishing the right to sue for the excess in an appropriate court if his claim exceeds that amount. In doing so, the legislator protected absolutely the jurisdictional limit of the Small Claims Court. In order to do so, however, he felt compelled to waive the usual prohibition against splitting claims. We should note also that the required result of this compromise is that in a later suit on the excess of the defendant's claim, the issues determined in the Small Claims Court action would have no preclusive effect whatsoever.

80. Another aspect of ancillary jurisdiction is found in section 76 of the Courts Law [Consolidated Version], 1984, providing a court with pendent jurisdiction to determine incidental questions arising from the main issue and necessary for its determination, even if such incidental issues are presumptively within the exclusive jurisdiction of another court. Thus, the jurisdiction of the Magistrates' Court is expanded such that it is not limited only to possession, use or partition of land, but it may also determine other matters concerning land, including title. Similarly, the jurisdiction of the District Court is expanded to include issues, which would not otherwise be within its jurisdiction. It may even determine matters of marriage and divorce which are within the exclusive jurisdiction of the religious courts.

Two examples may serve to illustrate the matter. An action to eject an alleged trespasser from the plaintiff's land involves possession of land and thus is in the exclusive jurisdiction of the Magistrates' Courts. What happens, however, if the defendant alleges that he, not the plaintiff, is the true owner of the land. Ownership of land, as distinguished from its possession, is presumptively within the exclusive jurisdiction of the District Courts.

In another case, an action for wrongful death is brought in a District Court by the plaintiff who alleges that she is the widow of the decedent. The defendant argues, however, that the plaintiff was never legally married to the decedent under the appropriate religious law of the parties and thus she has no capacity to sue as his widow. The validity of the marriage is, of course, presumptively within the exclusive jurisdiction of the appropriate religious court.

Prior to the enactment of the predecessor to section 76 in the Courts' Law, 1957, in both of the above examples, upon the raising of the defences, the actions in the Magistrates' Court and the District Court respectively would have been stayed until the relevant court of exclusive jurisdiction, i.e., the District Court as to the ownership of the land and the religious court as to the validity of the marriage, determined the validity of the defence in question.

Providing pendent jurisdiction as to these 'incidental' issues raised by the defence was the legislative response to this obviously inefficient and unsatisfactory situation. Thus, pursuant to this pendent jurisdiction, in the two examples above, the Magistrates' Court would determine ownership of the land and the District Court the validity of the marriage, both 'incidental' to the basic jurisdiction of these courts. The term 'incidental' here is, of course, a word of art, referring to the fact that the 'issue' involved is not itself within the jurisdiction of the court in question and the court's only authority to determine it is because such issue is incidental to the court's determination of the main issue, i.e., the right to possess the land which derives from its 'ownership' or the right to receive damages for wrongful death of the plaintiff's 'husband'. By no means is the issue necessarily 'incidental' in the sense of being of minor significance. Indeed, in the example of the Magistrates' Court ejectment action, ownership of the disputed land is the central issue in the case.

Finally as to the meaning of pendent jurisdiction, it should be emphasized that the jurisdiction involved is not as to claims or remedies, but as to *issues*. Thus, even though the Israeli rules of subject matter jurisdiction, as discussed above, are heavily dependent on the remedy sought by the plaintiff, lurking behind the system is the concept that the remedies are intimately involved with the determination of certain issues, e.g., ownership of land or the validity of a marriage, which issues are presumptively within the exclusive jurisdiction of specific courts.

In extending to other courts the authority to determine such issues 'incidentally', the legislator was still concerned to protect the court that had the heretofore exclusive jurisdiction as to such issues. It did so by limiting the effect of a court's decision on an incidental issue pursuant to this pendent jurisdiction only to the case before it.

That is, it limited the normal res judicata issue preclusion effect that stems from the decision of issues by the courts under Israeli law so as to protect the court of exclusive jurisdiction.

It should be noted that case law has ruled that the test for exclusive jurisdiction within the context of section 76 is jurisdiction pursuant to subjects in issue and not pursuant to the sum of the claim. Hence, the fact that the District Court has jurisdiction over claims above NIS 2,500,000 does not mean that it has 'exclusive' jurisdiction over such matters for purposes of the pendent jurisdiction rules. For example, a decision of the Magistrates' Court in an action for interest, in which the loan, which is the source of the interest, was negated, will preclude the lender in an action for the loan (the capital) in a District Court. The jurisdiction of the District Court over such an action would only be due to the sum of the claim and thus would not be exclusive in the above sense.

The courts have further restricted the exception from issue preclusion that stems from pendent jurisdiction by holding that the exception does not apply when a second action is brought in a court other than that which is seized of the exclusive jurisdiction. Thus, in the above example of the ejectment action in the Magistrates' Court that court's decision as to the ownership of the land would have exclusive effect in a second action also brought in a Magistrates' Court. Similarly, the District Court's conclusion as to the validity of the marriage would have preclusive effect in later actions in Magistrates' Courts or District Courts.

Indeed, while the issue has not been determined definitely, there is some authority for even further limiting the effect of the limitation on issue preclusion. Under this view, there would be preclusive effect to the determination of incidental issues pursuant to pendent jurisdiction even in the court of exclusive jurisdiction, so long, as the latter court was not seized of the action in question pursuant to the basis of its exclusive jurisdiction.

To illustrate this view, let us return to the example of the ejectment action in the Magistrates' Court. In this case, there is no doubt that the Magistrates' Court decision as to the land ownership would not preclude parties in a later District Court action for a declaration as to ownership. However, what if the later action is one in the District Court not for a declaration as to ownership but rather a monetary action against the trespasser for the value of his unlawful use of the land, which monetary value is within the jurisdiction of the District Court since the claim exceeds NIS 2,500,000. In this latter case, as distinguished from the former, it can be argued that the District Court is seized of jurisdiction not through the subject or issue of its exclusive jurisdiction, but merely because of the happenstance of the sum involved and thus should be precluded.

This result is, indeed, logical. Moreover, it has the beneficial effect of limiting the exception to issue preclusion, thereby diminishing the possibility of conflicting judgments as to issues such as the ownership of land. Such conflicting judgments may present very serious problems, both theoretical and practical, concerning the continued validity and effect of the first judgment.

Yet it also has a major detriment: it allows the manipulation of the claim presented to the court of exclusive jurisdiction so as to achieve preclusion or not according to the will of the plaintiff. In the example given above, if the Magistrates' Court decision as to ownership was favourable to the plaintiff, he will choose not to bring an action in the District court for a declaration as to ownership, but rather only one for monetary relief. This way the Magistrates' Court decision will be preclusive in the District Court. However, if it was unfavourable to him, he can avoid its preclusive effect in the District Court by bringing an action for a declaration as to ownership. And, if he still wants monetary compensation, can he avoid the preclusive effect by bringing one action both for a declaration of ownership and monetary relief?

Indeed, what if he wants the preclusive effect and, therefore, only brings the monetary claim. Can the defendant force non-preclusion by counterclaiming for a declaration as to ownership?

On the other hand, a contrary rule providing for no preclusive effect on the exclusive jurisdiction court regardless of the basis of the action in that court would also allow manipulation, this time between the different courts. In the example of a monetary action for unlawful use of the property following the Magistrates' Court decision as to ownership in the ejectment action, under such a rule the plaintiff, if he so desires could achieve preclusion by tailoring his claim to the jurisdictional limit of the Magistrates' Court or achieve non-preclusion by tailoring it to that of the District Court. This, indeed, may be relatively easy to accomplish in cases of continuing trespass in which the accumulated monetary sum allegedly due is related to the timing of the litigation.

As this discussion suggests there is no good resolution to these problems created by the issue preclusion limitation to pendent jurisdiction. However, whatever the ultimate solution reached as to the relationship between the two first instance courts in the general judicial system, the Magistrates' Courts and the District Courts, it is clear that the main purpose of the issue preclusion restriction on pendent jurisdiction was not to protect the District Courts from encroachment on their exclusive jurisdiction by the Magistrates' Courts. Rather, it was to protect the religious courts from encroachment by the general courts.

In light of this, it would seem that incidental decisions pursuant to pendent jurisdiction by the general courts where the exclusive jurisdiction is within the religious courts, e.g., the validity of the marriage in the wrongful death example above, should never preclude the relevant religious court no matter how the matter reaches that court.

III. Future Directions

81. As we have seen, the Israeli judicial system is quite fractionalized and, indeed, consists of a number of separate systems. In our view, this situation is not desirable. Yet the existence of the religious court system in Israel is such a highly complex matter involving such great historical and political forces that any discussion of changes concerning them would be far beyond the confines of this book. Nor will we discuss further herein the question of the justification for the continued existence of separate Labour Courts in Israel.

82. This brings us to the general court system. For more than twenty years, there has been a reform movement in Israel concerning the general court system. The object of this reform is the unification of the two first instance courts, the Magistrates' and District Courts, into one first instance court and the creation of a new intermediate Court of Appeals between that unified first instance court and the Supreme Court.

In 1982, Prof. Stephen Goldstein first advocated the unification of the Magistrates' and District Courts into one unified first instance court; in his view, the arguments for this position still are persuasive today. Without unduly prolonging the discussion on this point, the arguments will be summarized as follows: on the one hand, there is no benefit in the continuing division of first instance jurisdiction between Magistrates' and District Courts; such division does not contribute, in practice, to the efficient use of judicial expertise and in any event is not necessary for the achievement of this goal; it does not at all result in adapting special processes to particular types of actions and does not, in practice, result in judges of lesser experience or expertise being assigned to matters of lesser importance. On the other hand, the division of jurisdiction causes actual damage to the judicial structure as it results in duplication, burdens the efficient use of judicial manpower and creates needless litigation over questions of jurisdiction. Moreover, the very attempts to alleviate these problems, such as by means of pendent jurisdiction, create new problems of their own.

We have no doubt that the current first instance split jurisdiction contributes to the inefficiency of the general court system. Moreover, the unification of the first instance courts would have the beneficial effect of permitting the creation of an intermediate Court of Appeals, which would relieve the Supreme Court of the present burden of first appeals as of right from cases tried in the District Court.

This reform movement seemed to gain impetus when, in 2001, the monetary limit of the Magistrates' Court was raised from NIS 1,000,000 to NIS 2,500,000. This one act brought a great majority of first instance cases within the jurisdiction of the Magistrates' Courts thereby also increasing the percentage of the time the District Courts spend on their appellate jurisdiction.

Finally, in this regard, in 1997 a public committee chaired by a justice of the Supreme Court (Justice Theodore Orr) recommended the immediate basic unification of the Magistrates' and District Courts into one trial court. The existing District Court, under this recommendation would still retain some very limited original jurisdiction as to a few specific types of actions, such as forced dissolution of corporations and class actions, as well as its new Administrative Law Division. However, it would become essentially an appellate court, thereby solving the problems of the split trial court jurisdiction described above, as well as relieving the Supreme Court of the burden of appeals of right.

Following the publication of these recommendations, there was great debate within legal circles as to their desirability. And, as of this writing (March 2013), it seems that the likelihood of their implementation in this respect is very low. Given that the split remains, other measures were adopted in order to tackle the court system's major challenge of case load. One measure, as was proposed by the Orr Committee, has been the development of specialized divisions within the courts, in which judges accumulated expertise in their field of specialization.

In this respect, special note should be taken to the establishment of the special Financial Division for Corporate Affairs in the District Court of Tel Aviv. Unlike other specialized divisions, which were formed through the internal organization of the court system, this Financial Division in the result of a legislative amendment from 2010 to the Law of the Courts [Consolidated Version], 1984. The amendment specifically formed the Financial Division in the District Court of Tel Aviv, which is Israel's financial centre and also hosts the only stock exchange and the Israeli Securities Authority. However, the amendment did not preclude the formation of financial divisions in other District Courts, in fact it foresees such a possibility. According to the amendment, jurisdiction in financial matters, including all matters of Corporate Law and Securities Law, with the exception of matters of proceedings of corporate dissolution and restructuring, is given exclusively to the District Courts. However, section 42D and 42E provide for the formation of a special Financial Division in the Tel Aviv District Court and further provides that the exclusive venue for such matters in this district shall be granted to the Financial Division. The Division currently consists of three judges. The amendment provides that judges deciding financial matters shall be appointed by the President of the Supreme Court, after consulting with the Presidents of the District Courts, for a term of four years that may be further prolonged. The President of the District Court is not barred from allocating non-financial cases to the judges of the Financial Division, however the central purpose of the division is to elect judges with business and financial understating and unburden their case load so as to enable them to adjudicate financial and corporate cases with the timeliness fitting the pace of the business community. The Financial Division in the Tel Aviv District Court was formed in December 2010 and is so far considered to be quite successful in fulfilling its objectives. It is however doubtful whether other District Courts will have reason to emulate this format, as most of the case load involving corporate financial matters is naturally located in the jurisdiction of Tel Aviv.

Another measure in the footsteps of the Orr Committee recommendations was the adoption of internal guidelines to judges regarding continuance requests, thereby promoting the day-to-day hearing of cases. Judges have recently called on the legislature to establish a Court of Appeals as a fourth instance between the District Court and the Supreme Court in order to alleviate the Supreme Court's burdensome case load of civil and criminal appeals, however to date this call remains unanswered.

As with the guidelines regarding requests for continuance, it seems most of the proposals for change in the general court system to date are focused on surmounting the case load problem and increasing the efficiency of the courts. For example, in 2012 the Minister of Justice proposed a bill enabling the Presidents of the Magistrates Courts to compel plaintiffs who filed claims within the subject matter jurisdiction of the Magistrates Court to resolve their dispute by compelled arbitration held before an appointed attorney. The proposal was met with harsh criticism, including that of the President of the Supreme Court, for several reasons. First, the proposed bill contradicts the fundamental consensual idea of arbitration. See Part X, *infra*. Second, it imposes a private dispute resolution mechanism on a party who particularly sought to resolve a dispute before a State court. We doubt whether the proposed bill will be legislated as it is, or at all. However, this proposal stands as an illustration of the magnitude of the burden on the Israeli general court system and the length to which administrative, judicial and political decision makers may be willing to go in order to relieve this burden.

§2. VENUE (TERRITORIAL JURISDICTION)

I. Basic Principles

83. The State of Israel is divided into six judicial districts for purposes of venue or territorial jurisdiction. Each district comprises one District Court and a number of Magistrates' Courts. The venue of the Magistrates' Courts is the same as that of the District Courts, and a plaintiff filing an action in a Magistrates' Court may choose any one of the Magistrates' Courts within the appropriate judicial district. It should be noted in this regard that there are many more Magistrates' Courts than District Courts.

The number of District Courts was five since the creation of the system, until 2007 in which time the sixth District Court was established by splitting the overburdened Tel Aviv District and creating the Central District and its court. The number of Magistrates' Courts has changed from time to time. As of this writing there are thirty-one Magistrates' Courts as compared with six District Courts and thus in each judicial district there are a number of Magistrates' Courts.

84. The basic rule is that parties may agree as to venue, either as to a permissible venue or an exclusive one. In both cases, the agreement is binding.

85. In the absence of agreement of the parties as to exclusive venue, the basic provisions concerning venue relating to actions not wholly concerning land are found in Rule 3 of the RCP, which provides the following five alternative venues for such actions:

(1) The place of the defendant's residence or business. Case law has held that a defendant need not intend permanently to reside in the place. It has been held that a person is deemed 'resident' in a given judicial district for the purposes of this rule if he came there for an unspecified period of time and has no clear intention, whether linked to a date or to an event, of returning to his former place or residence. The place of the defendant's 'business' does require a certain measure of permanency and continuity. However, it is not limited to a primary or principal place of business, but includes any place of business. Thus, major companies with places of business throughout Israel, such as banks, insurance companies, sick funds, etc. may in practice be sued in every judicial district. It has also been held that the State of Israel 'resides' throughout the country and thus, it may be sued in any judicial district.
(2) The place where the obligation was created. In a written obligation, this is the place where the document was signed. Where the document states the place of signature, such a statement may be seen as an agreement as to local judicial jurisdiction.
(3) The place assigned or intended for fulfilling the obligation. It has been held that this provision applies both to consensual obligations and to those imposed by law. In addition, as to obligations to pay money, unless otherwise provided, it is assumed that the debtor is to pay the creditor at the latter's residence. Thus, for example, in an action for the duty of support of a minor, the action may be brought at the place of the minor's residence since this is the place intended for the fulfilment of the obligation.
(4) The place of the delivery of the property concerning which the action is brought.
(5) The place of the act or omission concerning which the action is brought.

Where there is more than one possible venue available under the above provisions, the plaintiff may choose among them as he desires.

In addition, the Supreme Court has held that the above provision that the action may be brought in 'the place assigned or intended for fulfilling the obligation' applies also to obligations to pay damages for breach of contract (as contrasted for paying money due under the contract) or for tort injuries and that, under the relevant substantive law provisions that place is the residence or place of business of the injured party.[8] This interpretation effectively provides an additional venue for monetary actions: the place of residence or business of the plaintiff. In so holding, the Court recognized that this was not the intent of Rule 3 and that the result greatly expands the choice of venue available to the plaintiff. However, the Court was not disturbed by this result since it currently believes that in such a small country as Israel, there is no great significance to venue restrictions. In addition to the specific decision in this case, it may be expected that this general attitude will result in

8. *Levi v. Poleg*, 49 (2) P.D. 731 (1995).

increasingly liberal interpretations of the venue provisions so as to lessen greatly the restrictions they impose on the plaintiff's choice of venue. This expansive interpretation also underlies the Magistrates Courts adoption of the approach that internet-related claims may be filed at the plaintiff's choice of venue because, as many such rulings point out, the end users of internet activities may reside anywhere in the country. There is no clear definition in the case law as to what exactly are internet-related claims and the issue of internet-related claims has not been discussed by the Supreme Court.[9] In our view, the expansive interpretation of the rules regarding venue overlooks the difficulties imposed thereby on socio-economically weak parties, especially given that trial costs imposed on the losing party do not account for the prevailing party's travel expenses, which may be significant in spite of the small dimensions of the country.

Under Rule 3(b), an action against several defendants may be brought in any district in which it may have been brought against any one of them.

86. Rule 4 of the RCP provides that an action wholly involving land shall be brought in the district in which the land is situated.

87. A further special provision relating to venue is found in the Inheritance Law, 1965. This Law provides that matters of inheritance be brought in the district in which the decedent resided immediately before his death. If he was not then a resident of Israel, venue is in the district in which his property is situated.

88. In all events, residual jurisdiction as to venue is in the judicial district of Jerusalem. That is, if there is no venue in any judicial district pursuant to the above rules, or pursuant to any other applicable provisions, the venue is in Jerusalem. The Jerusalem court may then, however, transfer jurisdiction to another district if it finds that another venue would be more convenient.

II. Changing the Venue

89. The above rules of venue provide a great deal of latitude to plaintiffs to choose a court. The rules are themselves broad and the multiple residence of multisite companies, as well as the State, may give the plaintiff virtually unlimited choice. Moreover, where the Magistrates' Courts are seized with subject matter jurisdiction, the plaintiff has an unrestricted choice as to any Magistrates' Court within an appropriate district.

This great latitude provided to plaintiffs has created the need for the development of discretionary authority to change the venue of particular actions in order to counteract abuse of the system by plaintiffs.

90. As to the choice of the particular Magistrates' Court within an appropriate district, section 49 of the Courts Law authorizes the President of the Magistrates'

9. See generally A. Tabeka, *Venue in Internet Related Litigation*, 52 Hapraklit 365 (2013) (Hebrew).

Court, at the request of a party or on his own motion, to transfer an action in which proceedings have not yet begun to another Magistrates' Court in the same district.

91. More generally, section 78 of the Courts Law authorizes the President of the Supreme Court to order the transfer of any action to another court of the same subject matter jurisdiction. This provision is obviously a special version of forum non conveniens designed to prevent abuse by the plaintiff of the great latitude offered him by the venue rules.

A most interesting group of cases has arisen concerning this rule in which actions are filed in districts that have no connection at all either to the parties or to the cause of action, but as to which there is venue because the defendant is a large multisite entity or the State itself, and, therefore, can be sued in every district. In these actions the plaintiff has filed his action in an 'inappropriate' forum not in order to harass the defendant, who is well equipped to defend the action anywhere in the State, but rather to take advantage of the fact that in one or two rural districts there is less of a waiting time for cases to be heard and determined. Doing so is particularly attractive to plaintiffs where the 'appropriate' forum involved, in terms of residence of the plaintiff himself and the cause of action involved, is that of the Tel Aviv District (particularly when the Tel Aviv and Central Districts were still adjoined), where there were significant delays.

The practice in such cases had been for the President of the Supreme Court to transfer these cases, at the request of the defendant, to the 'appropriate' district even though the clear consequence would be much greater delay for the action involved. However, in recent years there has been an acknowledged change in this practice and in recent instances, the President, or his alternate, has refused to transfer such actions if the action has been filed in a court seized with territorial jurisdiction and there is a reasonable chance that the action will be tried sooner there than in the court to which it is sought to be transferred.

92. A further and more specific transfer provision is found in Rule 7 of the RCP, which provides that if a number of actions concerning the same subject are filed in several courts, concerning venue, the President of the Supreme Court may determine which of the several courts should have exclusive jurisdiction in the matter, and transfer the actions to that court for consolidation.

It should be noted that the transfer provisions discussed herein apply only to cases in which the relevant actions have been filed in courts seized with jurisdiction. The following section will discuss cases filed in courts *not* seized with jurisdiction.

§3. The Results of Lack of Internal Jurisdiction

93. In terms of internal jurisdiction, historically there has been a clear distinction between subject matter and venue.

The latter has always been conceived as solely a matter of the defendant's interests. Thus, the defendant can explicitly agree to venue either before or at the time the action is filed. Moreover, the court may not raise the issue of venue on its own motion and, indeed, the defendant may be deemed to have waived his defence of lack of venue if he does not raise the issue early in the proceedings.

In contrast, subject matter jurisdiction is conceived as the result of legislative policy as to which the parties have no right of determination. The parties to a dispute are not capable by agreement of endowing a court with subject matter jurisdiction where the legislative has not so endowed it, nor is the absence of subject matter jurisdiction a personal defence of the defendant which he can waive.

94. This historic view of subject matter jurisdiction led to the rule that the defence of lack of subject matter jurisdiction could be raised by the defendant at any stage of the proceedings, even on appeal. Moreover, the court, again even on appeal, was obliged to raise it on its own motion if the defendant did not do so.

However, in recent years this view has been changed. It is now the rule that an appellate court should not overturn a final decision on the merits by a trial court when the issue of lack of subject matter jurisdiction is raised for the first time on appeal by the losing party.

In addition, the 1997 Report of the public committee on the reform of the judiciary, discussed, *supra*, paragraph 82, specifically recommended changing, by statute, the rule concerning lack of subject matter jurisdiction so to equate its effect to the lack of venue, with the exception that the trial court would still be authorized to raise it on its own motion, but only before the start of the trial on the merits. However, despite the fact that there does not seem to be any opposition to this suggestion, it has yet to be implemented.

95. Whatever may be the differences between territorial and subject matter jurisdiction, once a court determines that it lacks jurisdiction, either subject matter or territorial, the result is the same.

Section 79 of the Courts Law [Consolidated Version], 1984, states that if a court has found that it lacks jurisdiction over an issue, whether territorial or subject matter, it may order the issue to be transferred to the appropriate court. The wording of the section is not obligatory ('may'), but case law has held that the section must be interpreted as an obligatory command leaving no discretion to the judge. Moreover, due to the structure of the judicial system, both concerning territorial and subject matter jurisdiction, as long as the matter is justifiable, there is always an appropriate court to which the issue may be transferred, whether within the general court system or one of the special systems.

A court to which an action has so been transferred may not transfer it further to another court or return it to the original court. Consequently, case law has held that the very act of transferring an action to another court gives that second court jurisdiction over the action, even if the transfer itself had been on mistaken grounds. The remedy of a party wishing to return an action to the original court is only through the regular channels of appeal.

Chapter 2. International Jurisdiction

§1. Introduction

96. In relation to international jurisdiction, there is no significance in Israel to international treaties. All the developments in this field have developed, therefore, in the absence of such treaties. The basic principle in this regard is that international jurisdiction is based either on service of process on the defendant (either personally or through construed service of process) or on his agreement to adjudicate in the State.

§2. Service of Process within the State

97. International jurisdiction, i.e., the authority of a State's judicial system to assert jurisdiction over defendants, is based on English law and thus premises such authority on proper service of process on the defendant. A defendant found within the territorial limits of the State, may be served with process thereby seizing the Israeli courts with international jurisdiction. This is so even if he is only temporarily in the State, e.g., as a tourist, and the action itself has no connection with Israel.

It should also be noted that due to special regulations in this regard, for purposes of service of process the territorial limits of the State of Israel include the territories administered by Israel since the 1967 Six Day War.

98. In the past, although such service afforded the court international jurisdiction, if there was no real connection either between the parties and the State or the transaction sued upon and the State, the action could not be prosecuted if the defendant objected since the court would lack territorial jurisdiction. That is, none of the alternative venues provided in the RCP were applicable. However, in 1979 the Rules of Civil Procedure were amended to grant territorial jurisdiction in Jerusalem when there was no venue in any other district.

In order to respond to this new problem of actions being brought solely on the basis of service of process with no real relationship either between the parties and the State or the underlying transaction and the State, Israeli case law adopted gradually the principle of forum non conveniens. According to this principle, although the Israeli court may have jurisdiction based on the principle of service of process, it may use its discretion to decline the exercise of such jurisdiction. Amongst the factors which the court may take into account when declining the exercise of jurisdiction are where the natural forum for hearing the case may be, where the claim of action was founded, the place where the evidence is situated, where witnesses can be summoned, where costs can be reduced, and the ability of the parties to serve an action abroad. Factors such as the possibility of effective interim procedures (e.g., where possessions of the defendant are situated) or the forum of the substantive laws governing the action may also be considered. In addition, the principle of *lis alibi pendens* – that is, that another trial is in progress in a different State, must also be considered when determining whether to decline to exercise jurisdiction.

The result of the application of the rule of forum non conveniens is a stay of proceedings.

99. In addition to serving a defendant personally in the State, there are various provisions in the Rules of Civil Procedure, allowing service in the State on someone in lieu of the defendant (construed service of process), which service has the same effect as if it were on the defendant personally.

These include:

(1) service on the defendant's attorney;
(2) service on the manager of the defendant's business where the suit is related to such business and the defendant does not live in the judicial jurisdiction;
(3) service on the manager of the defendant's real property in a suit related to such property where it is impossible to serve the defendant personally; and
(4) service at the defendant's home on an adult member of his family, if the defendant cannot be found.

In paragraph 126, the effect of these provisions will be discussed on providing notice of the proceedings to the defendant. In this section, however. it is important to emphasize that such service suffices to provide international jurisdiction.

Indeed, in recent years, case law has increased greatly the availability of such provisions for this purpose. This has been accomplished by two developments. First, the courts have given these provisions a wide interpretation. For example, it has been held that for purposes of service upon him in lieu of the defendant, the attorney need not be authorized by the defendant to receive process. Rather, in the words of the Supreme Court in the 1984 *Yochimak* case, it is sufficient that the attorney 'is acting at the time as an attorney of the defendant'.[10] The meaning of the term 'acting as an attorney of the defendant' is not clear from the decision. On the facts of the case, however, the attorney had acted for the defendant in the transaction, which was the basis of the action against him and had continued to act on his behalf.[11]

Second, there has been a recent development concerning the use of these provisions for serving process in Israel on someone instead of the defendant when the defendant is a foreigner. Earlier case law was very hesitant about using these provisions against foreign defendants as distinguished from Israeli residents who were abroad temporarily. The hesitancy was prompted by the fact that there are other, special provisions of the RCP designed for asserting international jurisdiction over foreign defendants, which provide for service out of the jurisdiction with permission of the Court.

However, in the *Yochimak* Case it was held unequivocably that the provisions for service in the jurisdiction on persons in lieu of the defendant are applicable fully against foreign defendants and may be used, at the option of the plaintiff and without the need for any judicial permission, alternatively to the special provisions for service out of the State. This reflects the view that when a service of process is

10. *Yochimak v. T. Kedem*, 38(4) P.D. 309 (1983).
11. See, *AEG Aktiengesellschaft v. Alutaas Elektrovistu Industries, Ltd.*, 44 (1) P.D. 758 (1990) in which the *Yochimak* decision was limited to just such an attorney.

possible through a person in lieu of the defendant, particularly if this person is the manager of the defendant's business in Israel, then such a defendant has interests or business activities in Israel and should reasonably expect to litigate in Israel.

It should also be noted that the courts have given a broad interpretation in this respect to Rule 482, which allows the service on the manager of the defendant's business where the suit is related to such business and the defendant does not live in the judicial jurisdiction. The Supreme Court held that service can be made to a person (or entity) with whom the defendant has a business relationship and not necessarily to a manager. The Supreme Court further held that the validity of the service shall be examined according to the intensity of the relationship, whereby the court shall rely on indications as to the relationship between the defendant and the serviced person or entity, including *inter alia* whether the names of the defendant-entity and the serviced entity are similar, whether same personnel are employed by both entities, whether marketing and other business activities are performed jointly, etc. The court emphasized that the examination should focus on verifying that the nature of the relationship between the defendant and the serviced person is such that it was likely that the serviced person shall inform the defendant about the claim.[12]

§3. Service of Process without the State

100. As contrasted with service of process within the State, whether on the defendant personally or on someone else in his stead, service of process without the State is deemed to be an extraordinary event that involves interference in the affairs of foreign States. As such, it is possible only with express prior permission of the court.

101. The plaintiff must file a motion, supported by an affidavit attesting to the relevant facts, requesting such permission. This motion is usually filed along with, or shortly after, the filing of the complaint. Since the intention of the motion is to compel the defendant to appear in an Israeli court, the original granting of the motion is by necessity ex parte. A defendant wishing to challenge the granting of this ex parte permission usually files a motion to vacate the decision. The court then hears the defendant's motion to vacate, as if the ex parte permission never had been granted. That is, this hearing between the two parties proceeds with the full burden on the plaintiff to justify the granting of permission for him to serve process on the defendant abroad.

102. The conditions governing the granting of permission to serve process abroad are laid down in the RPC, Rules 500–503. These Rules contain three cumulative elements: the first is contained in Rule 500 which sets forth 10 situations in which a defendant may be served with process outside the jurisdiction. The second and third elements add to the above provisions the discretion of the court to allow or not to allow service on a foreign defendant based on such factors as the

12. *Tendler v. Le Club Mediterane (Israel) Ltd*, Israeli Supreme Court Leave to Appeal 2652/94, 25 Aug. 1994 (unreported).

competing equities and conveniences involved, as well as its evaluation that the plaintiff has, at least, a prima facie (or a good arguable) case on the merits.

The situations contained in Rule 500 pertain alternatively to the status of the defendant, for example whether or not he is domiciled in Israel; or to the relationship of the claim to Israel, for example, if it concerns land situated in Israel, a contract 'made' or 'created' in Israel, or an act or omission in the State; or to the fact that the foreign individual is a 'necessary' or 'proper' party to litigation that has been properly instituted against another party based on service of process within Israel. The decisional trend in the Israeli courts has been to construe broadly the situations covered in Rule 500 so as to allow for jurisdiction as widely as possible, relying on the use of judicial discretion not to employ that wide authority in inappropriate cases. Such a trend is in keeping with the increasing complexity and interdependence of international trade and commerce.

The other two necessary conditions are the court's determination that the plaintiff has, at least, a prima facie (or good arguable) case on the merits and a determination that Israel is an appropriate forum.

As to the former, it is clear that the court will examine the complaint most carefully and, may, indeed, enter into detailed study of legal issues. It is less clear to what extent the court will require the plaintiff to support his factual allegations with some level of evidence showing that such allegations are true or will enter into questions raised by conflicting factual allegations.

As to the latter, i.e., that Israel is an appropriate forum, the court will weigh the same type of issues described above as to forum non conveniens. However, until recently Israeli law clearly distinguished the two situations. In the case of forum non conveniens the court is already seized of international jurisdiction and the burden is on the defendant to convince the court that Israel is such an inappropriate forum that the litigation should not proceed in the State.

However, in seeking permission to serve process without the State, the plaintiff is required to convince the court, *inter alia*, that Israel is a convenient place for the litigation. Thus, the two situations differ both concerning the issue involved and as to the party bearing the burden of proof. Moreover, concerning service of process abroad the courts continually emphasize that this is an extraordinary power that involves intervention in foreign states and thus should be performed with great caution and only in cases where all doubts in granting the permission have been resolved.

However, as hinted above, in recent years the Israeli courts have both been much more receptive to plaintiffs who seek to serve without the State and, in doing so, have blurred the historic distinction between forum non conveniens and the determination that Israel is a convenient place for the litigation in the context of service abroad. Indeed, in some cases, they have even put the burden on the defendant in such cases as if the situation were one of forum non conveniens. *A fortiari,* they have been less inclined to stay cases on the basis of forum non conveniens. In attempting to justify this increasing receptivity to plaintiffs as to international jurisdiction, the courts have emphasized that in the current age of technology witnesses may not have to come physically to court and thus the argument that there will be a great burden on foreign defendants if the case is tried in Israel loses much of its force. While we have some doubts as to the correctness of this new trend, it does appear to be the current Israeli law on the subject.

Perhaps a contradicting trend to the one described above is the adoption by the Supreme Court of public considerations in weighing forum non conveniens assertions. In the past, Israeli case law conformed with English case law in the approach that only private considerations of the parties should be considered in examining the issue of forum non conveniens. As explained above, the resulting effect of this approach was increased receptivity to plaintiffs. Consequently, Israeli courts find themselves burdened with claims that are less connected to Israel. The Supreme Court has countered this phenomenon by adopting the American case law-developed doctrine of public considerations in forum non conveniens. According to Grunis P., in the *Katziv* case, a court may decline service without the State or stay a claim following a forum non conveniens assertion when considerations such as the overall burden on the Israeli judicial system justify such a result.[13] It is interesting to observe that although the original purpose of public considerations in the American jurisprudence seems to have focused on ejecting claims from the local jurisdiction, Israeli courts have sometimes used public considerations to tilt the balance of considerations in favour of entertaining the case in the Israeli forum. For example, Danziger J. held in the *Uri Arbel* case that protecting the right of Israeli tourists to file claims against tourist service providers in popular locations among Israeli tourists is a public consideration which justifies rejecting a forum non conveniens assertion.[14]

The American leading case on the matter adopted a list of public factors including congested courts, imposing jury duty on a community which has no relation to the litigation, holding a trial in the view of the public to which it is related, the local interest in having localized controversies decided at home, and holding a trial in a forum that is at home with the State law that must govern the case.[15] The Israeli Supreme Court's adoption of this doctrine did not directly address the types of considerations that should be adopted. In our view, the adoption of public considerations without duly attending to the implications of this doctrine and listing the adopted considerations, or at the very least proposing criteria for such considerations, yields undesirable procedural uncertainty and potential for policy conflicts. Indeed, the policy underlying the systemic burden consideration adopted in *Katziv*, which echoes the congested courts consideration in the American case law, conflicts with the protection of Israeli tourists' consideration in the *Uri Arbel* case.

§4. Agreement as to International Jurisdiction

103. A third and independent basis for international jurisdiction is the agreement of the parties. That is, a defendant's prior agreement that given litigation may

13. *Yosef Katziv v. ZAO Reiffeisen Bank*, Israeli Supreme Court Leave to Appeal 10250/08, 18 Mar. 2010 (unreported).
14. *Uri Arbel v. TUI AG*, Israeli Supreme Court Leave to Appeal 2737/08, 29 Jan. 2009 (unreported).
15. *Gulf Oil Corp. v. Gilbert*, 330 US 501, 509 (1947).

take place in Israel in and of itself provides Israeli courts with international jurisdiction. To be sure, there is a possibility that a court will decline to exercise this jurisdiction in a manner similar to that discussed above concerning the use of forum non conveniens as to service of process within the jurisdiction. Yet in the case of agreement, there is even a heavier burden on the defendant to convince the court of the inappropriateness of maintaining the litigation in Israel; for he, himself, has consented to international jurisdiction in the State.

The rule that a plaintiff who initiates an action in Israel thereby 'agrees' to international jurisdiction as to any counterclaim of the defendant, whether or not there is a connection between the claim and counterclaim, may be seen as a special instance of implied consent to international jurisdiction.

104. In addition to agreements that provide for international jurisdiction, there are others that negate such jurisdiction. That is, the parties may agree that any litigation arising from a given transaction be litigated exclusively in a State other than Israel. The question arises as to the effect of such an agreement in cases where Israel would otherwise be seized of international jurisdiction.

First, there is a presumption of interpretation providing that ambiguous provisions in this regard are to be construed as not purporting to deny international jurisdiction to Israeli courts. Second, the courts have held that when, despite this presumption, the agreement does purport to deny international jurisdiction in Israel, it does not bind the Israeli courts. That is the parties do not have authority to preclude de jure, international jurisdiction that would otherwise be operative.

However, and most important, despite this lack of de jure authority of the parties, the courts *generally* will decline, de facto, to exercise international jurisdiction if the parties have agreed that another State has exclusive international jurisdiction, pursuant to the principle *pacta sunt servanda.*

Only in exceptional circumstances will a court aid a party in dishonouring his agreement by asserting jurisdiction in the face of a clause providing exclusive jurisdiction in another State. Such could occur, for example, in the extreme situation where the court is convinced that the plaintiff would not have a fair trial in the State of agreed exclusive jurisdiction.

§5. Raising the Issue of Lack of International Jurisdiction and its Determination

105. As to international jurisdiction based on permission to serve process outside of the jurisdiction, as we noted previously, the issue is raised usually by a motion to rescind the permission which has been granted ex parte. However, the Rules of Civil Procedure also expressly permit raising the matter in the defendant's answer to the complaint.

In both cases, the court will address the issue of service outside the jurisdiction as if the ex parte order had not been granted, thus laying the full burden of persuasion on the plaintiff.

However, Rule 502(b) of the RCP provides expressly that whether the issue is raised by motion to rescind the permission or in the defendant's answer, it must be raised no later than the day the defendant first pleads to the merits of the complaint.

Since in his answer, the defendant must plead to the merits of the action, if he has not raised the issue of international jurisdiction in the answer, he cannot later raise it by motion to rescind the permission. Moreover, the case law suggests that he also cannot raise it later by amending his answer. Finally, even before filing the answer the defendant may plead to the merits of the action, for example, by filing a motion to dismiss the complaint on grounds of res judicata. In such a case, after filing such a motion, the defendant would be precluded from later raising the issue of international jurisdiction either by motion to rescind the permission or in the answer.

Thus, not only may a defendant agree in advance to international jurisdiction, but he may lose his defence as to international jurisdiction if he does not raise it in a timely manner. This is in direct contrast to the treatment of subject matter jurisdiction, but is in accord with the law governing venue, as discussed above.

There are no express provisions in the Rules of Civil Procedure concerning the requirement of timely raising other issues concerning international jurisdiction such as improper service of process within the jurisdiction, the enforcement of an exclusive jurisdiction agreement, or forum non conveniens. However, it would seem that these must also be raised at a very early opportunity or will be deemed to have been waived.

In keeping with the requirement of raising issues concerning international jurisdiction at an early stage of the proceedings, is the expectation that, no matter how raised, these issues also will be disposed of by the court at a preliminary stage of the proceedings. And, indeed, such is the rule.

106. A determination that the court lacks international jurisdiction will result in dismissal of the action without prejudice to the plaintiff who may bring it again in a court that is seized properly with international jurisdiction.

A determination that the court has international jurisdiction will, of course, allow the case to proceed. Under Israeli procedure interim decisions generally are not final, and are subject to change at any time until judgment is rendered in the case. However, the Supreme Court held in the 1986 case of *Ra'ad v. Chai*,[16] that this general rule does not apply to decisions sustaining international jurisdiction. In the words of the court:

> Once the defendant's motion to rescind [the permission to serve without the jurisdiction] has been denied (subject to the possibility of appeal), the international jurisdiction of the court becomes final ... Even if it becomes clear during the course of the action that a given factual allegation [on which the international jurisdiction rests] is completely base-less ... the international jurisdiction of the court remains in existence.

This is so, since the very maintenance of the litigation is based on the decision that the court is seized of international jurisdiction. It would be inefficient in the

16. *Ra'ad v. Chai*, 40 (2) P.D. 141 (1986).

extreme for a court to dismiss an action for lack of international jurisdiction after it has heard the entire case on the merits with the full participation of the defendant.

However, as the above quote expressly states this finality is not absolute, but is subject to the possibility of appeal. For purposes of appeal, a decision of a first instance court sustaining international jurisdiction is an 'other decision', as that term is discussed in paragraph 39, and thus is subject to appeal at the time of its rendering only with leave of the appellate court. If the defendant seeks such leave and it is in fact granted, the appellate decision will determine the matter finally at the same early stage of the proceeding as did the trial court and thus will not create the problem of a later decision denying international jurisdiction upsetting a proceeding that has already been maintained on the merits of the action.

However, as also discussed in paragraph 39, the Rules of Civil Procedure expressly provide that if 'other decisions' are not appealed at the time of their rendering, either because leave to appeal was not requested or because such leave was requested and denied, they are appealable as of right at the time of final judgment as part of the appeal on the judgment.

This Rule, if applied without any restrictions or limitations as to the issue of international jurisdiction, would seem to allow a defendant whose argument as to lack of international jurisdiction has been rejected, to defend fully the case on the merits and, if he loses, then to appeal as to the issue of international jurisdiction as of right as part of the appeal on the judgment.

The overturning on appeal of a judgment on the merits on the grounds that the court lacked international jurisdiction would seem to undermine the rationale of the *Ra'ad* decision as to the desired finality of the determination on international jurisdiction in the first instance court, since it would have the same highly undesirable effect that the *Ra'ad* decision sought to prevent: overturning an action for lack of international jurisdiction after such action has been heard on the merits with the full participation of the defendant.

The effect of the appellate process on the desired finality of decisions sustaining international jurisdiction was not addressed expressly in the *Ra'ad* decision. Nor has it been addressed in any other case since that decision.

We would suggest the following as to this problem. First, in the light of the *Ra'ad* decision and based on its *rationale*, it would be expected that appellate courts generally would grant leave to appeal as to decisions sustaining international jurisdiction if such is sought at the time of their rendering. Second, because of the unique status of the defence of lack of international jurisdiction as expressed, *inter alia*, in the *Ra'ad* rationale, a defendant who has not sought leave to appeal, but has defended the action on the merits following the rejection of his argument as to lack of international jurisdiction may be deemed to have 'waived' the defence or to have 'submitted' to the jurisdiction. Under either view, the defendant would be estopped from raising the issue of lack of international jurisdiction as part of his appeal against an adverse judgment on the merits.

Finally, if the issue can be raised in the appellate court as part of the appeal of the judgment on the merits – either because the defendant's leave to appeal was denied or because he did not seek such leave and his failure to do so is not deemed to estop him from later raising the defence as part of his appeal on the judgment – it does not necessarily mean that the judgment on the merits will be overturned in every case in which the appellate court believes that the trial court erred on the issue of international jurisdiction.

This is so since, as will be discussed more fully in paragraph 211, Israeli jurisprudence holds that even if the first instance court has erred, its decision will not be overturned on appeal if the appellate court determines that such error has not caused a 'miscarriage of justice'.

Applying this principle to the issue of international jurisdiction it would seem that an appellate court could sustain a judgment on the merits against a defendant even if it determines that the trial court erred in rejecting his argument as to lack of international jurisdiction, if it finds that, the maintenance of the litigation in Israel, on the particular facts of the litigation in question, did not prejudice the defendant.

Part III. Actions and Parties

Chapter 1. Actions

§1. General

107. According to the Rules of Civil Procedure, the plaintiff's complaint should disclose a cause of action , i.e., a factual situation that, based on the application of a relevant legal rule, gives the plaintiff a right to judicial relief. The relevant elements of such a cause of action are determined by substantive law.

§2. Types of Actions: Declaratory Relief verses Substantive Relief

108. Israeli procedure inherited declaratory judgment proceedings from English equity jurisprudence. According to section 75 of the Courts Law (Consolidated Version) 1984, a court that hears a civil action has the jurisdiction to award a declaratory judgment. In essence, every judgment includes a declaration and, indeed, a judgment for the defendant is typically only a declaration of non-liability. However, in a substantive relief action, the plaintiff seeks more than a declaration of a right to relief; he seeks monetary or in rem relief, as to which the declaration of his legal right is only a necessary, preliminary condition. In contrast, in a claim for a declaratory judgment, such a declaration is the only relief sought by the plaintiff.

Declaratory judgments may be sought in three different situations:

(1) Before a claim for substantive relief has arisen, a plaintiff seeks a declaration of rights and obligations vis-à-vis a defendant in order to guide him in his future actions. A typical situation is where parties to a contract disagree as to its interpretation. Such a case represents, perhaps, the clearest situation in which the use of a declaratory judgment would be most efficient in that it would aid the parties to avoid violating legal rights, e.g., breaching the contract the interpretation of which is in dispute, and thereby avoid all the transaction costs involved in post breach relief. However, such a case also represents the clearest deviation from the traditional role of common law courts, which is to adjudicate as to past events as distinguished from giving legal advice as to future actions. Such legal advice is generally thought to be the prerogative of attorneys, not judges.

(2) After an alleged claim for substantive relief has arisen but before the potential plaintiff has brought his action. In such a case, the potential defendant may bring an action for a declaration of non-liability. Generally, the Israeli system, like

other procedural systems, allows the alleged injured party the advantage of the initiative in bringing an action both in terms of the time (subject to limitation provisions) and place (subject to jurisdictional requirements). Frustrating this advantage by allowing the potential defendant to seize the initiative would seem to be justified only in extraordinary circumstances. One such justification may be the threat of inconsistent judicial determinations if the potential plaintiff is not joined with others who are suing the potential defendant. This situation has given rise to the specific device of interpleader which will be discussed later in paragraph 121. There may also be other extraordinary circumstances in which the threat of potential liability presents such an economic burden to the potential defendant, that it is just to allow him to precipitate the determination of the issue despite the fact that the plaintiff's delay in initiating the action is counterbalanced by the relevant limitations provisions.

(3) After an alleged claim for substantive relief has arisen and the plaintiff could bring an ordinary action for substantive relief, but chooses to bring only one for a declaratory judgment. In this case, the plaintiff is 'splitting' his action in a way that may unduly burden both the defendant and the system. Thus, allowing him only declaratory relief while retaining the option of later implementing the declaration by an action for substantive relief would seem to be justified only in extraordinary situations. Such may be the case, for example, in a very complicated situation involving numerous potential remedies which may even have to be brought in different courts due to subject matter jurisdiction rules, the resolution of which might be expedited by a relatively quick and simple declaration of rights. Another such case may be one in which the possible substantive relief of compensation for damages may have concretized for purposes of the existence of a cause of action but the full extent of the damages may in fact not be known for a long time; in the interim it may be justified to provide only a declaration of the plaintiff's rights.

109. Unlike an action for substantive relief, as to which the plaintiff has a right to have his action determined on the merits, there is no such right to declaratory relief. Thus, in all the above situations, the provision of declaratory relief is a matter of judicial discretion. The following considerations should be weighed by the court: the benefits of providing declaratory relief to the plaintiff versus its pitfalls; does the plaintiff have a legitimate interest in obtaining declaratory relief; and finally did the plaintiff apply to the court in good faith.[17] The jurisprudence has emphasized that, in exercising this discretion, judges should be quite reluctant to grant declaratory relief in the third situation described above, i.e., that of a plaintiff who has a right to seek substantive relief. There would also seem to be reluctance to grant declaratory relief sought by a potential defendant. In addition, the courts do not allow declaratory relief in actions relating to rights that have not yet arisen, i.e., theoretical or academic actions.[18]

---

17. *Lual v. Levis*, 34 (4) P.D. 286 (1980); *Muati v. Income Tax Assessor, Tel Aviv*, Israeli Supreme Court Petition 2801/2006, 19 Sep. 2007 (unreported).
18. *Snob v. Snob*, 35 (1) P.D. 401 (1980).

However, the courts have been relatively receptive to the granting of declarative relief in the first situation. i.e., before a right to substantive relief has arisen. Indeed, the Israeli legal culture is, in general, relatively receptive to declaratory judgments. This relative receptivity is, in the authors' view, the result of four factors:

(1) A general lack of sympathy with so-called procedural limitations that prevent adjudication on the merits of the issues.
(2) The accepted utilization of declaratory relief actions against the State in order to circumvent the legislative prohibition on the granting by the general courts of injunctions against the State has helped create a receptive climate also to other uses of declaratory relief.
(3) A claim for declaratory relief may enjoy the procedural advantage of being able to be filed by originating summons, discussed in paragraph 136, a process which may not be available for the relevant substantive relief.
(4) Finally, as will be discussed in paragraph 220, the court filing fee may be substantially lower, if the only relief sought is declaratory, particularly as contrasted with monetary relief.

Chapter 2. Parties

110. All persons and other entities having legal capacity may sue or be sued. Persons who lack legal capacity, such as minors (under the age of 18) and those who have been declared incompetent may sue by means of a 'close friend', e.g., parent of a minor, or guardian, either general or appointed *ad litem*.

Filing a claim as a representative is permitted according to Israeli law in other circumstances. Thus, for example, according to the Succession Law, 1965, an heir can file a claim as a representative of all heirs, as long as they have given their consent or the court has given its approval in advance or retroactively. In addition, although Israeli legislation does not formally recognize the legal term 'amicus curiae', the court may permit the joinder of a party as 'amicus curiae' as a matter of discretion.[19]

Unincorporated associations that lack legal personality are able to sue and be sued by means of class actions. See Part VIII; however, unincorporated associations that hold rights or are subject to duties in a specific context (e.g., ownership of land), according to law, are considered to have legal capacity to sue or be sued, as long as the action refers to those rights or duties.[20]

Finally, the Law for the Amendment of Civil Procedure (the State as a Party), 1958 states that for the purpose of civil law proceedings, the status of the State is equivalent to that of a person, and it may sue or be sued.

19. *John doe v. Migdal Insurance Company*, Israeli Supreme Court Petition 11152/2004, 4 Apr. 2005 (unreported). In addition, legislation accords several institutes and bodies a special status and permits them to join certain claims as parties, despite not having a direct interest in the proceedings. *Kusli v. The State of Israel*, 53 (1) P.D. 529 (1999).

20. *The Greek Orthodox Patriarch of Jerusalem v. Ramla Municipality*, 36 (3) P.D. 670 (1982).

Chapter 3. Joinder of Actions and Parties

§1. VOLUNTARY JOINDER BY PLAINTIFF OR PLAINTIFFS

I. Uniting of Actions by the Plaintiff against the Defendant; Rule 46

111. A plaintiff (or several plaintiffs) is able to unite in one complaint all claims, whether cumulative or alternative, that he has against a defendant or jointly against several defendants, whether or not those claims are related factually or legally.

This right of a plaintiff to unite all claims against the defendant is, however, subject to three limitations:

(1) The court has discretion to order the severance of the claims for trial or even eliminate one or more of them from the united complaint if, in its view, there is no convenient way to adjudicate them together. It would seem, however, that in most cases severance of the claims for trial would be able to resolve any difficulties involved in the united litigation and thus eliminating one of the actions should be reserved for the extreme case in which the plaintiff has united the actions in order to harass the defendant.

(2) An action by or against a person in the capacity of administrator of an estate, trustee or other representative may not, except with the leave of the court, be united with an action by or against him personally. However, such leave of court is not required for personal actions by or against an administrator of an estate if such actions are related to the estate which he administers or are concerned with a right or liability jointly held by the administrator and the decedent whose estate he administers.

(3) Rules of jurisdiction may prevent the uniting of claims that would otherwise be permissible. In paragraph 77, this was discussed in detail as to subject matter jurisdiction. As to venue and international jurisdiction, the traditional understanding has been that to the extent that these are based in the given case on the connection of the action to the State or to the venue district, each joined action must have its own jurisdictional basis.[21]

II. Joinder of Parties; Rules 21–22

112. A number of plaintiffs may join in one complaint if they claim relief, jointly, severally, or alternatively, because of one occurrence or transaction or one series of acts or transactions, and there is at least one question of law or fact common to the several actions. Similarly, one or more defendants may be joined in one

21. *Ashborn Insurance & Trading Ltd. v. CAE Electronics Ltd.*, Israeli Supreme Court Petition 9725/2004, 4 Sep. 2007 (unreported).

complaint if they are alleged to be liable to the plaintiff or plaintiffs, jointly, severally, or alternatively because of one act or transaction or one series of acts or transactions and there is at least one question of law or fact common to the several actions

As with claims joined by one plaintiff against one defendant, the court has discretion to sever the actions for trial or to order a different method of trial, if it believes that the joinder may complicate or delay the proceedings. However, unlike the situation of joined claims, it would appear that the court is not authorized to dissolve a joinder on the grounds of complications or delay, if such joinder is proper under the rules set forth above. The difference as to judicial discretion between joined claims and joinder of parties in this regard is due to the fact that the basic joinder of parties requires a connection between the actions whereas joinder of claims does not. As with joined claims, however, joinder of parties otherwise permissible under the RCP may be limited because of jurisdictional limitations.

Plaintiffs who join together and defendants who are joined by the plaintiff or plaintiffs are normally joined in the complaint that opens the proceedings. Parties may also be joined at later stages of the proceedings; such late joinder requires court permission.

§2. Joinder Imposed on the Plaintiff

I. General; Counterclaims; Rule 24

113. The basic principle of Israeli procedure is that the plaintiff is the master or sovereign of the proceeding, which he has initiated, including decisions as to what actions will be adjudicated and what parties will be involved. While, as discussed above, the plaintiff may quite freely unite several actions against the defendant, he is not compelled to do so even if such actions arise from the same transaction or occurrence. This situation, of course, must be distinguished from the problem of a plaintiff splitting one action, which will be discussed at length in the section of res judicata in paragraphs 170–171.

The defendant is also deemed to be the master of any action that he may have against the plaintiff and thus he is not compelled to bring such action as a counterclaim even if it arises out of the same transaction or occurrence as the plaintiff's action. However, the defendant may freely bring such action as a counterclaim if he so desires, whether or not it is related, factually or legally, to the plaintiff's claim. Again, as with the joinder of claims by a plaintiff, if a party convinces the court that it is not efficient to litigate the original action and the counterclaim together, the court may order them to be severed for trial.

In paragraph 79, we discussed in detail the jurisdictional problems concerning counterclaims as to subject matter jurisdiction. We would only note herein that simple counterclaims present no problems as to venue or international jurisdiction as the rule is clear that by bringing his action in the State or relevant district, the plaintiff has thereby consented to jurisdiction in the forum as to the counterclaim or, alternatively, has waived any objection thereto.

We have restricted the above statement to simple counterclaims, referring thereby to counterclaims in which the only defendant is the original plaintiff. However, Rule 54 allows the defendant to join in the counterclaim persons additional to the plaintiff if 'the counterclaim raises questions between him [the defendant] and the plaintiff together with such other persons'. This language is both awkward and ambiguous and it is not clear that it allows the same liberal joinder of additional defendants to a counterclaim as does the general rule of joinder of defendants discussed above.

It would seem clear, however, that as to such additional defendants there would have to be bases for venue and international jurisdiction other than the consent or waiver of the original plaintiff. As to venue, while it is not absolutely clear, it would seem that the original plaintiff and the additional defendant to the counterclaim should be viewed as joined defendants such that the fact that there is venue in the forum as to the original plaintiff should suffice to provide such jurisdiction also as to the additional defendant.

As to international jurisdiction, the additional defendant would have to be served properly with process either within or without the State pursuant to the provisions discussed in paragraphs 96–102. A difficult, and unresolved, issue in this regard is the application of Rule 500(10) concerning a foreign person who is necessary or proper to an action filed against a defendant who has been served within the State. While it is clear that a counterclaim is an action for purposes of this provision it is questionable whether the original plaintiff has been served with process within the State where the basis of international jurisdiction over him is his presumed consent or waiver and, indeed, in fact he will not have been served with process within the literal language of Rule 500(10). On the other hand, may not such consent or waiver be viewed as the equivalent of being served within the State?

Where the original plaintiff is local and could have been served with process within the State had the counterclaim been brought as an independent action, it would seem that Rule 500(10) should be applicable as to the additional defendant. Otherwise, the defendant would be penalized by having brought his action as a counterclaim. The issue is more problematic in a case in which the original plaintiff is not local and thus could not have been served with process within the State in an independent action.

Returning to the basic principle discussed in this section, that of a plaintiff being master of his litigation, the rules as to counterclaim do reflect this principle as to the defendant and his action. However, as to the plaintiff they represent an infringement of his absolute sovereignty over the litigation since he is compelled to litigate as to the defendant's action. The counterclaim rules represent, therefore, a prime instance of the principle of plaintiff sovereignty succumbing to countervailing factors of efficiency and fairness to the defendant, as already discussed in paragraph 75.

114. As to the selection of the parties to the litigation the principle of plaintiff sovereignty has influenced the courts in adopting, traditionally, a narrow construction of the general compulsory joinder provision contained in Rule 24 of the RCP, which provides that, at all stages of the proceedings, the court, either at the application of a party or on its own motion, may order the joinder of a person 'who ought to have been joined as a plaintiff or defendant or whose presence in the litigation is necessary in order to allow the court to adjudicate and determine efficiently and fully all the issues involved in the matter'.

The accepted interpretation of the phrase concerning a person who 'ought to have been joined' is that it refers only to what are today very unusual situations in which the relevant substantive law provides for joint (as distinguished from joint and severable) rights or liabilities.

More significantly, following the English precedent, the Israeli courts have held that the very broad language concerning a person whose presence is necessary to adjudicate efficiently and fully all the issues in the case should be construed narrowly so as to apply only to a few, specified situations.

The first situation is one in which the joinder of a party is necessary in order to bind that party to the res judicata results of the judgment and obligate him to act in accordance with the court's ruling, so that the court's decision will fully and efficiently resolve all the issues involved in the matter.[22] This might be the case, for example, when the plaintiff requires the defendant to restitute his personal belongings and the defendant claims that he passed the belongings to a third person. In this case, joinder of the third person as an additional defendant is required in order for the plaintiff to recover his belongings.

The first situation concerns protection of the defendant from the possibility of inconsistent judgments against him. Inconsistent judgments for this purpose, however, are limited to those that require inconsistent performance by the defendant, e.g., to act and not to act simultaneously, and do not include inconsistent monetary judgments that result in multiple liability or the inability to enforce rights of indemnification or contribution.

The second situation concerns third parties who may be adversely effected by the litigation and wish to join it in order to protect their interests.[23] In these cases, Rule 24 acts essentially as an intervention provision there being no express intervention provision in the Rules of Civil Procedure.

However, in keeping with the plaintiff mastery principle, this intervention traditionally has been limited primarily to cases in which the intervenor claims a specific property interest, as distinguished from a mere monetary interest, in the litigation. A common example is that of an intervenor who claims that he is the true owner of property that has been attached in the litigation on the basis of its being that of the defendant. In addition, it has been held that one who will be bound by the litigation through res judicata also has a right to intervene.

While this narrow traditional interpretation of Rule 24 is, indeed, consistent with the plaintiff sovereignty principle it creates serious problems as to fairness concerning the defendant who may be faced with the possibility of inconsistent monetary judgments against him and third parties who may have a legitimate interest in intervening in litigation despite the fact that they neither claim an interest in specific

22. *The Greek Orthodox Patriarch of Jerusalem v. Rabinovich*, Israeli Supreme Court Petition 9360/2011, 8 Jan. 2011 (unreported).
23. *Ibid.*

property involved therein nor will be bound by res judicata as to the results. Moreover, the tendency of Israeli procedure today is to value very highly interests of efficiency and completeness that would be promoted by allowing broad discretion to the court to join parties, as suggested by a literal reading of Rule 24 in order to determine finally the entire matter involved.

As to the protection of the defendant, even before the British mandate over Palestine, the restrictive reading of the English equivalent of Rule 24 had prompted the creation of third-party practice (impleader) and interpleader proceedings, which proceedings were adopted in Mandatory Palestine and are retained in Israeli procedure.

As to the intervention of third parties and the general expansion of the possibility of forcing joinder on plaintiffs so as to allow the court more efficiently to adjudicate as to the entire matter involved, the major developments in the English rules occurred after the creation of the State of Israel and, therefore, are not reflected in the Israeli Rules of Civil Procedure.

However, there are a number of indications in recent judicial decisions that suggest that in the future Rule 24 will be interpreted more broadly and in accord with its broad language so as both to better protect third parties who may have a legitimate, albeit a non-specific property interest in intervening in litigation and to better enable the courts to determine matters fully and completely.

We will now discuss the defendant protective devices currently in Israeli procedure: third-party practice and interpleader.

II. Third-Party Practice (Impleader)

115. Third-party practice, or as is sometimes termed, impleader, allows a defendant to join to an action a third party whom the defendant claims is liable to him for all or part of the plaintiff's claim against him. It is a conditional claim against the third party, dependent on the defendant's liability to the plaintiff, which liability the defendant may well be disputing.

The advantage of joining the third party to the original action instead of the defendant awaiting the result of the action and then bringing an independent action against the third party is primarily that of binding the third party to the res judicata results of the findings against the defendant that will be relevant to the defendant's action against the third party. This binding of the third party is of utmost importance to the defendant in order to avoid the possibility of conflicting judicial decisions that would effectively nullify his substantive rights against the third party. Additionally, the device may allow for the efficient resolution of the entire matter at one time.

However, the joining of an additional party who may be liable to the defendant may adversely effect the plaintiff in conducting his action and thus there are limitations on the device in order to protect the plaintiff.

116. Rule 216 provides three alternatives for the serving of a third-party notice. These alternatives are based on the similar English rule and are primarily the result of the history of that rule rather than logical analysis. Thus, the exact purpose of each alternative and the relationships among them are not clear. The first, and primary, alternative concerns a claim by the defendant for contribution or indemnity from the third party for any or all of the sum he will have to pay as a result of the main claim. Since the provision includes both contribution and indemnity, it is not necessary to distinguish between them absolutely herein. The term contribution is usually used, as the word itself suggests, for a claim for partial relief against the third party whereas indemnity usually refers to a claim for total relief. Contribution is usually used concerning claims between tortfeasors whereas indemnity usually results from a contractual relationship between the indemnitor and the indemnitee.

It should be noted that as to contribution among joint and several tortfeasors who have already been joined as defendants by the plaintiff, the Rules of Civil Procedure provide two possibilities. First, without the serving of a third-party notice one or more of the joined defendants may simply request the court to determine the contribution percentages among the defendants in the course of determining the main action. Alternatively, one of the joined defendants may serve a third-party notice on the others; this is so since the Israeli Rule, unlike its English counterpart, allows the serving of a third-party notice on all relevant persons, including on those who are already parties to the litigation.

The advantages of serving a third-party notice in such a situation are twofold: first, it will require the court to determine the contribution ratios whereas a mere application for the court to do so without the filing of a third-party notice is subject to the court's discretion; second, it will produce a judgment between the defendants which can be entered as such so as to allow a defendant who is compelled to pay to the plaintiff more than his proportional share of the liability to recover the excess from the other defendants. However, a third-party notice is an action as to which a court filing fee, which may be quite substantial (see paragraphs 220–223), must be paid. This is not true as to a mere application to determine the contribution ratios between joint and several tortfeasors.

The second alternative that allows the serving of a third-party notice applies when the defendant claims relief against a third party which relief is connected to the subject of the original action and which is essentially the same as the relief requested by the plaintiff. The primary purpose of this provision was to expand the first and allow the use of third-party practice in cases in which the defendant claims a right of reimbursement from the third party as to his liability to the plaintiff, but which do not come within the technical definitions of contribution or indemnity. Such cases would include, for example, situations in which the third party's alleged actions, intentionally or negligently, caused the defendant's liability to the plaintiff.

The third alternative concerns situations in which a question or issue between the defendant and third party is essentially the same as that in dispute between the plaintiff and the defendant and it is desirable that this issue be determined in the same action.

This provision is most problematic. Its language is very broad and it would seem to allow the use of third-party practice in many cases, which do not involve the purpose of this type of action, i.e., a defendant's claim for some type of reimbursement from the third party as to his possible liability to the plaintiff. It appears to be a general joinder provision, which is more applicable, therefore, to Rule 24 than to third-party practice. Indeed, while this paragraph does appear in the parallel English rule as to third-party practice, a very similar provision was added in 1971 to the English equivalent of Rule 24 in order to broaden the application of that rule.

As discussed above in the discussion of Rule 24, such a provision was not added to the Israeli Rule 24; however, recent jurisprudence indicates a tendency to broaden the application of Rule 24 even without it being amended.

In our view the proper place for this provision, therefore, is not in third-party practice, but in Rule 24. There, it would serve the purpose of broadening the ability of third parties to intervene if they so desire. There is no reason for such broadening to be the initiative of the defendant, which is the result of the placement in third-party practice.

Thus, it is not surprising that we have found no cases, either in Israel or in England, that rely on this provision concerning third-party practice.

117. There is one other matter that should be mentioned in this regard. The Israeli Rules of Civil Procedure, like their English counterparts, do not specifically provide for non-reimbursement actions between joined defendants as, for example, does the cross-claim rule of the American Federal Rules of Civil Procedure.[24] which Rule allows a party to claim against a co-party *inter alia*, as to any action that arises out of the transaction or occurrence of the original action.

Such a cross-claim is possible, for example, in the case of a three-party accident in which one defendant claims against the other not only contribution as to his possible liability to the plaintiff, but also compensation for his own damages in the accident.

Such a situation would seem to be covered by the very broad language of the third alternative. And, indeed, such an interpretation of this alternative would provide for a device, which may be quite useful in a system that seeks to allow the disposition of all issues arising out of the same transaction or occurrence in one litigation.

However, there is no doubt that the rules of third-party practice in the RCP when considered in their entirety as a comprehensible unit view this device as allowing actions for reimbursement that are conditional on the ultimate determination that the defendant is liable to the plaintiff. An independent, unconditional damage action by the defendant is clearly inconsistent with this view, and thus should be rejected.

118. As stated above, while a third-party action may be most important to the defendant, it also forces on the plaintiff an additional party to the action. The balancing of these two interests is accomplished as follows. First, in actions conducted by the pleading proceedings, as will be discussed in paragraphs 129–134, the defendant has an unqualified right to serve a third-party notice, if the matter is within one of the first two alternatives discussed above. However, where the main action is conducted by the special expedited process of an originating summons, see paragraph 136, the defendant must receive permission of the court prior to serving a third-party notice. The same is apparently true as to actions conducted by expedited judgment proceedings, see paragraphs 138–143.

Moreover, in any case, where the court believes that the determination of the third-party action at the same time as the original action is liable to complicate

24. Rule 13 (g).

unduly the determinations, it may order the third-party action to be tried after the hearing of the original action or even after the rendering of judgment in such action (Rule 222).

119. A third-party action is initiated by the serving of a third-party notice on a relevant third party. Where the main action has been initiated by the ordinary process, such notice must be served by the defendant prior to the time set for the serving of his answer to the original complaint, usually thirty days following the serving of the complaint on him. In cases in which the defendant must receive judicial permission to serve the third-party notice, such permission also must be requested within thirty days of the service of the complaint on the defendant. If permission is granted the third-party notice must be served by the defendant within the period of time set by the court. It should also be noted that if the complaint was amended the defendant is entitled to serve an amended answer and therefore he is also entitled to serve a third-party notice even if the period of time set by the RCP has passed.

The third-party notice is equivalent to a complaint initiating proceedings and thus must comply with the requirements of such a complaint as will be discussed in the next chapter. Also, the defendant must attach to the third-party notice a copy of the plaintiff's complaint against him.

The third party may then defend both against the third-party complaint against himself and also against the plaintiff's original action against the defendant by filing an answer within thirty days after the service of the third-party notice on him. If the third party does not file an answer, he is deemed to have admitted the validity of any judgment that may be obtained against the defendant, including even a consent judgment, as well as to the right of the defendant claimed against himself.

Rule 219 provides expressly that the third party can himself serve a further third-party complaint and so on *ad infinitum*. However, the RCP do not further define expressly the relationships among the plaintiff, the defendant and the third party. In our view, the thrust of the Rules is that the defendant and third party should be viewed as plaintiff and defendant respectively as to the third-party action, with all the rules concerning plaintiff and defendant applying to them. Thus, for example, the third party may file a counterclaim against the defendant.

However, the plaintiff and third party should not be viewed as plaintiff and defendant respectively, unless the plaintiff has chosen to amend his complaint so as to join the third party also as a defendant to his action. Thus, for example, absent such an amendment of the complaint, the third party could not file a counterclaim against the original plaintiff. This result is consistent with the basic principle of not forcing third parties on the plaintiff except as necessary to protect the interests of the defendant.

120. As with other multiple party situations, issues of jurisdiction arise also as to third-party practice. In the leading 1976 case of *Cherkelevitz v. Olenbolsi*, the Supreme Court held that by its nature a third-party action is ancillary to the main action and thus does not require independent venue.[25] In so holding, the court referred both to English and American cases concerning the nature of third-party actions and their relationship, therefore, to various types of jurisdiction.

The main English authority referred to was the speech of Lord Justice Williams in the 1902 decision of the Court of Appeals, in the case of *McCheane v. Gyles*.[26]

In this case, the English Court of Appeal held that the English Rules of Procedure expressly required independent international jurisdiction grounds for third-party actions. Moreover, the English equivalent of Rule 500(10) did not apply to third party actions since the third party, while necessary and, perhaps, crucial to the protection of the defendant, is not necessary or proper to the original action of the plaintiff, which is the action referred to in the Rule.

However Lord Justice Williams emphasized, in dictum, that a third-party action is inherently ancillary to the main action and, therefore, had not the English Rules clearly required independent international jurisdiction as to third-party actions, he would have held that such independent international jurisdiction was not required. In the *Cherkelevitz* case, the Israeli Supreme Court relied on this dictum rather than on the holding of the *McCheane* case.

The Court also relied on American authority holding that for purposes of subject matter jurisdiction of federal courts, third-party actions are viewed as ancillary to the main action and thus independent subject matter jurisdiction is not required. On the other hand, the Court ignored other American jurisprudence holding that this is not true as to international jurisdiction and venue.

Cherkelevitz clearly settled the law as to venue. However, its implications as to international jurisdiction and subject matter jurisdiction are less clear.

As to the former, there are two relevant decisions. The first is a 1978 District Court decision, *Olin Matheon Co. v. Boeing Corp*.[27] In this case the widow and children of a deceased El Al Airlines employee who had been killed by an explosion while testing the emergency evacuation system in an airplane brought an action against the Israeli employer, El Al, and two American companies, the manufacturer of the airplane and the manufacturer of a certain aspect of the evacuation system. The defendants sought to bring a third-party action against another American company that had allegedly manufactured the specific part of the evacuation system that caused the explosion.

This is, of course, a classic third-party action situation. The District Court did not refer to the possibility that independent international jurisdiction was not required for third-party actions. Rather, it addressed only what was presented to it: the plaintiff's petition for permission to serve process outside the State; and stated that Rule 500(10) did apply. This is so, said the District Court since the ancillary nature of third-party actions as determined in the *Cherkelevitz* case resulted in the third party being necessary or proper to the original action. In so stating, the court rejected the contrary holding of the English court in *McCheane*.

The view of Rule 500(10) stated by the District Court in *Boeing*, while clear, and, indeed, convincing, did not, create binding precedent. This is so for two reasons:

25. 30 (3) P.D. 102.
26. [1902] 86 L.T. 1 (C.A.).
27. 1980–1981 (2) P.M. 502.

first, it was a statement not of the Supreme Court but of a lower court. Second, it was dictum; the *Boeing* Court vacated the authorization to serve process outside the State on the grounds that the non-particularized third-party notice was not sufficient to show that the defendant had a good, arguable case against the third party.

However, the *Boeing* opinion does represent a persuasive statement that the Israeli rule should be based on the *Cherkelevitz* decision. However, in a 1990 decision by a single justice of the Supreme Court, S. Levin, J., the *Boeing* view as to Rule 500(10) was rejected.[28] The case, was similar in structure to that of *Boeing*.

As in *Boeing*, S. Levin, J., did not discuss the possibility that independent international jurisdiction was not required at all as to third-party actions. Rather he referred only to the issue of the applicability of Rule 500(10) to third-party actions.

In rejecting the *Boeing* view of Rule 500(10), S. Levin, J., relied exclusively on the English decision on this point in the *McCheane* case. Indeed not only did he not attempt to justify the rejection of the *Boeing* view on policy grounds, but he stated expressly that the result he had reached was undesirable and suggested that Rule 500(10) be amended so as to allow authorization to serve process out of the jurisdiction as to third-party notices in such cases.

This issue was finally resolved by the Supreme Court decision, *Weinberg v. Biels*. In this case, the court ruled that third-party notices are ancillary proceedings to the main procedure and therefore should be considered as a part of it for the purpose of interpreting Rule 500(10). Interpretation of Rule 500(10) as applicable to third-party notices, so the court explained, is compatible with the goal of the rule, which is to fully and efficiently resolve all the issues relevant to the matter. It follows that according to current Israeli procedural law, Rule 500(10) allows authorization to serve process out of the jurisdiction as to third-party notices. In our view, such an approach is justifiable for three reasons: First, in a *Boeing* type case, which involves a local defendant who seeks contribution or indemnity from a foreign manufacturer, it is quite important to the defendant to bring the foreign manufacturer into the action so as to prevent the possibility of his being the victim of inconsistent judgments. Second, in such a case, the plaintiff, if he had so desired, usually could have joined the foreign manufacturer as a defendant by availing himself of Rule 500(10). His decision not to do so should not prevent the defendant from effecting the joinder by filing a third-party action. Third, as the court noted in *Weinberg v. Biels* this Rule enables the court to fully and efficiently resolve all the relevant issues to the matter being heard.

To the best of our knowledge the only case dealing with the ancillary nature of third-party actions concerning subject matter jurisdiction is the recent, 1999, decision of the Supreme Court sitting as the High Court of Justice in *Delta Co. v. The Municipal Court of Ariel*.[29] In this case, the regional council brought an action against a group of citizens in the municipal court, concerning the payment of certain tax charges. The defendants sought to bring a third-party action against Delta Co., alleging that it was obliged to pay these taxes. Delta Co. sought to dismiss the third-party action for lack of subject matter jurisdiction. The matter eventually reached the High Court of Justice which held that for reasons of 'efficiency' and

---

28. *Alba Machines for the Metal Work v. Clogar S.P.A.*, 45 (1) P.D. 353 (1990).
29. *Delta Co. v. The Municipal Court of Ariel*, 55 (3) P.D. 246 (2001).

'justice' the third-party action should be determined with the original action, thereby implying that for purposes of subject matter jurisdiction, third-party actions are viewed as ancillary to the main action and thus independent subject matter jurisdiction is not required.

However, it should be noted that in the *Delta Co.* case, both the issue of subject matter jurisdiction and the issue of third-party notices were settled by regulations. This was one of the considerations that led the court to hold that the rules of third-party notice may expand the court's subject matter jurisdiction. However, the court believed that rules of third-party notice may not expand the court's subject matter jurisdiction if the issue of subject matter jurisdiction is settled by law. Since the court's ruling dealt only with the first case (i.e., a case in which the issue of subject matter jurisdiction as well as the issue of third-party action were both settled by regulation), Israeli law has not yet resolved the general question of the relationship between rules of third-party notices and rules of subject matter jurisdiction. Finally, one should remember that the *Delta Co.* case is quite unique and that the issue of the ancillary nature of third-party actions for purposes of subject matter jurisdiction will only arise in rare and unique cases. This is so since the basic criterion for subject matter jurisdiction in the general court system is the amount in controversy. The common third-party practice action is a monetary claim against the third party for reimbursement of the sum that the defendant may have to pay to the plaintiff. By the nature of such reimbursement, it will not exceed the sum of the original claim and thus will be within the jurisdiction of the court, which has jurisdiction over the original claim.

However, in addition to a situation such as the *Delta Co.* case, it is possible that the issue might arise under the following hypothetical circumstances.

The issue of subject matter jurisdiction will arise only in one of two situations. First, if third-party actions are allowed to include independent damage claims, as distinguished from reimbursement claims, of the defendant. As discussed above, in our view third-party actions should not include such independent damage claims.

The second possibility is that of a monetary 'reimbursement' claim by the defendant against a third-party who has agreed to indemnify him if the defendant is compelled to evacuate certain real property. In such a case, the evacuation action will be in the Magistrates' Court whereas the third-party reimbursement action may be for a sum in excess of the limit of the Magistrates' Courts.

In our view, in light of the *Cherkelivitz* and *Delta Co.* opinions, and by analogy to the rule as to counterclaims, the third-party action should be allowed in the Magistrates' Court if this rare situation should arise.

III. Interpleader; Rules 224–233

121. The rules of procedure concerning interpleader proceedings are intended to aid a person sued or about to be sued by several persons whose claims are adverse to each other. Such a person may petition the court for interpleader relief either before or after an action has been filed against him. In these proceedings, the plaintiff and persons about to sue (hereinafter referred to as claimants) are made parties to the action; the question before the court is to which of the various claimants the defendant owes his debt; the point of departure being that he owes it to only one of them. The goal of this proceeding is to clear contradictory claims against a person and reach a conclusive decision that will guide that person as to whom he is liable.[30] While the subject matter of interpleader proceedings is usually contradictory monetary claims, there is no limitation as to the possible subject matter of interpleader proceedings. Therefore, it is also possible to use interpleader proceedings to resolve contradictory claims regarding land.

An application to the court to allow interpleader proceedings must be supported by an affidavit. If the applicant is already a defendant, the affidavit must be submitted within ten days of his being served with process. The applicant must declare in his affidavit:

(1) That he claims no benefit in the subject matter of the claims other than for compulsory payments made or costs incurred.
(2) That he is not in collusion with any one of the plaintiff or claimants.
(3) That he is prepared to bring the disputed asset to court or handle it in accordance with the court's orders.

A court receiving an application to allow interpleader proceedings will send a summons to the claimants, at least fifteen days before the date set for the proceedings, accompanied by a copy of the applicant's affidavit. Where an action has already been filed against the defendant, a copy of the pleadings will be included with the summons, and the plaintiff will be sent a summons to the proceedings, along with the defendant's affidavit. The court will send the applicant a notice of the implementation of interpleader proceedings.

Upon receipt of this summons, an applicant may file a statement of claim against the defendant or applicant, in a form similar to that of a plaintiff's complaint. Alternatively, he may file a 'declaration of withdrawal', stating that he claims nothing from the defendant or applicant. If a claimant does not respond at all, he will suffer the limited result of a default, as discussed below. Interpleader proceedings in which the plaintiff (if indeed a complaint had already been filed) and all the claimants who contest the action appear for trial, will proceed whether or not the defendant or applicant appears, and, after a full trial on the merits of the claims, judgment will be given determining the claims of all the parties.

If, in a case in which the interpleader action was filed by a defendant after an action was brought against him, the plaintiff does not appear for trial, the court will dismiss his complaint with prejudice, and dismiss the interpleader action, unless it decides otherwise, i.e., either to postpone the entire trial to a later date or to allow the interpleader action to proceed as to the claimants despite its dismissal with prejudice of the original action.

However, if a claimant does not appear and the court does not postpone the trial, it will determine the claims of the parties who do appear and issue a 'curtailing decree' against the defaulting claimant.

30. *Arad municipality v. Satar*, Israeli Supreme Court Petition 5168/2004, 7 Jun. 2005 (unreported).

A curtailing decree creates a res judicata against the defaulting claimant in favour of the defendant or applicant thereby estopping the defaulting claimant vis-à-vis the plaintiff and the other claimants. However, if the defaulting claimant has not filed a declaration of withdrawal, i.e., he has filed a statement of claim or has not responded at all to the summons, he will not be estopped from claiming later against the plaintiff or other claimants.

In terms of jurisdiction, the Rules expressly provide that as to subject matter jurisdiction and venue, if an action has already been filed against the defendant, the court also has jurisdiction as to the interpleader action. If no action has yet been filed, the interpleader proceedings may be maintained in any court in which an action in the matter could be brought against the defendant. There are no specific provisions in the Rules as to international jurisdiction and we know of no jurisprudence on the issue. In our view, the issue should be treated in a similar way to that which we advocated above as to third-party actions.

§3. Consolidation of Actions filed Separately

122. The Rules of Civil Procedure also authorize the consolidation of separate actions that are pending in the same court if they involve similar issues of law or fact. Rule 520 states that such consolidation is in the discretion of the court which may act either at the application of a party or on its own motion, and which may attach such conditions to the consolidation as it sees fit.

According to Rule 7, if a number of actions concerning the same subject are filed in several courts with the same subject matter jurisdiction, then in relation to venue, the President of the Supreme Court may determine which of the several courts should have exclusive jurisdiction in the matter, and transfer the actions to that court for consolidation.

Since the consolidation applies to actions pending in the same court, either originally or as a result of transfer, the consolidation raises no questions of international or local jurisdiction. Nor will there generally be a problem of subject matter jurisdiction. The only exceptional case is that of two monetary actions pending in a Magistrates' Court, each of which is separately within the jurisdictional amount of that court, but where if taken together the total sum would be above the jurisdictional amount.

As discussed in paragraph 77, where separate monetary claims against the defendant are consolidated in one action by the plaintiff or in a case of monetary claims with multiple plaintiffs or defendants, the jurisdictional amount is determined by the total of the separate claims. Should this principle be applied, therefore, to prevent a consolidation, which would produce a total jurisdictional amount in excess of that of the Magistrates' Court? There are no judicial decisions on this point, but the prevailing view is that these actions can still be consolidated and remain in the Magistrates' Court in which they were pending separately. This view may be explained by the rule according to which the subject matter jurisdiction is determined according to the relief claimed by the plaintiff on the day in which the claim was filed.

Chapter 4. Sanctions for Procedural Irregularities

123. Based as it is on the English system, Israeli procedure is characterized by rules setting rigid time limits and set orders of proceedings. The application of such rules, in practice, demonstrates the essential clash between the conflicting interests and values involved. On the one hand, it is felt necessary for adjudicating parties to file pleadings on time, appear at hearings as required, respond to interrogatories and applications to disclose and examine documents and the like. Thus, the sanction of default judgment and other forms of preclusion must be available in order to enforce these obligations. And so they are in the Rules of Civil Procedure.

On the other hand, there is a strong reluctance to determine issues against an adjudicating party if he has not had his day in court, even if his failure resulted from his own faulty conduct. One source of this reluctance is the importance attributed to the right of access to the courts according to Israeli law. Although there is a dispute regarding the legal origin of this right, it is considered to be one of the basic and fundamental rights to which a person is entitled.[31] This reluctance is further strengthened by the fact that in the vast majority of cases, it is not the party himself who was at fault but rather his attorney.

Therefore, for example, along with the rule providing for default in the event that the defendant does not file a timely statement of defence or non-appearance by a party at a hearing, the Rules of Civil Procedure contain provisions for opposition that include the discretionary setting aside of an even validly entered judgment so as to provide a defaulting party with another chance to have his day in court. See *infra* paragraphs 202–204.

Other examples of judicial discretion to excuse non-compliance with the apparently strict rules include relatively liberal provisions for the amendment of pleadings, as well as for amending any other 'defect or mistake in any proceedings' (Rule 524). Furthermore, as noted in Rule 154 of the RCP, a plaintiff may be allowed a voluntary non-suit, which permits him to cease, without prejudice, a proceeding in which he has erred and to renew the action by filing a new complaint. All these provisions may be seen as a desire that, in the words of Rule 92 concerning amendment of pleadings, ' … the court will be able to determine the issues that are in fact the issues which are in controversy between the parties.' And, this, despite the fact that one of the parties, or in practice his attorney, has erred and defaulted in performing his obligations.

It is true that these Rules permitting corrections of mistakes are all discretionary; a party who has not complied with a given Rule has no right to have his non-compliance excused and must rely on the court to exercise its discretion in his favour. However, this discretion is generally employed in favour of the non-complying party, so long as the immediate damage caused to the other side by the fault sought to be excused can be remedied by the payment to him of appropriate monetary compensation. And, as noted by the then Deputy President of the Israeli

31. *Cohen v. Speaker of the Knesset*, Israeli Supreme Court Petition 2171/2006, 29 Aug. 2011 (unreported).

Supreme Court, in a 1984 decision, 'the situations in which the wrong [to the other side] cannot be rectified by monetary compensation are extremely rare'.[32]

This lenient attitude toward procedural irregularities is also demonstrated by changes made in the 1984 RCP as compared with prior Rules. Thus, in the prior Rules there were a number of situations in which the failure of a plaintiff to comply with the Rules resulted in a dismissal of the action, with prejudice, i.e., res judicata would bar reinstitution of the action. Such was the sanction as to a plaintiff who failed to comply with discovery orders, failed to appear for trial, or failed to prosecute his action. The 1984 Rules changed the sanction as to these situations from dismissal of the action with prejudice to dismissal without prejudice.[33] That is, despite the plaintiff's non-compliance with the Rules, he is not barred from re-instituting the action.

124. The generally lenient attitude toward procedural irregularities is subject to two main exceptions:

(1) specific rules that require a stricter attitude; and
(2) the imposition of financial sanctions for procedural irregularities.

The first specific rule in this regard concerns the extension of time limits. Rule 528 of the RCP distinguishes between time limits that are set by the court and those set by statute or rule. As to the former, the general, lenient approach applies, i.e., they may be extended from time to time, even after the time period has expired, and generally are so extended even if a party has been negligent in not complying with a time limitation. As with other types of procedural irregularities, monetary compensation is viewed as the remedy due to the other side.

As to time limits established by statute or rule, while they may also be extended even after the time period has expired, any extension can only be for 'special reasons which shall be recorded'. Such special reasons are generally considered to be causes beyond the control of the offending party.[34] Thus, if a party was negligent in not adhering to the time limit, it will not be extended if such limit has been set by statute or Rule as distinguished from having been set by the court.

It should be noted, however, that the concept of time limits set by statute or rule has been narrowly construed to apply only to time limits set absolutely by statute or rule. Thus, for example, if a statute or rule provides for a given time limit 'unless otherwise provided by the court', or expressly provides that the court may extend the time limit, the time limit is not considered to have been set by statute or rule and the lenient approach applies to its extension.

---

32. *The Arthur Rubenstein Music Society v. The Governmental Corporation for Medals and Coins*, 38 (1) P.D. 566, 568 (1984).
33. As to failure to comply with discovery orders or to prosecute the action, the exclusive sanction against a plaintiff in the 1984 Rules is a dismissal without prejudice. As to a plaintiff's failure to appear for trial, the court has discretion either to dismiss with prejudice or without prejudice, compared with the previous Rules where the exclusive sanction was a dismissal with prejudice.
34. *The Municipal Committee for Planning and Construction, Rishon Lezion v. Mihkashvili*, 50 (3) P.D. 209 (1996).

An example of a purposeful use of this principle is found in the 1984 change in the Rule concerning the time in which a plaintiff must file a reply to the defendant's answer, if, indeed, he must do so. Prior to the 1984, RCP the Rule provided absolute time limits: in the District Courts fifteen days after the filing of the defendant's answer, and eight days in the Magistrates' Courts. In 1984, however, the Rule was amended by adding the words 'if the judge or registrar has not extended the time'. This addition changed the approach as to the plaintiff's failure to comply with the time limit from that of the strict standard to that of the lenient one. This, of course, was consistent with the changes in Rules concerning dismissals (from with prejudice to without prejudice) to the benefit of erring plaintiffs.

The second specific rule requiring a strict attitude toward the correction of a mistake is Rule 149, which concerns the decisions taken at the pre-trial conference. See the discussion on the pre-trial conference, paragraph 160, *infra*.

125. As an alternative to other sanctions for procedural irregularities, the recent tendency has been to employ financial sanctions.

As previously noted, it is customary to condition permission to amend pleadings, extend time limits, and the like upon payment by the applicant of the other party's costs, including attorney fees, incurred as a result of the mistake sought to be corrected.

In addition, the basic principle in Israel in regard to taxing costs is that the losing party is generally required to pay the winning party's costs, including attorney's fees. However, the court has discretion not to award costs to a winning party if, for example, he has unduly prolonged the litigation. Indeed, the Supreme Court has even indicated that in an extreme case of abuse of process by the winning party, costs may not only be denied to the winning party but may even be awarded to the losing party.[35] Moreover, courts have held that they have the discretion to impose all or part of the costs of a proceeding not on the party involved but on his attorney when such costs were caused by a negligent act or omission of the attorney or by other improper conduct of the attorney without the knowledge of the party represented.[36]

In addition a long standing Rule of Civil Procedure, now Rule 514, provides that if the court finds that a party has unnecessarily prolonged any proceeding by raising frivolous arguments or by other means, it may impose on that party the cost of that proceeding in such amount as it determines appropriate in light of the specific circumstances, regardless of the final results of the litigation.

In recent years, as a result of both a reluctance to use other sanctions for procedural misconduct and a growing frustration with such misconduct, which causes court delays and backlogs, there has been a growing tendency of the courts to use these financial sanctions more frequently.

This tendency is seen in three main areas. The first is the amount of costs awarded to winning parties. Despite the accepted Israeli theory that a winning party should generally be reimbursed in full for his costs, historically Israeli courts have frequently awarded sums that are clearly insufficient. Today, courts more regularly

35. *Shviki v. The State of Israel*, 62 (3) P.D. 806 (2008).
36. *Nir v. The State of Israel*, 49 (2) P.D. 639 (1995).

award higher costs. This change may be due to the frequent admonitions of the Supreme Court in this regard, as well as the example set by the Supreme Court in awarding costs on appeal.

The Supreme Court's attitude in this regard has been expressly based not only on the desire to make winning litigants 'whole', but also on the presumed deterrent effect of high cost awards on the filing and pursuing of frivolous claims and defences. In recent years, there has been a number of Supreme Court decisions in which the costs awarded were clearly in excess of the actual costs incurred by the prevailing side, and therefore can only be explained as a sanction imposed on the losing side for pursuing a frivolous claim or defence.

The second aspect of this new tendency has been the increasing willingness of the Supreme Court to deny costs to a winning party if he has unduly prolonged the litigation.[37]

The third aspect is the amendment of the previously discussed Rule 514 to provide that in cases of costs awarded because the party has unnecessarily prolonged the proceedings, the court may award 'costs to the State Treasury', in such amount as it sees fit in lieu of, or in addition to, awarding costs to the other party.

It is, of course, clearly a misuse of terms to speak of awarding 'costs' to the State in a case in which the State is not a party, where the sum awarded is not based on any calculation as to the expenses incurred by the State as operator of the judicial process, and where the payment is imposed on a party because of his faulty conduct.

It is doubtful, therefore, that the Minister of Justice had the authority to adopt this amendment. However, without ever discussing this issue on the merits, the courts have employed the amendment extensively so as to impose substantial 'costs' to the State Treasury.[38]

---

37. See for example: *Garbi v. Ben David*, 45 (5) P.D. 661 (1991).
38. For an extreme example, see *Super Medic v. Anton Hubner GmbH*, Israeli Supreme Court 615/11, 27 Mar. 2011 (unreported), in which the court imposed costs on both the appellants and the respondents for submitting what the court deemed to be unnecessarily long appeal submissions in spite of the fact that the briefs by the parties were not preceded by any delimitation of their length by the court. For a fuller discussion of the issue of awarding costs to the State, see S. Goldstein, *Reflections on the Possibilities and Problems of Accelerating the Civil Litigation Process*, 7 Tel Aviv Stud. L. 50, 64–66 (1986); Z. Zylbertal, *Costs Awarded to the State*, 15 Mishpatim 389 (1986).

Part IV. Proceedings

Chapter 1. Proceedings in First Instance

§1. Adversary Proceedings

I. Ordinary Proceedings

A. Notice

126. No matter what method of initiating proceedings is employed, the Rules require that notice of such initiation of proceedings be provided to the defendant. As discussed in paragraphs 96–102, international jurisdiction generally is based on effective service of process, including the document that initiated the proceedings, on the defendant. This service of process, whether within or without Israel, serves the dual purpose both of effecting international jurisdiction and of providing notice to the defendant of the initiation of the proceedings.

When service of process is not made personally on the defendant but is made on someone in his stead, such as a manager of his business or property in relevant cases, or on an adult member of his family living with the defendant (see paragraph 99 *supra* for details of such provisions), the courts have emphasized that the service must be such that it will be virtually certain that the defendant will receive the notice via the person served.

The Rules also recognize, however, that this rightful emphasis on providing notice to the defendant may have to be tempered by the right of the plaintiff to pursue his legal remedies. Thus they provide that in a situation in which the defendant is a resident of Israel but despite the diligent efforts of the process server, he has been unable to locate the defendant or to serve notice on someone in his stead pursuant to the Rules, or such a person has refused to receive the notice, the notice of the proceedings may be posted on the outside door or other conspicuous place of a building in which the defendant regularly lives or works.

In addition, they also provide that when absolutely none of the above methods are available for serving notice, the plaintiff may apply to the court to authorize 'substituted service'. Such substituted service may be effected:

(1) by posting at the court or at the building in which the defendant has recently lived or worked;
(2) by publication in a newspaper; or

(3) by any other method which the court deems reasonable under the circumstances.

It should be pointed out, however, that this provision provides for 'substituted service'; not for 'constructive service'. That is, in order to permit such service the court must be of the opinion that under the circumstances involved there is a reasonable likelihood that notice of the proceedings will, in fact, reach the defendant.

127. Finally, in terms of protection of the defendant, reference should be made to the possibility of setting aside default judgments that may have been entered due to the fact that the defendant did not receive notice of the proceedings and thus did not file a defence. Where the defendant has not been properly served with notice, a default judgment must be set aside as a matter of law. Where the notice has been proper, however, a default judgment may also be set aside at the discretion of the court. In a case in which despite proper notice – such as by substituted service as described above – the defendant did not in fact receive notice of the proceedings and he has a prima facie defence to the action, the court will use its discretion so as to set aside the default judgment.

B. The Different Types of Actions

128. Regular proceedings in the general courts may be initiated either by complaint or by originating summons. In addition, the Rules of Civil Procedure provide for a special expedited judgment process.

1. Pleading proceedings

a. Complaint; Rules 9, 14, 72-82

129. The primary method of conducting proceedings is by way of pleadings, the first of which is the complaint. The complaint must include the essential facts (as distinguished from conclusions, principles and provisions of law and evidence) which constitute the plaintiff's cause of action (claim), as well as the date on which the claim arose.

While, at times, it may be difficult to distinguish 'essential facts' from conclusions and evidence, the emphasis in the Rules is on relatively particularized factual accounts of the transaction or occurrence which forms the basis of the plaintiff's claim for relief. In certain situations, e.g., claims of fraud, deceit, malice or improper influence the Rules require even more detailed factual statements than are required generally.

The complaint should present a coherent version of the facts, and the plaintiff cannot base his claim on contradictory facts, unless he states that the facts are unknown to him. While, according to the RCP, this rule applies only to factual allegations, several decisions handed by the Supreme Court have expanded this prohibition to contradictory legal allegations, as well.[39] Generally, principles and provisions of law do not need to be set forth in the complaint, but may be included if the plaintiff so desires. Furthermore, reference to a provision of law in the complaint does not preclude the plaintiff from using other provisions of law at a later stage in the proceedings. Nonetheless, if the complaint includes a claim of breach of statutory provision the plaintiff is obliged to indicate in the complaint the statutory provision that was allegedly breached.

As stated above, generally, evidence, as distinguished from facts, should not be included in the complaint. The Rules do, however, contain a number of exceptions to this principle, for example, a plaintiff seeking to prove a matter involving medical issues must attach a medical document or expert opinion concerning the matter to his complaint.

A plaintiff must also list in the complaint all the documents upon which he relies and attach them to the complaint.

As discussed in paragraph 23, despite the recommendations of the Advisory Committee, as of this writing, the complaint need not be verified by affidavit.

The complaint must also specify the relief requested by the plaintiff. In addition, it must include the value of the subject matter of the action, so far as this is determinable. Where the claim is for a sum of money the complaint must specify the amount claimed, or the estimated amount if the exact sum will be clarified only during the proceedings. However, in a claim for damages due to personal injury, the plaintiff is not required to specify the amount of his general damages. In a claim involving land, the complaint must describe the land so as to enable its identification.

It should be noted that if specific relief is not requested or if the plaintiff has agreed to waive it, the court cannot order that relief, subject to the following exceptions:

(1) the parties implicitly agreed that the court would order that relief. The implied consent of the parties may be concluded from their behaviour during the proceedings;
(2) the relief results directly from the relief that is requested, or justice or efficiency compels the grant of such relief; and all the needed evidence for ordering the relief has been adduced before the court;
(3) it is a general remedy, i.e., interest, index-linked payments and costs.

The plaintiff may request cumulative or alternative remedies.

In addition to the essential facts and the requested relief, the complaint should include the name of the court in which the claim is filed and the basis for the court's jurisdiction in the case; the personal details of the plaintiff and defendant, including whether one or the other is incompetent, or is a corporation, and if so, what kind of corporation. A 2012 amendment to the RCP stated that if the plaintiff is an Israeli

39. *Beit Sason Ltd. v. Shicoon Ovdim and Investment Ltd.*, 59 (6) P.D. 625 (2005).

resident he must specify his Israeli identification number and if he is not an Israeli resident he must specify his passport number and country of issue of the passport. The amendment has been strongly criticized on the ground that it is expected to prevent persons who do not hold an Israeli citizenship or a valid passport from filing a claim in Israeli courts and consequently will deny their right of access to the courts. Following this criticism the Israeli Ministry of Justice published a clarification to the amendment. According to the clarification, these rules should not be interpreted as preventing Palestinians, refugees and stateless persons from filing a claim to a court in Israel, but as requiring the specification of an identification number or a passport number when the plaintiff holds one. Moreover, a later amendment to the RCP explicitly states that if the plaintiff does not have an Israeli identification number he should indicate this in his claim as well as the reasons for the lack thereof. In this case, the Chief Secretary of the court may approve the application of the complaint.

130. Following service of the complaint on him, the defendant must file an answer within the time set forth in the process, usually thirty days. The result of a failure to file an answer will be described *infra*, paragraph 196 in the section on default judgments.

In general, the defendant's failure to deny a factual allegation of the complaint is taken as an admission. Rule 85 provides expressly that a defendant may not file a general denial but must respond specifically, by a denial or admission, to each factual allegation of the complaint, except that of damages. Rule 86 makes it clear that the defendant's denial should not be evasive, and that he must present a full factual version of his position.

In practice however, these Rules are often ignored and defendants regularly file vague answers, which deny all the plaintiff's allegations in general language. In such a case, the court may ignore the defendant's denial and deal with the factual allegations as if they have been admitted by the defendant.

131. In addition to denying the factual allegations contained in the complaint, the defendant also has to allege affirmative defences if he intends to rely on such at trial. It is often most difficult to determine which defences the defendant must raise affirmatively, as distinguished from merely denying the allegations of the plaintiff.

In general, Rule 81 provides that a party need not raise in his pleadings matters as to which the burden of proof is on the other party. That is, the burden of pleading is derivative from the burden of proof. As discussed in paragraph 229, in most cases the burden of proof is on the plaintiff, therefore, if the plaintiff has not alleged a fact in his complaint, it is not part of the litigation. If he has raised it, the defendant may attempt to prove the falsity of the fact at trial if he has merely denied it in his answer. There are however certain matters concerning which the burden of proof at trial is on the defendant and thus he must raise their factual basis in his answer if he intends to prove them at trial. Rule 80 provides that the plaintiff need not claim in his complaint that a pre-condition for the existence of a cause of action was fulfilled. It further states that if the defendant wishes to claim that the pre-condition was not fulfilled, he should affirmatively claim so in his answer.

In addition, Rule 88 provides specifically that a mere denial of an allegation that there exists a contract between the parties is taken only as a denial of the existence of the contract, as distinguished from its legality or its legal sufficiency. If the defendant wishes to raise the latter, he must do so affirmatively. Similarly, a contention that the person who purportedly signed the contract on behalf of the defendant was not authorized to do so must be raised affirmatively.

Rule 89 provides further that the defendant must raise affirmatively anything that shows that the complaint is not well founded or that the transaction in issue is legally void or voidable, as well as any matter which, if not so raised, may surprise the plaintiff or raise factual questions which do not arise from the complaint, such as fraud, limitations, release, payment, performance, or facts that disclose an illegal action.

It should be noted that the defendant must raise affirmatively such matters as payment or performance if he wishes to rely on them at trial, despite the fact that in his complaint the plaintiff must effectively allege the opposite, i.e., that a monetary obligation is due and owing or that the defendant has violated his obligation by failing to perform.

The requirements discussed above as to the complaint concerning essential facts, conclusions, evidence, specificity, principles of law, etc., are also applicable to the affirmative allegations of the answer.

132. Finally, a defendant who wishes to raise a counterclaim must do so in his answer. See paragraph 113 concerning counterclaims.

b. Reply

133. In the vast majority of cases filed according to the ordinary procedure, the pleadings consist only of the complaint and answer. In such a case, the plaintiff is deemed to have denied any affirmative allegations in the defendant's answer, which relate to the plaintiff's claim. A plaintiff need only file a *reply* to the defendant's answer in two situations. First, when he wishes not only to deny the affirmative allegations in the defendant's answer but also to refute them with his own affirmative allegations, which were not included in the previous pleadings. Second, when the defendant has filed a counterclaim. In this latter event, the plaintiff's reply serves as an answer to the counterclaim and must comply with the requirements of an answer as set forth above. It should be noted that the plaintiff may not include in the reply a new cause of action or include a factual allegation that contradicts factual allegations previously set out in the complaint.

c. Further Particulars and Admissions

134. The pleadings filed by a party may omit a necessary particular or may not specify sufficient details. In such a case, if the omission is sufficiently grave the opposing party may have the pleading struck out. However, Rule 65 states that if the omission is less serious the court, either on its own initiative or at the application of the opposing party, may order the filing of further and better particulars of any matter mentioned in the pleadings.

The two main purposes of an application for further particulars are to limit the field of controversy and to clarify it. The further and better particulars aid in defining a general claim made in the pleadings, thus limiting the questions in controversy and preventing the opposing party from widening the controversy. They also clarify the controversy, thus allowing the party applying for the particulars to prepare more efficiently for trial and preventing surprises during the proceedings.

We should note that the 1991 amendments to the RCP, in accordance with their general aim of requiring greater clarity and reliability in the pleadings, revised and expanded the prior Rule as to particulars. Thus, since 1991, Rule 65 authorizes the court to order greater particularity not only as to any matter in the pleadings but also as to any matter 'related thereto'. Moreover, it may order that the factual matters be particularized by affidavit.

2. Originating summons and motion practice; Rules 248-258

135. The sources of originating summons proceedings are also derived from English procedure. As discussed above, ordinary pleading proceedings are designed to prepare the way for the determination of disputed factual matters on the basis of oral testimony based on first-hand knowledge, as distinguished from hearsay, and subject to cross-examination. This procedure, which is very costly and time consuming is only justified, if at all, when the case involves significant factual disputes.

Thus the originating summons proceeding was developed originally as an alternative proceeding for those types of cases which did not involve such factual disputes.

136. Today, originating summons proceedings may be used in lieu of ordinary proceedings in certain types of cases, at the option of the plaintiff. The first pleading in this type of procedure is a document called an 'originating summons', filed by a plaintiff who is designated the 'petitioner'. The originating summons must contain all the information required of an ordinary complaint, but, as distinguished from such a complaint, the petitioner must append to it an affidavit (based on first-hand knowledge) verifying the factual allegations contained in the originating summons. In addition, the petitioner is obliged to include in the originating summons the legal allegations and references upon which the action relies. The defendant, termed 'respondent', may, if he so desires, file a reply, however, must do so at least fourteen days before the hearing on the originating summons. Like the originating summons, the reply must contain all the information required of an ordinary answer, as well as the legal allegations and references upon which the reply relies, and the respondent must append to it an affidavit (based on first-hand knowledge) verifying the factual allegations. A respondent who has not filed a reply is not prevented from appearing at the hearing, presenting legal arguments in his defence or cross-examining the affiant on behalf of the petitioner. However, a recent amendment to the RCP (Rule 256A) as of 2013 states that when the respondent has not filed a reply or requested to hold a hearing within the time set out for filing a reply, the court can give a decision based on the originating summons, if under the circumstances of the case the court finds that it is justified to do so. It follows that the rule that applies to originating summons proceedings is different from the rule that applies to ordinary pleading proceedings. As will be explained hereinafter, in ordinary pleading proceedings the court cannot give a decision based on the complainant on its own initiative.

At the hearing of the originating summons, the parties have a right to cross-examine each other on their respective affidavits. They may, however, only introduce oral evidence with the permission of the court. Such permission will be given in cases where a party cannot, by himself or through another person, verify the factual allegations on which he relies on the basis of first-hand knowledge. This would be the case, for example, when the person who has first-hand knowledge regarding the facts refuses to cooperate with the party and is not subject to his control.

Procedures of disclosure and examination of documents are also applicable to originating summons proceedings, if the court believes that using these procedures will make the proceedings shorter and more efficient.[40] The Rules of Civil Procedure contain a list of matters as to which an originating summons may be used. They are:

(1) administrators of estates, guardians, or other fiduciaries who seek judicial approval of transactions or determinations of other issues relating to the relevant estates, as well as actions by heirs, beneficiaries, etc. for directions to fiduciaries;
(2) actions by buyers or sellers of land for declarations as to the meaning of a sales contract, as distinguished from the existence or validity of the contract;
(3) an action for dissolution of a partnership as long as the existence of the partnership is not itself in dispute;
(4) an action for a declaration as to the meaning of any document and the rights pursuant thereto;
(5) any action for a declaratory judgment.

137. The generally accepted view is that this list, however, is not closed and other types of actions may also be brought by an originating summons if they are appropriate for such a proceeding, that is, they do not involve complex and disputed factual matters that require the hearing of multiple or long and complex oral testimony or a determination of the credibility of oral testimony.[41] Indeed, there is authority to the effect that, in an appropriate case, an originating summons may be used even in a case specifically excluded from the above list, such as that concerning the validity of a contract for the sale of land.[42]

As noted above, use of an originating summons is originally at the option of the plaintiff-petitioner. However, if he does use an originating summons, the court may transfer the proceeding to the ordinary process if, in the view of the court, the specific case is not appropriate for the originating summons procedure. This may be

40. *Ragumi 1978 Ltd. v. Shelus*, Israeli Supreme Court Petition 2284/2005, 22 May 2005 (unreported).
41. *Bublil v. Indig*, Israeli Supreme Court Petition 10227/2006, 5 Feb. 2007 (unreported).
42. *Haim v. Habaiov*, 41 (1) P.D. 716 (1987).

carried out by the court either at the application of the defendant-respondent or on its own motion.

It should be noted that filing an application to transfer the proceeding to ordinary process, based on the claim that the specific case is not appropriate for hearing as an originating summons, would not serve as a justification for the extension of time prescribed in the rules to file a reply. A party who plans to file a reply in the event that his application for the transfer of proceedings is denied should file that reply within the time period prescribed in the RCP. This rule is subject to one exception: where prima facie there is a reasonable likelihood that the application for transfer will be upheld and filing a reply would require excessive resources to be invested.[43]

3. Expedited Judgment Proceedings; Rules 202-214

138. Rule 202 of the RCP provides as follows:

> A plaintiff may bring the following claims by summary judgment procedure:
>
> (1) Claims for a liquidated sum of money, with or without interest, as follows:
> (a) Claims based on an express or implied contract or obligation, provided there is written evidence thereof;
> (b) Claims based upon a commitment to pay a liquidated sum of money, arising out of an express provision of law;
>
> (2) Claims of a local government authority for the payment of a liquidated sum due it by law as a local government authority for municipal taxes, levies, fees or participation charges;
>
> (3) Claims for eviction from land, or eviction from rental premises to which the Tenants' Protection Law [Consolidated Version], 1972 does not apply, provided there is written evidence regarding the same.

139. The plaintiff's right to bring a claim for an expedited judgment is limited to the above causes of action. Joining a cause of action that is not included in this list to a cause of action that may be filed in expedited judgment proceeding would make the whole claim inappropriate for hearing in expedited judgment proceedings.

Except in the last case that deals with claims for eviction from land, all other claims that may be filed in expedited judgment proceedings are claims for a liquidated sum of money; that is a fixed sum of money or one that can be mathematically calculated, i.e., liquidated damages or interest. Therefore, a claim for declaratory judgment or a claim for personal injury compensation cannot be filed in expedited judgment proceedings.

If the plaintiff files an expedited judgment proceeding, the defendant has no right to defend the action unless and until he receives the court's leave to do so; a defendant's application for leave must be filed within the time set forth in the process (usually thirty days); it must include the defendant's contentions, the references

43. Bublil, *supra* n. 41.

upon which the application is based and it must be supported by an affidavit showing that the defendant has a prima facie defence on the merits and verifying the facts upon which this defence is based.

Other than in exceptional cases, for example, where the facts are in the knowledge of another person; the defendant's affidavit should support the application.

The status of a defendant who does not file a motion for leave within the period set in the Rules is identical to that of a defendant who does not file a reply. Therefore, in such a case the plaintiff is entitled to a default judgment.

In accordance with the general rule as to affidavits in support of interlocutory motions, set out in Rule 521, the affidavit does not need to be based on the personal knowledge of the affiant, but may be pursuant 'to the best of his belief' provided that the reasons for this belief are set out.

A hearing is held on the motion for leave before a judge or registrar, during which, the plaintiff may cross-examine the affiant on his affidavit. However, Rule 205 provides that the judge or registrar may accept the application based solely on the written application and may, for reasons that are to be recorded, reject the application without conducting a hearing on the matter. This rule is similar to the general rule concerning interlocutory motions, set out in Rule 241(d), according to which the court or the registrar is authorized to decide on the motion without cross-examination of the affiant, that is to say, solely on the basis of the pleadings filed by the parties.

The plaintiff's limited right to cross-examine the defendant on his affidavit may be understood in light of the narrow issue presented to the court by a defendant's motion for leave to defend, that is whether or not the defendant has demonstrated that he has a prima facie defence.

Israeli courts have adopted a lenient attitude toward applications for leave to defend, on the ground that rejecting the application would deny the defendant the right of access to the courts. Thus, the defendant's motion for leave will be rejected only in cases where it is clear beyond any doubt that his defence has no chance of succeeding. In other words, it is sufficient for the defendant to prove that he has a prima facie defence.[44] Therefore, the court should not examine the quality of the defendant's evidence nor how he would succeed in proving his defence. Furthermore, in determining this issue the judge or registrar will not enter into issues of credibility but instead will determine the matter on the presumption that the facts set forth in the defendant's affidavit are true.

It is the plaintiff's choice whether or not to utilize an expedited judgment proceeding; if he chooses to pursue such a proceeding, the proceeding may nonetheless be transferred to an ordinary process if, in the view of the court, the specific case is not appropriate for filing in the expedited judgment procedure. The court may transfer the proceedings as aforesaid either upon the application of the defendant or on its own motion.

It should be noted that like the legal position regarding originating summons, filing an application to transfer an expedited judgment proceeding to an ordinary process, based on the ground that the specific case is not appropriate for the expedited

44. *H'amerkava parking, Holon Ltd. v. Municipality of Holon*, 53 (1) P.D. 390 (1999).

judgment proceeding, would not serve as a justification for an extension of time prescribed in the rules for filing an application for leave to defend. A party who wishes to file an application for leave to defend in the event that his application for transfer is denied should file the application within the time period prescribed in the RCP. This rule is subject to one exception: where prima facie there is a reasonable likelihood that the application for transfer will be upheld and filing a reply would require excessive resources to be invested.[45]

140. The origin of this Israeli expedited judgment procedure is found in Order 14 of the Rules of the Supreme Court of England, as this Order was then in force when the Rules of Civil Procedure based on such English Rules were introduced into the District Courts (1938) and Magistrates' Courts (1941) of Mandatory Palestine.

The expedited judgment procedure as adopted in Mandatory Palestine was limited to what is now section 1(a) of Rule 202. The other sections of the Rule were added after the establishment of the State of Israel; sections 1(b) and 2 in 1953; section 3 was not added until 1976.

More important, however, than these additions are the fundamental changes that occurred in the Israeli procedure since the Mandatory rules, which have brought the procedure far from its English origin and have resulted in its now being the functional equivalent of procedures existing in some civil law systems.

The first and most significant of these relates to the requirements of the complaint filed by the plaintiff. Under the Mandatory rule, in order to invoke this expedited judgment procedure, a plaintiff had to attach to his statement of claim an affidavit verifying the facts on which his claim was based and stating that in the plaintiff's belief the defendant has no defence to the claim. Only after such an affidavit had been filed by the plaintiff did the defendant need to apply for leave to defend, pursuant to which he filed his counter-affidavit.

This situation of affidavit and counter-affidavit still applies under Order 14 of the English Rules of the High Court. However, the Israeli Rules of Civil Procedure of 1963 introduced a major change into the Israeli procedure. The necessity for a plaintiff's affidavit verifying the facts of his statement of claim and stating his belief that the defendant has no defence was abolished. Instead, if the claim meets the requirements of what is now Rule 202, it may be filed in the expedited judgment procedure without any requirement of additional affidavits or other documents. The only factor, therefore, distinguishing a complaint filed today in the expedited judgment procedure from one filed in the pleading procedure is the title of the complaint which reads: 'Expedited Judgment Procedure.'

Thus, the Israeli expedited judgment procedure, as set forth in the 1963 Rules of Civil Procedure, applied to specific types of claims for liquidated sums for which there was a justifiable presumption that the defendant had no defence. The essential purpose of the procedure was to expedite 'debt collection'.

45. *Bar-Lev (Arcadi Gaydamak) v. Balram Chainrai*, Israeli Supreme Court Petition 1206/2009, 21 Jun. 2009 (unreported).

141. Even further expedition of debt collection was achieved in 1963 when the Execution Law, 1967, was amended to confer the force of a judgment upon all negotiable instruments. Previously actions on negotiable instruments, such as bills of exchange, promissory notes and cheques, were among the primary uses of the expedited judgment procedure described herein.

However since 1968, the holder of a negotiable instrument need not initiate any judicial action at all; rather he may directly execute upon the negotiable instrument through the Execution Offices. If the debtor seeks to deny his liability, he must file an opposition in the Execution Office, setting forth his defence and verified by an affidavit. This opposition serves the same purpose as a motion for leave to defend filed in a proceeding under Rule 202. Indeed, when such an opposition is filed, the Execution Office must stay the execution and refer the matter to the court, which then deals with the opposition as an application for leave to defend in an expedited judgment procedure. That is, upon the filing of an opposition, the claim is treated as if it had been filed originally as an expedited judgment procedure. Thus the special execution procedure for negotiable instruments is, in effect, a subprocedure of the expedited judgment procedure providing a super-expedited debt collection process as to negotiable instruments.

The basic nature of the expedited judgment procedure, i.e., its limitation to 'debt collection' type claims as to which there is a justifiable presumption that the defendant has no defence, was not affected significantly by the addition, in 1976, to Rule 202 of subsection (3) relating to ejectment and eviction claims; these claims are quite specific and delimited and are, in effect, in the field of real property, the functional equivalent of debt collection claims as to monetary obligations.

142. However, along with its retention of the requirement that a plaintiff file an affidavit as to the facts and his belief that the defendant has no defence, the English Order 14 was greatly extended in 1962, and now applies to almost all types of claims, including claims for unliquidated damages. Due to these separate and divergent developments in Israel and England, it is clear that in its present form the Israeli expedited judgment procedure no longer resembles Order 14 in England.

This independent development of the Israeli procedure necessarily raises the question of whether the procedure is justified. It should be noted in this regard that while the procedure has been subject to criticism and, indeed, in 1984, was changed as a result of such criticism, the criticism has not been directed primarily at the heart of the procedure – the need for the defendant to receive permission to defend – but rather at an ancillary aspect of this process. The 1963 Rules of Civil Procedure, provided, *inter alia*, that when leave to defend is granted, 'a date for the hearing [on the main action] will be set immediately, in the Court's order granting leave to defend'. While this was not the only possible interpretation of the above language, the clause was interpreted to mean that not only was the date for the hearing to be set immediately, but that the hearing itself was to be held as soon as possible.

The effect, therefore, was that although in principle, following the granting of leave to amend, an action that originated as one for expedited judgment was to be maintained thereafter as an ordinary action, such action continued to enjoy a great advantage over ordinary actions, i.e., an earlier trial date, queue jumping preference.

Nor was this advantage merely theoretical; it was of great practical importance, particularly since Israeli courts have been increasingly plagued by lengthy delays in the litigation process. These delays caused ordinary actions in some judicial districts to wait years for a judicial hearing at the first instance. Moreover, the situation was exacerbated further by Israel's high inflation that could result in the reduction of the real value of the plaintiff's claim during the long waiting period.

This practical advantage of filing claims by expedited judgment procedure even when leave to defend was granted, was not lost on plaintiffs or potential plaintiffs, but rather was much appreciated by them. Thus, plaintiffs had a great incentive to try to file their claims by the expedited judgment procedure, even if they knew that it was almost certain that the defendant would apply for and be granted leave to defend. The result was continuing attempts by plaintiffs to expand the use of the expedited judgment procedure.

This process was further encouraged by that fact that if a plaintiff files a claim in a expedited judgment procedure and it turns out that he has attempted to expand the process further than the judge or registrar before whom the matter is brought is prepared to go, the plaintiff suffers no real set-back. A claim improperly brought in an expedited judgment procedure is not subject to dismissal on that account. Rather the only result is the striking out of the heading of the complaint, which describes it as having been brought in the expedited judgment procedure. Following that striking out, the claim proceeds as an ordinary one, with no loss even of its place in the regular queue for a judicial hearing; that is, the same result as if it had been originally filed as a regular action. Therefore, there was no reason for a plaintiff not to try his luck by attempting to file a doubtful action as an expedited judgment procedure.

In most cases, of course, the defendant would object. However, as noted above, no real penalty would be imposed on the plaintiff if he lost on this point. Moreover, in some cases the defendant may not be opposed to providing the claim with an early hearing, queue jumping, preference by having it filed in the expedited judgment procedure. In such cases, the plaintiff and defendant may agree in advance that the plaintiff will not oppose the defendant's motion for leave to defend in return for the defendant not raising the issue of the appropriateness of filing the claim in the expedited judgment procedure.

Thus, it is clear why plaintiffs continually attempted to expand the use of the expedited judgment procedure. It is less clear why the courts acquiesced in this expansion.

As we have noted above, it would appear that the principal, if not exclusive, purpose of the expedited judgment procedure as adopted in 1963 was that of the enforcement of debt collection, primarily those debts involving negotiable instruments such as cheques, and municipal tax claims. A major function of the expedited judgment procedure was, therefore, removed from its direct application when, in 1968, claims based on negotiable instruments became enforceable directly through the Execution Offices. It may have been expected that this would have resulted in the expedited judgment procedure, as such, losing much of its importance. However, this did not occur.

Even prior to 1968, the courts had begun to acquiesce in the desire of plaintiffs to expand the use of the expedited judgment procedure well beyond that of 'debt collection' claims. This was accomplished through a wide interpretation of the elements of Rule 202, primarily those relating to the definition of 'an expressed or implied contract or obligation', and as to the necessity that the claim be based on 'written evidence'.

In so expanding the use of the expedited judgment procedure, despite the criticism directed against such expansion, it seems that the courts also were influenced by the very long delays often involved in filing claims in the regular proceedings and thus were sympathetic to the plight of plaintiffs who attempted to avoid these delays by widening the use of the expedited judgment procedure. As a result, however, the courts not only failed to alleviate the basic problem of the severely long delays involved in the regular process, but, by giving preference to expedited judgment claims, indeed, exacerbated the situation as to ordinary claims.

143. This matter finally came to a head in 1980 when a special committee that had been appointed by the Minister of Justice to study the structure and jurisdiction of the courts recommended that the expedited judgment procedure be abolished altogether. However, the recommendations of the Committee were based only on the negative aspects of the procedure that derived from giving cases filed in the expedited judgment procedure expedited trial dates after leave to defend had been granted.

When, therefore, this recommendation was considered by the Advisory Committee to the Minister of Justice on the Rules of a Civil Procedure, this latter committee recommended not to abolish the expedited judgment procedure completely, but rather to abolish only that clearly unjustified part of the procedure, i.e., the expedited trial date, queue jumping, preference given to cases filed in this procedure after leave to amend has been granted.

This recommendation was accepted by the Minister of Justice and in the new 1984 Rules of Civil Procedure the expedited judgment procedure was retained, but without the Rule that had been interpreted to provide for expedited hearings. In the authors' view, it is clear that in omitting such a rule, the intention was that, following the granting of leave to defend, actions filed in expedited judgment proceedings would be treated in the same manner as all other claims in terms of the queue for trial.

However it has been argued in Y. Sussman, *The Law of Civil Procedure*, edited by Dr Shlomo Levin, the Deputy President of the Israeli Supreme Court, that this was not the necessary result of the omission of this rule.[46] In this view, while, 'the Rules abolished the automatic preference that had been given to claims filed in the expedited judgment procedure, the question of whether to expedite them in preference to other claims is now given to the president of each court'.[47]

Moreover, Justice Levin adds that the presidents of the courts 'should continue to give a preference to such claims. Unless they do so, the expedited judgment proceeding will lose – to a great extent – its meaning and the justification for its existence'.[48] He provides, however no justification for his view either as to the intention

46. Yoel Sussman, *The Law of Civil Procedure* 656 (7th ed., Dyonon Publishing 1995).
47. *Ibid.*
48. *Ibid.*

of the drafters of the 1984 Rule in omitting the early hearing rule or as to the normative desirability of continuing to grant queue jumping preference to expedited judgment proceeding except to state, laconically, as to the latter, that such a preference is justified 'on grounds of desirable judicial administration'.[49]

In our view, as we have already noted, it is clear that the 1984 Rule intended to abolish the queue preference given to expedited judgment proceedings over regular proceedings. This, of course, is not to say that in an expedited judgment proceeding, as in a regular proceeding, it may not be justified to grant a queue preference as a matter of the discretion of the president of the court in the circumstances of a specific case. Yet, that is a far cry from a general rule that presidents of the courts should use their discretionary powers to grant automatic queue preferences to all expedited judgment proceedings, *qua* expedited judgment proceedings. If this were to be done, it would be hard to understand what meaning would be given to the omission of the queue preference rule in the new Rules of Civil Procedure.

Moreover, as already indicated, in the authors' view, the abolishing of the queue preference rule was clearly correct. Early trial dates for expedited judgment proceedings, *qua* expedited judgment proceedings, after leave to appeal has been granted, are not justified. Moreover, the granting of this preference has served as an incentive to distort the basic purpose of the expedited judgment procedure.

4. Case allocation departments and the fast track

143(a). Both case allocation departments and the fast track are very recent innovations in Israeli civil litigation, which were inspired by the new case management reforms adopted in the English Civil Procedure Rules 1998, as a result of the recommendations of the well known Wolff Report.In 2001, the Courts Law was amended so as to authorize the Minister of Justice, in consultation with the President of the Supreme Court, to create in the courts 'departments for case allocation'. The Minister exercised this authority in enacting, in 2002, special rules entitled 'Court Rules (Case Allocation Department), 2002'. While neither the Courts Law nor these Rules limit the creation of the departments only to certain courts, in fact they have thus far been created only in the Magistrates' courts.

While many aspects of these case allocation departments have yet to be implemented, the 2002 Rules are quite clear as to the ultimate aims of these departments, which is case management similar to the new English procedures. Thus, the Rules provide that the Administrator of the Courts, with the approval of the Minister of Justice, is to design a national case allocation department plan which will include the following activities of these departments:

(1) sorting, classifying and evaluating cases with the aim to insure that judicial time will be expended only where judicial judgment is required;
(2) allocating cases to the appropriate track in order to expedite their treatment;

49. *Ibid.*

(3) preliminary approaches to parties or their attorneys in order to insure honest and expeditious proceedings;
(4) approaches to parties, in appropriate cases, in order to receive their consent to referring cases for alternate dispute resolution proceedings, including mediation, arbitration, and preliminary neutral evaluation of the chances of success of the parties (hereinafter 'ADR');
(5) allocating cases in a given court to a 'control centre' judge or other judges according to their subjects and the fields of expertise of the judges;
(6) creating and operating follow-up and oversight procedures in the courts concerning the treatment of cases, including those referred to ADR;
(7) advising parties who are not represented by counsel so as to insure equal access to the courts, more expeditious proceedings and savings in resources.

Following the creation of this national plan, which to the best of our knowledge has yet to be implemented in full, the chief judge of each court is to create a more detailed plan for the court over which he presides. In addition, the Administrator of the Courts, with the approval of the Minister of Justice, is to determine in which courts there will be a 'control centre judge', who then will be appointed from the judges of that court by the court's chief judge. Each such control centre judge 'will be responsible for the administration of the case allocation department, as well as for other preliminary proceedings, including defining the issues in dispute between the parties, disposing of interim motions, referring cases to alternate dispute resolution proceedings, preparing cases for trial either before himself or other judges, all of which [is to be done] with the aim of improving the efficiency of the treatment of the case at trial'.

While the control centre judge, if one exists, is to have ultimate responsibility for the case allocation department, this department is to be administered on a daily basis by a newly created court employee, entitled the 'Legal Secretary'. The criteria to be appointed legal secretary are set out in the Rules quite explicitly and clearly indicate the function to be performed by the Legal Secretary. The appointee must be an attorney who has completed a course for mediators, or is committed to do so within a year of the appointment. Also, he or she is to be knowledgeable in the Rules of Civil Procedure as well as in the administration of courts, including the use of computers in the courts.

Without going into the very detailed provisions as to the functions of the control centre judge and Legal Secretary, their direction is very clear: case management as adopted by the English reform based on the Wolff Report. The basic aim of the case management recommendation of the Wolff Report is to transfer major aspects of the management of the pre-trial proceedings from the parties and their attorneys to the court. On the other hand, it should be noted that in accordance with Israeli theory, if not practice, referrals to ADR are still officially suggestions to the parties rather than orders of the court.

143(b). As stated above, also in accordance with the English-inspired case management reforms, the Israeli Rules of Civil Procedure, 1984, were amended in 2001 to add a 'fast track' procedure (Rules 214A-214Q). This is not the place for a detailed study of the English case management reforms. Suffice it to note, however, that an integral part of those reforms is the allocation of all cases to one of three tracks: the small claims track, the fast track and the multi-track. On the face of it, Israel adopted, in 2001, only one of these tracks, the fast track. However, such a view is misleading. In reality, Israel now has a complete track system similar to that of the English.As discussed in paragraph 65, *supra*, Israel has long had small claims courts which, despite being entitled 'courts' are not separate courts, but rather divisions within the Magistrates' Courts.

As to the multi-track, actually under the English scheme this track is a catch-all which includes all cases falling outside both the small claims track and the fast track. The result is a situation which is not dissimilar to that in Israel. While there is no name in the new Israeli procedure for cases that are not pursued in either the small claims division or the fast track, they are subject to case management under the rules described above in paragraph 143(a) concerning the case allocation departments, the control centre judges and the Legal Secretary. Such case management, if and when it is fully implemented, will not be dissimilar to the case management provisions of the English multi-track process.

In both the English and Israeli procedures the primary rationales for using the fast track are the relatively small amounts involved, the goal of shortening proceedings and reduction of administrative costs. In Israel the fast track is designed for claims that are filed in Magistrates' courts in the form of regular claims or that are transferred to Magistrates' courts from the Small Claims courts and do not exceed NIS 75,000. Excluded from this category are claims where an application to approve a class action has been filed and claims based on the Road Accident Victims Compensation Law, 1975. A claim that is filed within the framework of an expedited judgment proceeding will be routed to the fast track path only if an application for leave to defend has been filed and approved. It turns out that claims that do not exceed NIS 75,000, filed within the framework of expedited judgment proceedings, will not automatically be routed to the fast track path. It follows that in claims that do not exceed NIS 75,000 the plaintiff has a choice whether to file the claim within the framework of an expedited judgment proceeding or as a regular claim which means that it will be assigned to the fast track path.

The Israeli rules automatically assign all cases to the fast track which fall within the NIS 75,000 limit stated above. Subsequently, however, a court is authorized to transfer a fast track case to the regular proceedings if it finds that it is not suitable for the fast track. In making such determination the court is to consider such factors as the complexity of the facts and evidence involved, the number of parties, complications caused by the existence of counterclaims and third-party actions, the extent of oral evidence and expert testimony involved, and the effect of the determination of the case on the public at large. Moreover, upon the application of all the parties, and if the court believes that the claim is suitable for the fast track path, a court may order a case to proceed in the fast track even if it is above the monetary limit.

We will not further compare the details of the Israeli fast track proceedings with its English parent as such a comparison would go well beyond the confines of this monograph. We would point out, however, one major difference in the general approach between the two systems. The English rules leave very wide discretion to the judges in managing the fast track, as they do with regard to the entire case management process. In contrast, the Israeli version of the fast track, while still leaving room for some judicial discretion, is determined to a greater extent by specific rules.

143(c). In contrast to most regular proceedings, the pleadings in fast track cases must be verified by affidavits. This requirement is a continuation of a general trend in Israeli procedure concerning the use of affidavits, as discussed in paragraph 23, *supra*.

In addition to affidavits verifying the facts pleaded, the parties in the fast track must attach legal authorities and expert opinions to their pleadings, if they have any.

It follows that there is another difference between pleadings in the fast track and pleadings in the regular track. In the latter case, the plaintiff should not attach his legal authorities to his pleadings and should only attach expert opinions relating to medical matters.

In addition, the parties must attach to their pleadings a list of all documents relevant to the case, not only those on which they intend to rely. If such documents are in the possession of the pleader, they are to be attached to the pleading. If they are not, the pleader is to state in an affidavit in whose possession they are, to the best of his knowledge.

These provisions concerning the disclosure and attachment of documents as part of the pleadings are termed in the fast track rules 'early disclosure of documents'. This term indicates clearly the unusual aspect of these rules as compared to regular proceedings, which is the timing of the disclosure of documents. Whereas under the ordinary proceedings disclosure of documents is part of the discovery process, which takes place after the close of the pleadings, in the fast track it is part of the pleading, process itself. Moreover, whereas in the ordinary process such disclosure takes place only at the application of another party, here there is a direct disclosure obligation on each party without the need for an application. Yet the essence of the disclosure obligation remains the same.

Another innovation in the fast track procedure is the requirement that, within forty-five days from the close of the pleadings, all parties must file witness affidavits, which will serve as the direct testimony of such witnesses. A witness as to whom such an affidavit has not been filed is precluded from testifying at trial, except if the court allows him to do so due to the extraordinary situation involved in a given case. Such an exchange of witness affidavits was also part of the 1988 reform proposals discussed in paragraph 23, *supra*, which were rejected at the time. Instead, as discussed in paragraph 247, *infra*, the court at the pre-trial conference or the trial was merely authorized to require such affidavits. The fast track rules, therefore, return to the original concept of requiring such witness affidavits of all parties shortly after the close of the pleadings. In the attempt to expedite the fast track process, certain restrictions are placed on the filing of counterclaims, third-party actions and preliminary relief. A counterclaim may only be filed if it does not involve parties other than those already part of the action and, if filed as a separate claim, either it would itself be filed in the fast track procedure or, alternatively, it arises out of the same transaction or occurrence as the original claim. The restriction that a counterclaim not involve other parties is unique in Israeli civil procedure but its practical effect is quite limited. More significant is the restriction that the counterclaim itself either be a claim suitable for the fast track or arise out of the same transaction or occurrence as the original claim.

Generally, in Israeli civil procedure a defendant may file any claim he has against the plaintiff as a counterclaim with no requirement of any connection between the two claims. However, the requirement of a connection between the two claims is not unprecedented. Thus, when the plaintiff's claim has been filed in a Magistrates Court, i.e., the lower level first instance court and the defendant's claim would ordinarily be filed in a District Court, i.e., the higher level first instance court, he may file it as a counterclaim in the action in the Magistrates Court if, and only if, it arises out of the same transaction or occurrence as the original claim. The analogy is clear. In an attempt to prevent the fast track process from being burdened by unrelated counterclaims which themselves are not suitable for fast track proceedings, the Rules equate the fast track to a separate first instance court which is below an ordinary Magistrates' Court.

Third-party actions are also limited, but again not uniquely so. In Israeli procedure, the defendant in an ordinary action has a right to file a third-party action without the necessity of receiving judicial permission to do so. However, where the plaintiff's action has been filed by the issuance of an originating summons, rather than by the ordinary process, the defendant may file a third-party action only with permission of the court. This rule is aimed at preventing originating summons actions, which generally involve claims, which do not involve complicated factual questions, from being burdened by third-party actions, which may be of an entirely different character than those suitable for the originating summons procedure. Analogously, the same principle has been adopted for the fast track process.

As to preliminary relief, the restrictions apply neither to the forms of such relief available to the plaintiff nor to the criteria for granting them, but rather only to the timing of the applications for such relief and the process for their determination. Thus, the fast track rules provide that a written application for preliminary relief be filed 'as early as possible after the reason for such relief has arisen'. In dealing with an application for preliminary relief, the court has great flexibility. Thus, it may deny the application summarily if it believes it to be unfounded. If it believes the application requires a response, the court may order the plaintiff to send the application to the defendant who will then ordinarily have seven days in which to respond in writing. The court may then determine the issue on the written statements. If it does so, it is to render its decision within seven days after the defendant's response. Alternatively, it may order an oral hearing to be held as part of the preliminary hearing, as will be discussed below, at the trial on the merits or at some other early date. In such a case, the court is to render its decision within seven days of the oral hearing.

As can clearly be seen, the fast track procedure retains the substance of the preliminary relief provisions while expediting the determination of preliminary relief applications so that they will not impede the basic objective of the fast track process, taking straightforward cases to trial within a limited but reasonable timescale.

This brings us then to the heart of the process: the timetable. The Rules provide that following the close of the pleadings the court shall set the date for trial, which date shall not be later than six months after the close of the pleadings.

Rule 214L also authorized the court to hold one preliminary conference if it sees that it is necessary to do so 'in order to expedite, simplify and accelerate the proceeding and to clarify the most suitable way of determining the case'. This preliminary conference is quite similar to the traditional pre-trial conference in Israeli procedure which, as noted in paragraph 158, *infra*, was adopted by Israel from American procedure in 1963. However, it has been adapted to the requirements of the fast track. Thus, the preliminary conference is to be held, if possible, within thirty days after the close of the pleadings. The matters to be dealt with at the preliminary conference include the following: determining that the case is suitable to the fast track process and transferring it to the regular process if it is not; insuring that the parties have complied with all the requirements of the fast track process; determining the questions that are truly in dispute between the parties; determining applications for preliminary relief as discussed above; appointing agreed upon or court appointed experts; determining the dates for the filing of witness affidavits if this has not yet been done; determining the list of witnesses who will be called at trial; presenting suggestions to the parties for compromise settlements, for determining the case by a 'compromise judgment', or for referring the case to arbitration or mediation; and imposing costs or fines on parties who have not complied with the provisions of the fast track rules or who have otherwise unnecessarily delayed the proceedings.

One of the most important objects of both the regular pre-trial conference, see paragraphs 158, 161, *infra*, and the fast track preliminary conference, is to try to induce the parties to settle. In order to facilitate this purpose the Israeli rules as to the pre-trial conference specifically authorize the court to summon the parties themselves, in addition to their attorneys, to the conference. Yet the summoning of the parties is not required, but is merely within the authority of the court. Moreover, case law that preceded the adoption of the fast track rules held that such summoning cannot be automatic, but must be the result of a particular determination of the court in each individual case.

In order to overcome this case law the preliminary conference fast track rules provide specifically that the parties themselves must attend the preliminary conference unless the court has determined otherwise.

Yet most curiously, these Rules also provide that, if possible, the judge who presides at the preliminary conference should not be the same judge who will later decide the case at trial. There is no similar provision in Israeli procedure as to the regular pre-trial conference or other aspects of pre-trial procedure. Not only does this provision detract from the efficiency of the preliminary conference vis-à-vis the later trial, it also greatly reduces the power of the judge in the preliminary conference in his attempts to persuade the parties to settle the case or to use ADR. As such, it is clearly inconsistent with the general trend of Israeli procedure in these regards.

The Rules further provide that the trial in fast track cases should normally take no more than one day. In the unusual event that the trial is not finished in one day, the examination of witnesses should continue on a daily basis without interruption until completion. In any event any trial session, including that involving legal arguments as distinguished from the testimony of witnesses, should be held no more than fourteen days after the previous session.

These apparently curious and somewhat contradictory provisions must be understood in light of the fact that there is generally no continuous trial in Israeli litigation practice. Rather, as discussed in paragraph 255, *infra*, the trial, both as to oral testimony and legal arguments, is generally held in short sessions which may last over months or even years. These Rules suggest strongly that fast track cases should be determined in one day and, if not, by a continuous process.

In order to encourage this result the court is given express authority to limit the examination of a witness, if it thinks that the examination is not relevant to the issues involved, is not fair or is more burdensome and complicating than constructive.

Further, in keeping with the aim of this short and concise trial process, the Rules provide that if the parties wish to present written arguments to the court they should submit them no later than seven days before trial. Oral summations are to be made immediately following the conclusion of the taking of testimony.

Immediately following the trial or within fourteen days thereafter, at the latest, the court is to render its judgment. While this judgment is to be reasoned, it also is to be concise, 'unless the court believes that the reasoning should be more detailed because the judgment contains an innovation in the law, or is of special importance to the public at large or because of other unusual circumstances which must be recorded' (Rule 214Q).

All of these provisions concerning the trial and judgment are at great variance with regular Israeli litigation practice. Again, we would emphasize that this fast track procedure is the exception and the norm of Israeli civil procedure remains as described in the other paragraphs of this monograph.

C. *Summary Dismissal*

144. An action may be dismissed summarily by the court in one of two ways: the first, with prejudice, that is the plaintiff is barred by res judicata from reinstating the action; the second is without prejudice, that is, the plaintiff may reinstate the action. It should be emphasized that the courts have ruled that extreme care must be taken before a case is dismissed summarily whether with or without prejudice.

145. Rule 100 authorizes the court to dismiss an action summarily, without prejudice, in a number of situations. The first and most important is where the facts alleged in the complaint or originating summons do not show a cause of action. That is, even if the plaintiff were to prove all his factual allegations, he would still not be entitled to relief as a matter of law. In most circumstances, an action will only so be dismissed at the application of the defendant, but in exceptional situations, the court may act on its own motion. It should be emphasized, as mentioned above, that the courts are most reluctant to dismiss an action summarily: they will do so only where it is absolutely clear that the plaintiff cannot succeed on the merits and after he has been provided with an opportunity to amend the complaint or originating summons, if the defect is correctable by amendment.[50]

An action may also be dismissed summarily pursuant to Rule 100 if the court finds it to be frivolous or vexatious. Here again, however, dismissal is warranted only in extreme cases and subject to the right of the plaintiff to try to correct the defect by amendment.

Finally, an action may be dismissed without prejudice where the plaintiff has not paid the required court filing fee. See paragraphs 220–223.

146. Rule 101(a) applies to summary dismissals with prejudice and specifically authorizes such dismissals where the action is barred by res judicata or for lack of jurisdiction. In addition, the court is authorized to dismiss summarily for any other reason for which the action may be dismissed at the outset.

This last clause allows the defendant to raise, either by motion for summary dismissal or in his answer, preliminary defences such as limitation. It should be remembered that such defences as is the case with issues of jurisdiction (and res judicata), should be raised and determined at an early stage of the proceedings.

The classification of lack of jurisdiction as a Rule 101 dismissal with prejudice seems clearly wrong; it should be classified as a dismissal without prejudice. However, there is very little practical significance to this misclassification. This is so since, as discussed in paragraph 95, where a court believes that it lacks either subject matter or territorial (venue) jurisdiction, it does not dismiss the action; rather it transfers it to the appropriate court. This result is also required by a specific reference in Rule 101(b). Where a court believes it lacks international jurisdiction, it does, indeed, dismiss the action. However, in such a case a later action on the same cause of action will presumably be brought abroad. In such a case, it would seem inconceivable that the foreign court would hold the action barred by res judicata due to the Israeli misclassification.

D. *Progress of Proceedings*

1. Preparatory measures

a. General

147. As discussed above, the detailed factual nature of the pleadings and, particularly, the requirement that the parties plead expressly any fact that might otherwise 'surprise' an opposing party, as well as the use of further particulars might seem to be all that is required in order for the parties to prepare properly for trial. Yet, in addition to those pleading requirements the RCP contain additional discovery devices.

The explanation for this is threefold. First, in actual practice the pleadings are not nearly as detailed as the Rules would seem to require. Second, even if the pleadings were so detailed, in order to defend properly against the opposing party's case, a

50. See for example: *Chukit H'acarmel Projects Ltd. v. Micha Chah General Contracting Ltd.*, Israeli Supreme Court Petition 5634/2005, 4 Jun. 2007 (unreported).

party might need other devices. Thus, for example, in terms of documents the Rules only require parties to attach to their pleadings documents upon which the claim is based. This means that a party will usually only attach documents that support his allegations. Yet, an opposing party obviously might want to see other documents before trial, that is documents that support his allegations and documents that contradict or weaken the other party's allegations.

Third and most importantly, even if the pleadings were as detailed as possible they would only serve to help a party prepare his defence against the adversary's case. They would not help him discover information or documents known to his adversary, which the latter does not intend to use, precisely because they would help the case of the party who does not have knowledge of or access to these documents.

The discovery devices are designed to achieve, therefore, two purposes: first, to help a party to prepare properly his defence against the opponent's case and, second, to assist a party in preparing his own case by allowing him access to information and documents known or in the possession of other parties. Additional goals of the discovery devices are more of a public nature: to reduce administrative costs, shorten proceedings and expose the truth.[51]

The primary discovery devices set out in the RCP are written interrogatories, disclosure and examination of documents and inspection of property.

It should be emphasized that all these devices may be used only incidentally to pending proceedings and none of them may be utilized unless and until an action has been filed. The RCP do not provide for any pre-action discovery. Moreover, there is no discovery against non-parties; that is, all of these devices may be used only against parties to the litigation. Excluded from this rule are cases in which documents that are relevant to the proceedings are in the possession of a company, which is not a party to the claim, but is under the control of a party to the claim.[52]

Subject to these limitations, and others that will be discussed below, the scope of discovery, in terms of the subjects covered, is quite broad. Discovery is permitted concerning any fact or document relevant to the action, whether or not the particular fact or document will be admissible in evidence. It is sufficient that the item as to which discovery is sought may lead to evidence that is helpful to a party in defending against his opponent's allegations or in supporting his own allegations. In addition, the relevance of the information to the claim should not be certain at this point of time, and the party may only prove that the information has some relevance to the claim. Moreover, while discovery is, indeed, limited to parties, the party against whom discovery is sought need not be a party adverse to the seeker of the discovery; it is sufficient that he be a party to the action.

---

51. See, for example: *Academic Arab College For Education in Israel, Haifa v. Kna'an*, Israeli Supreme Court Petition 10538/2008, 12 Apr. 2009 (unreported); *Sonol Israel Ltd. v. Lizerovich*, Israeli Supreme Court Petition 3068/2008, 20 Aug. 2008 (unreported).
52. *Leviev v. Refaeli*, Israeli Supreme Court Petition 11126/2008, 7 May 2009 (unreported).

b. Interrogatories, disclosure and examination of documents and Inspection of Property; Rules 105–124.

148. A party may serve on another party interrogatories, i.e., a list of written questions, which must be answered by affidavit within thirty days. He may also apply for another party to disclose by affidavit the existence of any documents relevant to the action, which are, or once were, in the possession of the disclosee.

The object of the Rules is to allow such discovery to be conducted without judicial intervention. Thus, a party seeking discovery must apply for it in writing from the other party within thirty days after the filing of the final pleading, either the answer or reply if there is one. It is only after the requestee has not responded within thirty days of the request, that the requesting party may petition for a court order.

As to interrogatories, in such a petition the requesting party must set forth the exact questions to which he wants the other party to respond. As noted above each of these questions must be relevant to the substance of the action, but the test for such relevance is very broad.[53]

However, the Rules view compelling a party to respond to interrogatories as a greater intrusion on him than some of the other devices. In determining whether or not to issue such an order, Rule 107 provides specifically that the court should consider any alternative suggestions made by the requestee concerning the provision of further particulars, admission of facts or inspection of documents if any or all of these would suffice in lieu of interrogatories.

Where an order to respond to interrogatories has been issued, the requestee must respond by affidavit within a specific time, usually seven days. If he objects to a particular question, he must set forth the objection in his affidavit.

If the requestee has not responded, or if his answer is not adequate, the requesting party may petition the court for a further order requiring the requestee to respond or to respond further, as is applicable, either by affidavit or by oral interrogation. Only following the failure of the requestee to respond adequately to this second court order may sanctions be employed against him.

Two points are worthy of note regarding this procedure as to interrogatories. First, it is very long and complex, consisting of three stages: a request outside of the judicial process and two court orders before sanctions may be employed. In our view, it would be desirable to shorten the process by eliminating the need for the second court order.

Second, the possibility of an order to answer orally if the affidavit is insufficient is unique in Israeli discovery procedure, which procedure does not include American-style depositions. It is limited, however, to situations where the responses to the first court order are found to be insufficient. Moreover, in practice it is not used. The reply to the interrogatory may be used as evidence in court only it if is submitted in evidence by a party, as is the case concerning any other evidential document. A party may submit all or only some of the answer to the interrogatory as evidence at the trial, but the court may look at all the answers and decide that other answers are so connected with the answers submitted in evidence that they too should be in evidence.

53. *Chiat v. Chiat*, 3 (1) P.D. 113 (1950).

149. As to disclosure of documents, following the refusal of a party to disclose the existence of relevant documents pursuant to the required out-of-court request, the requesting party may petition for a court order requiring the requestee to state, by affidavit, which documents relevant to the litigation are, or were in his possession or control, as determined by him after inquiry and investigation.

While the issuance of such a disclosure order is within the discretion of the court, the normal practice is to allow disclosure as a matter of course.

The responsive affidavit by the requestee must differentiate between documents in his possession or control and documents, which were in his possession or control but are no longer so. As to the latter, he must state when they left his possession and where they are now. A party claiming privilege as to a particular document must nevertheless list the document in his affidavit, and specify alongside the listing of the document that he claims privilege regarding it. See *infra* as to privilege concerning the examination of documents.

With two exceptions, the affidavit is final and no interrogation may be conducted concerning it. The first exception concerns privilege: where a party has claimed privilege as to a certain document the court may examine it in order to decide whether the claim of privilege is valid. The second exception is where the requesting party can prove from the affidavit itself or from documents mentioned in it that the affidavit is incomplete. In such a case, the court may order another affidavit to be served. Further, Rule 113 allows a party to request the court to order the disclosure of the existence of a particular document. In the course of time, the courts allowed requests for disclosure of a certain type of documents as well, as long as their relevance to the claim has been proved.[54] Such a request may be made in the circumstances described above, that is, where the affidavit was incomplete, or for any other reason, and need not necessarily be preceded by a general request for disclosure. Where a request in accordance with Rule 113 is founded on facts rather than on a logical conclusion arising from the pleadings or previous affidavit, it must be accompanied by an affidavit.

In addition to the sanctions discussed below a document that is not disclosed pursuant to a court order for disclosure may not be presented in evidence by the requestee unless the court authorizes its presentation after determining that there was justification for the requestee's omission. As the courts have clarified, the use of this sanction is limited to cases in which the omission to disclose a document was intentional or malicious. When a justification for the requestee's omission is found, the court may make an order for costs or other appropriate measures for the protection of the requesting party and will not use this sanction.[55]

150. As to examination of documents a party may request in writing any other party, at any time of the proceedings to allow him or his attorney to examine and copy any document which the requestee had mentioned either in his pleadings or in his affidavit filed in response to a disclosure request as described above. As with

54. *United Commercials Broadcasts Media (2003) Ltd. v. IBA*, Israeli Supreme Court Petition 3059/2012, 1 Jul. 2012 (unreported).

55. *Ragubi v. Tnuva Central Cooperative to market agricultural produce in Israel Ltd.*, 45(1) P.D. 620 (1990).

interrogatories and disclosure of documents, this first request is made only between the parties and without any judicial intervention.

While a request to examine and copy documents may be applied at any time and will usually take place at the beginning of the procedure (usually at the pre-trial conference), the court may postpone the examination of the documents if he believes that permitting a party to examine the documents at an early stage of the procedure will assist him to disrupt evidence and will not promote the discovery of truth.[56]

As with the failure to disclose a document, the failure of the requestee to comply with the out-of-court request to examine a document will result in a prohibition against the requestee submitting the document in question, unless the court authorizes its presentation after determining that there was justification for the refusal. In the latter case, the court may make an order for costs or other appropriate measures for the protection of the requesting party.

However, such a remedy will only be effective if the document was such that the requested party wishes to present it in court, that is, that the document was to his advantage. It is not helpful to the requesting party if he seeks to examine a document that may be used to his own advantage in court.

In such a case, he must apply for a court order to allow the examination. In addition to such an order concerning documents as to which the requestee has disclosed their existence, either in his pleadings or affidavit in response to a disclosure order, the court may order the examination of any other specific documents that the requesting party can show by affidavit to be relevant to the action and in the possession or control of the requested party.

A party may object justifiably to an order for examination for two primary reasons. First, that the document is no longer in his possession or control and thus he is not in a position to allow its inspection. Second, that the document is privileged. In this regard, two kinds of privilege may be distinguished.

The first is evidentiary privilege as set forth in the Evidence Ordinance [New Version], 1971 which provides either absolute or qualified evidentiary privileges on such grounds as State security, attorney-client communications, medical communications, etc. These privileges will be discussed further in paragraph 232. Herein, it is sufficient to note that any document that is privileged concerning its presentation in evidence at trial is thereby also privileged from examination during the discovery process.

The second form of privilege is specifically related to the discovery process and is not derived from evidentiary privileges at trial: the privilege concerning the examination of documents that were produced by or for a party in anticipation of legal action. This privilege from discovery of documents produced in anticipation of litigation is not based on any statutory rule. It is essentially a judge-made doctrine, which may, perhaps, be based on a specific interpretation relating to the examination of documents of Rule 120(b) of the RCP which provides that the court shall not order response to interrogatories, or the disclosure or examination of documents, 'unless it believes that such is necessary in order to provide a fair process or to save costs … '. This privilege presents a significant limitation on the purposes of

56. *Swisa v. Hachsharat Hayishuv Insurance Co.*, 55 (1) P.D. 515 (1999).

the discovery process, which is to assist a party both to defend against the allegations of his opponent and to prove his own allegations. Access to documents which the opponent has produced in anticipation of the litigation might be most important to either or both of these objectives.

The privilege has been justified on two grounds. The first is utilitarian: the fear that the opponent may gain access to a document produced in anticipation of litigation e.g., an investigating report as to the cause of an accident, may unduly deter a potential party to litigation from investigating the matter fully. The second is more abstract and ephemeral. There is a sense that it is not 'fair' for one party to litigation to obtain a 'free ride' on the preparatory work of his opponent.

In our view, both of these grounds are problematic. The first is not axiomatically obvious and demands empirical proof. Moreover, as will be discussed below, its application is particularly questionable as to public institutions.

The second is essentially an attack on the central concept of the discovery process. Moreover, if there is a particular concern as to the 'free rider' problem, this could be surmounted by an allocation of costs.

As will be discussed below, the scope of this priviledge in Israeli law was substantially limited in 1994. The first two leading cases on the issue are relatively old: from 1968[57] and 1974.[58] Both of these cases relied heavily on the then English rule concerning documents produced in anticipation of litigation. This rule provided an absolute privilege as to such documents even if at the time of their production the litigation had not yet commenced and the anticipation of litigation was merely one reason, not necessarily the dominant, let alone the exclusive, reason for their production.

However, the 1968 case, also referred to the American (Federal) rule in this regard which provides, *inter alia*, for only a qualified privilege, which may be overcome by a showing of necessity by the requesting party.

Even more significantly, in a 1979 decision the House of Lords changed the English rule so that the privilege is available only if the anticipation of litigation was the dominant reason for the production of the document in question.[59] The Israeli Supreme Court did not have occasion to consider changing its rule in light of the 1979 decision of the House of Lords until 1994, when it adopted the English rule, which limits the privilege to cases where the primary or dominant purpose of creating the document was the anticipation of litigation.[60] This greatly restricts the privilege, particularly as to public institutions.

This can be illustrated by the very similar facts of the 1974 Israeli case, and the 1979 English in which the House of Lords changed the English rule. Both cases involved actions for damages against public employees for injury or death to an employee resulting from work accidents allegedly caused by the employer's negligence. In both cases, following the accident, the public employer, in accordance with its normal practice, conducted an internal investigation to discover the cause

57. *Singer v. Bainun* 22 (2) P.D. 604.
58. *Gaunsher v. The Israel Electric Corp.*, 29 (1) P.D. 169 (1974).
59. *Waugh v. British Railways Board* [1979] 2 All E.R. 1169, HL.
60. *Haddasah Medical Association v. Gilad*, 49 (2) P.D. 516 (1994); *Bank Egud v. Azulei*, 49 (4) P.D. 54 (1995).

of the accident, which resulted in a report. The issue was whether or not this accident report was privileged from examination.

In the Israeli 1974 case, it was held to be privileged on the ground that one of the purposes of its production was anticipation of possible litigation. However, in the 1979 English decision, once the House of Lords determined that the privilege required that anticipation of litigation be the dominant purpose in producing the document in question, it was clear that the privilege would not apply. In such a case no public employer – and, indeed perhaps no employer, public or private – could argue successfully that the establishment of the cause of the accident so that proper safety measures could be taken was not, at least, as equally a significant purpose as that of preparing for possible litigation.

Such would be the result also in Israel today. In addition, there is also a hint in one of the 1994 cases that Israel might adopt the American view that this privilege, when it exists is not absolute but qualified and may, therefore, be overcome by a showing of necessity by the requesting party.[61]

Finally, in regard to this privilege it should be noted that Rule 120(b), which limits discovery orders to those necessary to provide a fair process or to save costs, applies in theory not only to examination of documents but also to their disclosure and to interrogatories. Further, the reasons given for protecting from examination documents produced in anticipation of litigation, would seem to apply also to facts or documents discovered by a party in anticipation of litigation. However, it has never been suggested that these are privileged. Thus, a party may not refuse to answer an interrogatory on the ground that he has discovered the information requested in anticipation of litigation. Nor can he refuse to disclose the existence of a document on the ground that he has discovered it in anticipation of litigation. Indeed, as to disclosure of documents Rule 112 expressly provides that the requestee must answer 'after investigation and inquiry'. This inconsistency between the treatment of examination of documents and that of interrogatories and disclosure of documents also raises questions as to the justification for the privilege as to documents produced in anticipation of litigation.

151. Rule 124 provides that the court may, at any time after the filing of an action, and on such terms as it prescribes, order a party to allow an opposite party, or his expert, to inspect any property or article in respect of which a question has arisen in the action. This inspection has not been the subject of substantial litigation and thus there is very little jurisprudence interpreting it. It would seem, however, that despite the somewhat peculiar wording of the relevancy condition, i.e., property as to which a question has arisen in the action, the broad view of relevancy generally applicable to discovery should apply here too.

152. Rule 122 of the RCP allows the following sanctions to be imposed on a party who has not complied with the second order to respond to interrogatories, or an order to disclose documents or allow their examination, or to allow the inspection of property: where he is a plaintiff, the action may be struck out (i.e., dismissed without prejudice); where he is a defendant the answer may be struck out and he

61. *Bank Egud v. Azulei*, 49 (4) P.D. 54 (1995).

will be considered as not having filed an answer (i.e., a default judgment will be entered against him); the court may however extend a party's time limit to comply with the discovery order in question.

As a general rule, the court will use this sanction only in extreme circumstances, given its implications for the parties. Therefore, if a party has not complied with the court's order in good faith, due to misunderstanding or even negligence, the court will not impose this sanction on him. However, if the court has been persuaded that the party's conduct was malicious or resulted from disrespect for the court it may implement this sanction.[62]

As discussed above, in paragraph 123, prior to the 1984 Rules of Civil Procedure, the dismissal of a plaintiff's action under this process was *with prejudice*. Today, as we have mentioned, the dismissal is *without* prejudice. This change was the result of the prevailing lenient attitude toward procedural faults and a desire not to determine actions against a party because of such faults.

Even prior to this change, the Rule was applied leniently. The courts allowed repeated extensions of time limits to comply with discovery orders and accepted compliance with the order even if such occurred after the required date, and the requested party had not requested an extension. Sanctions under the Rule were imposed only when it is was absolutely clear that a party continuously and purposefully refused to comply with an order.

It may be that the limitation of the sanction against plaintiffs to a dismissal without prejudice, may lead to greater use of the sanction than prior to 1984. However, it is doubtful that the ultimate sanction against a purposeful and continuously recalcitrant plaintiff should be only a dismissal without prejudice. Moreover, the new, lenient Rule discriminates against recalcitrant defendants as compared with recalcitrant plaintiffs. As to the former, striking out the answer results in a default judgment which, as is the case concerning all judgments against the defendant, is res judicata.

2. Amendments

153. The purpose of the pleadings is to define the issues for trial and thus they provide the framework for proof. Generally, the court will not allow a fact not alleged in the pleadings to be proved.

154. It follows that a party may wish to amend his pleadings in order to prove facts that he has so far not alleged. This may occur because of a mistake in the pleadings or the discovery of new facts, or even their occurrence, after the filing of the pleadings. A party may also wish to amend his pleadings in light of later pleadings by his opponent.

Rule 92 states that an amendment to the pleadings may be made only with leave of the court. However, the courts have adopted a liberal approach toward this issue.

---

62. *Club Hotel Management (1996) Ltd. v. Dagan*, Israeli Supreme Court Petition 9265/2006, 3 May 2007 (unreported).

As discussed in paragraph 123, the courts have emphasized that the aim of the procedural system is to allow the parties to put forward and develop their claims in the fullest possible manner and thus will almost always allow honest mistakes to be rectified, compensating the opposing party with the award of costs, if necessary.[63] Thus, an amendment usually will be allowed even if the party seeking the amendment was negligent.

Despite the adoption of a liberal approach towards requests for amendments of pleadings, the courts consider the following considerations and may decline the request based on them: The reasons for not originally filing the amended pleading; has there been a delay in filing the application; the stage at which the application was submitted; whether the applicant acted in good faith; is the amendment consistent with procedural fairness; and whether amending the pleading will deny the opposite party a defence that was available to him if the amended pleading would have been filed originally.[64]

Thus, the court may refuse to allow an amendment when the party's negligent delay in filing the correct (i.e., amended) pleading has caused serious damage to the opposing party that cannot be compensated by the granting of a continuance or the award of costs. This may occur, for example, where a key witness in terms of the amended pleading – but not the original one – has become unavailable to testify in the interim and had the amended pleading been filed originally the party could have been able to take appropriate steps to preserve his testimony for trial.

The court will usually also deny leave to amend when the mistaken pleading was not the result of a good faith; but rather was a result of conscious, tactical decision akin to bad faith. An amended pleading operates in most cases retroactively, i.e., it dates back to the date of the original, defective pleading. An exception to the retroactivity of amended pleadings concerns amendments that add or substitute parties. As to these, Rule 26(b) provides expressly that 'for purposes of limitations, the proceedings in respect of the new party are deemed to have commenced with the amended pleading'.

A similar result is reached by the judge-made rule whereby amendments are not allowed in cases where an attempt is made to use them in order to add new causes of action where the period of limitations as to such causes of actions has expired between the filing of the original pleading and the proposed amendment. However, when the requested amendment concerns the original cause of action, the court will not reject the request even though the period of limitations as to that cause of action has expired.[65]

As will be discussed later in this chapter a major objective of the pre-trial conference is to determine the need for, and to allow, amendments of the pleadings so as to permit the determination at trial of the real issues in dispute between the parties.

---

63. *Israel Discount Bank Ltd. v. Shimer*, Israeli Supreme Court Petition 6195/2012, 25 Oct. 2012 (unreported).
64. *Azrom Metal Industries Ltd. v. Netafim Ltd.*, Israeli Supreme Court Petition 5818/2012, 7 Aug. 2012 (unreported); *Market Place Systems Ltd. v. Teletel Communication Channels Ltd.*, Israeli Supreme Court Petition 3385/2008, 25 Sep. 2008 (unreported).
65. It should be noted that the term 'cause of action' has received a broad interpretation in this context, and was interpreted as 'the transaction or act presented for discussion'. *Ibid.*

A request to amend the pleadings after the pre-trial conference which is, in effect, a request to amend the pre-trial order will be met with the difficulty of having to comply with the strict standard for amending pre-trial orders, as will be discussed later in this Part.

155. The Rules authorize the court to order an amendment on its own initiative, without a motion to this effect by a party. However, consistently with the adversary procedure, it will very rarely employ this authority, but will await a motion for amendment filed by a party. According to Rule 241, a motion for amendment should be filed in writing. If the request is based on facts, the applicant should verify the fact by an affidavit.

156. Once an amendment has been allowed, the applicant may amend his pleading within fifteen days. An amendment or the addition of a factual allegation requires the filing of a new affidavit in support of the amended pleading. After the amended pleading is filed in court, the opposing party may amend his last pleading as a matter of right. i.e., without need to obtain leave, within the period of time set in the rules. Moreover, in such an amendment by right he may introduce new allegations, whether or not they have any relationship to the amended pleading to which, in theory, he is responding.

157. Finally, pleadings may be deemed amended by implication. This occurs when an issue not included in the pleadings is, in fact, litigated at trial. This situation, termed a 'change of front' is based on concepts of implied consent or waiver. Thus, a mere non-objection to an isolated piece of evidence concerning a point not raised in the pleadings will not, in and of itself, constitute such implied consent or waiver. While the line is often difficult to draw, a finding of implied consent or waiver should be based on such factors as the apparent significance of the evidence, its extent, whether or not the opposing party cross-examined the witnesses as to this evidence, whether or not he himself submitted contrary evidence on the same point, etc. If the court finds that a 'change of front' has occurred, it may find that the plaintiff is entitled to remedies resulting from the 'change of front', although these remedies were not expressly demanded in the claim.[66]

3. Pre-trial conference; Rules 140–149

158. The pre-trial conference was introduced into Israeli procedure by the first Israeli adopted Rules of Civil Procedure, i.e., those of 1967. While some of its aspects are in common with the English summons for directions it was inspired directly by the pre-trial conference of the American Federal Rules of Civil Procedure.

---

66. For example: *Ol Services Ltd. v. Mushitz*, 49 (2) P.D. 397 (1995).

The proclaimed purpose of the pre-trial conference is threefold:

(1) to complete the already ongoing process of discovery and preliminary relief if any;
(2) to prepare the case for trial by determining finally the issues which are in dispute, order of proof, form of proof, etc.; and
(3) to see if the parties can be induced to settle.

The Rules do not mandate the holding of a pre-trial conference in every action, but leave it to the discretion of the court. In practice, such conferences are held generally as a matter of course, shortly before the trial. The pre-trial conference may be held before a judge or a registrar who is himself a judge. This last category includes all the registrars in the District Courts but only some of those in the Magistrates' Courts.

159. The principle power of the court at this stage is to examine whether the pleadings have been lawfully drawn up, to allow or order their amendment, if this is necessary, to strike out anything not requisite to the issue, to ascertain which questions are really in dispute between the parties and to draw up a list of such issues. It may decide on the joinder or striking out of parties, on notices to third parties and may order the consideration or dismissal of an action brought by way of third-party notice. It may also decide with respect to giving further particulars, admissions of facts and documents, presentation of interrogatories, discovery and inspection of documents, making inquiries and taking accounts, inspection of property and appointments of experts, and interim relief.

The court may also determine, after an inquiry of the parties, matters such as the manner in which pleas are to be proved, the validity of evidence and even may order evidence to be taken outside the area of the jurisdiction of the court or outside the territory of the State. It may make any direction as to procedure, which may simplify or ease the trial, for example the order in which questions of fact and law should be considered and whether certain matters should be separately clarified.

The court may also order that a prospective witness first file an affidavit as to his testimony, or that a specific fact be proven by affidavits, as distinguished from oral testimony.

Finally, the court may determine the case before it by ordering the action to be dismissed summarily or by rendering a judgment for the plaintiff, either partial or full, if it is clear that the defendant has no defence to the claim.

It is important to note that the court is authorized to decide all the above matters on its own motion and without a motion to this effect by a party. In fact, the courts have emphasized that the judge in the pre-trial conference should take the initiative in order to prepare the claim for trial. It follows that the pre-trial conference is not conducted according to the adversarial system principles.[67]

67. *Sagy v. Rogozin Indistury Ltd.*, 52 (2) P.D. 706 (1998).

160. Matters determined in the pre-trial conference are not to be re-examined at a later date unless special reasons justifying their re-examination are shown and the court decides that this re-examination is necessary in order to avoid a miscarriage of justice. Moreover, the same principle applies to matters, which a party could have raised at the pre-trial conference but failed to do so. i.e., they cannot be raised later unless special reasons are shown and such is necessary in order to avoid a miscarriage of justice.

While the exact meaning of these expressions, as well as the relationship between the special circumstances and the avoidance of a miscarriage of justice are not clear, it is obvious that the intention of the Rules is to give a great degree of finality to the pre-trial conference and, therefore, to impose on the party seeking to deviate from its decisions or raise matters not raised therein a very heavy burden of justification. As noted in paragraph 124, this exceptional degree of finality given to the pre-trial conference contrasts with the generally lenient position of the Rules as to correction of mistakes.

161. In one major respect, the Israeli Rules as to pre-trial conferences even go beyond that of the American Federal Rules of Civil Procedure on which they are based, in that they authorize the court to order the parties to appear in person at the pre-trial conference and to testify personally at the conference as to the issues in dispute.

This represents a major exception to the prevailing rule in Israel, as well as in England and the United States that, generally, a party need not appear personally in legal proceedings but may be represented by counsel. Moreover, as will be discussed more fully in the next subsection herein, having the parties testify personally before third-party witnesses also presents a major exception to the usual order of testimony prevailing in Israel, as well as in England and the United States, pursuant to which the plaintiff presents all his evidence before the defendant presents any of his.

The power to order the personal appearance of a party at the pre-trial conferences strengthens greatly the ability of the court both to form a first-hand impression as to the true issues in controversy and to induce the parties to reach a settlement.

The failure of a party to appear personally at the pre-trial conference if he is so ordered by the court is equivalent, in terms of sanctions, to a failure of appearance (by counsel) at trial. See *infra* paragraphs 197–204 as to default proceedings.

The testimony and statements of parties at the pre-trial conference, as well as the decisions of the judge at the conference, are considered as if they are part of the trial itself.

4. The trial

a. Determination of the date

162. In most cases, a pre-trial conference is held and it is then that the trial date is set.

In the absence of a pre-trial conference, Rule 151 provides that the trial date shall be set thirty days following the filing of the last pleading; the court may, however, decide to set an earlier date.

Unfortunately, the backlog in the courts may result in a trial date more than a year after the filing of the action. Moreover, as discussed in paragraph 22, generally a 'trial' in Israel, unlike in England is not a single uninterrupted event, but rather a series of sessions spread over an extensive period of time.

In addition to the general calendar by which cases are listed for trial in the order of their filing, the president of each court has discretion to accelerate certain cases for trial.

In paragraphs 142–143, we discussed the acceleration of trial dates in relation to expedited judgment proceedings. In practice, actions filed pursuant to originating summonses may receive accelerated treatment. So may particular cases filed pursuant to the regular pleading process if there is special justification for their acceleration.

b. The trial process; Rules 158–160

163. In accordance with English practice, the usual procedure in Israel at trial is for the plaintiff to open the proceedings and present all his evidence before the defendant presents his evidence. Thus, the plaintiff begins by presenting an oral statement of what he intends to prove and then presents all his proof, both oral and written, following which the defendant does the same.

Following the defendant's proof, the court may, but is not so required, to allow the plaintiff to present rebuttal evidence. Following the presentation of all the proof, the parties then present their closing summaries, first the plaintiff and then the defendant.

The order of presenting evidence and closing summaries will be reversed when the defendant admits all the factual allegations in the statement of claim but nonetheless asserts that the plaintiff is not entitled to relief. This situation is called 'admission and dismissal'.

In recognition of the fact, as mentioned above, that the trial may be spread over an extensive period of time, the Rules provide that the closing summaries, which are usually oral, should be presented as soon as possible, after all the proof has been presented. However, in exceptionally complicated cases, the court may order the filing of such closing summaries in writing, in lieu of, or in addition to, the oral summaries.

If written summaries are ordered, they are to be filed by the parties within the period of time set by the court.

In certain cases, a party may wish to present evidence after the proper time for doing so has elapsed, for example where he forgot to present the evidence previously, or where new evidence appeared. The general principle is that a court will allow the rectification of mistakes if such rectification does not lead to a complete reopening of proceedings, and if it can be compensated for by the payment of costs to the opposing party. The courts have ruled that evidence may be presented even after the summing up, so long as judgment has not yet been rendered. The court may consider the following matters: whether the application has been filed late; whether the application is in fact an attempt to engage in a 'change of front'; and whether the application contravenes former decisions of the court.[68]

164. We should note that although the Israeli system generally follows this English based sequence of proof. i.e., one party presenting all its proof before the other party presents any of its proof, the Rules do recognize the possibility of using a different system of proof. Party testimony at the pre-trial conference has already been mentioned. Moreover, Rule 158(b) states expressly that the court, either at the request of a party or on its own initiative, may order the parties themselves (both plaintiff and defendant) to testify first at trial prior to hearing the testimony of third parties of either side.

This order of proof is used regularly pursuant to the special rules of procedure governing maintenance claims as well as those concerning periodic payments to traffic accident victims and actions brought pursuant to the Prevention of Family Violence Law, 1991. And, indeed, if the move toward greater use of party affidavits continues, see paragraph 23, such order of proof may also become more common in general litigation.

A great deal of the trial process in Israel is involved with evidence. This is since Israel has adopted the English practice of binding rules of evidence concerning the proof process. Thus, we will discuss the trial processes further in Part VII. *Evidence*.

E. Judgment

1. General

165. The Rules provide that at the conclusion of the trial or as soon thereafter as circumstances permit the court will render its judgment. Rule 190 provides expressly that a Court of First Instance shall give its judgment no longer than thirty days after the conclusion of the trial; if it has not given its decision by that time, the judge must submit a reasoned notice in writing to the president of the court. Unfortunately, these rules are ignored regularly in practice and judgments are, in fact, rendered long after the conclusion of the trial, either with or without the filing of a perfunctory notice to the president of the court, pursuant to Rule 190.

The Rules also require that a judgment be ceremonially pronounced orally. However such oral pronouncement is only necessary concerning the section of the judgment stating the operative decision of the court, as distinguished from its reasoning. A party has a right to be given notice of the date of the oral pronouncement of the judgment, and is free either to attend or not as he sees fit. This ceremonial oral pronouncement of the judgment appears to be a relic of the English tradition pursuant to which judgments are rendered orally regularly from the bench immediately following a continuous trial. Since this situation does not prevail in Israel, it would

---

68. *PazGaz Ltd. v. Pupic*, Israeli Supreme Court Petition 806/2008, 7 Sep. 2008 (unreported).

seem that the requirement of oral pronouncement of written judgments is an unnecessary expenditure of time and might well be eliminated.

The written judgment must contain a summary statement of the matter, the court's finding in respect of the material facts, the questions to be decided, the decision and the grounds thereof. See paragraphs 34–35 for a discussion of the insistence on reasoned decisions.

On the basis of the written judgment the court draws up a *decree* which, similar to the oral pronouncement, is a statement of the operative decision without the court's reasoning. The Rules require that the written judgment be served on the parties. However, they also provide that the service of the decree is sufficient for this purpose. In practice the parties do receive a copy of the full written judgment, including all of the reasoning.

2. Partial judgments

166. Rule 191 authorizes the court to render a partial judgment: where it appears to the court that part of the trial has reached a stage that does not justify delaying giving a judgment until the end of the trial. A partial judgment may be rendered, and the continuation of proceedings will be limited to the other points in controversy. Such a partial judgment may be rendered, for example, where the action contains multiple claims or multiple parties and judgment can be given on a portion of the claims or as to some of the parties without awaiting the result regarding all of them.

As will be explained later the issue of appeal requires that a distinction is drawn between a 'partial judgment' and 'other decision'. This distinction is somewhat vague.

However, as the courts have clarified the key criterion for ruling on this issue is the relief required from the court. If the court awarded a party a remedy which he requested, from among several remedies requested, and this remedy stands by itself, even though the proceedings have not been concluded, the decision should be considered as a 'partial judgment'. However, if the decision is only one layer of the final decision or an interim measure prior to reaching the final decision or a measure needed for the continuation of the procedure, it should be considered to be an 'other decision'. This would be the case, for example, when the court rendered a decision as to the defendant's liability before discussing issues of damages or other remedies.[69]

Following this discussion it should be noted that a partial judgment is a judgment in all respects:

(1) it is final, subject only to the rules of rectification of judgments (to be discussed below);

69. *Shansi v. Giladi*, 41 (4) P.D. 707 (1987).

(2) it must be appealed as a judgment at the time of its rendering (as discussed later in paragraph 206); and
(3) it may be enforced.

3. Consent Judgments

167. Where the parties have come to an agreement or compromise, the court may render its judgment according to the agreement. This may be achieved in one of two ways: the first, that the parties inform the court of the compromise, and the court may confirm the compromise and give it the validity of a judgment. The second, that the parties inform the court of the judgment they wish it to give, and the court renders the judgment. The court is not obliged to confirm a compromise or render an agreed judgment, but will act according to its discretion, taking into account amongst other factors, whether the parties came to a final agreement, whether the judgment can be executed, and whether the judgment is in the subject matter jurisdiction of the court.

A consent judgment contains two attributes: that of a consensual agreement and that of a judgment. Thus the judgment may be rescinded as a result of a defect liable to rescind an agreement per se: e.g., mistake, misrepresentation, or illegality.[70]

However, unless and until rescinded a consent judgment has the same force as any other judgment. A party wishing to rescind a consent judgment on the basis of a defect in the underlying agreement in most cases must initiate an independent action for this purpose; an appeal is not appropriate since on appeal he will not be allowed to introduce the new facts required to prove the defect in the agreement. Only in the rare case where such facts appear on the face of the consent judgment or in the protocol of a hearing would an appeal be the appropriate way of attacking the judgment.

A defect as to the judgment itself or concerning the process of rendering judgment on the agreement, as distinguished from a defect in the underlying agreement, may be rectified by the rendering court itself.[71]

4. Indexing and interest added to judgments

168. The Adjudication of Interest Law, 1961 entitled a successful plaintiff in a monetary action to interest on the amount awarded, at the prevailing legal rate, from the date of filing the action to the date of payment. However, when Israel entered a period of high inflation, the prevailing legal interest rate, determined by a governmental regulation, always lagged behind the inflation rate. The result was that the real value of the plaintiff's claim was eroded. This erosion took place from before the action was filed and while the action was pending, until judgment and, indeed, until final payment. The longer the time required to secure judicial relief and payment the greater the erosion of the value of the plaintiff's claim.

---

70. *Shohat v. Clal Insurance Company Ltd.*, Israeli Supreme Court Petition 5914/2003, 1 May 2005 (unreported).
71. *Arzchi Investment Company Ltd. v. Rahmani*, 43 (3) P.D. 489 (1989).

These effects of inflation provided strong incentives for debtors to delay payment of their debts as long as possible. Such a situation increased both the quantity and length of litigation, which in turn increased court delays, thereby providing debtors with even greater incentives not to pay their debts unless and until they were finally forced to do so by court decrees.

Such a vicious circle could be broken only by preserving the value of creditors' recoveries and, thereby, decreasing debtors' incentives not to pay their debts promptly. Thus, criteria both of fairness and of efficiency required remedial action aimed at preserving the real value of claims. The courts struggled with this problem developing such concepts as judgment date assessment of the value of tort claims.

However, the most important response was that of the legislature: the 1978 amendment of the Adjudication of Interest Law, 1961 authorized the courts to award indexing of the nominal monetary recovery to a cost of living index (the Consumer Price Index) plus 3% real interest in lieu of the prevailing legal interest rate. Moreover, in accordance with a prior 1974 amendment concerning interest, this indexing could be awarded from the date of the cause of action (i.e., injury or breach). Finally, the name of the statute was changed to the Interest and Indexing Law, although anachronistically retaining the date of the Law as 1961.

Despite the discretionary wording of the statute, the Supreme Court has made it quite clear that the courts are to index fully monetary awards, except in the very rare cases in which there are special reasons that justify proving less than full indexation. As stated by the then president of the Supreme Court. Justice Landau:

> It has already been explained in the decisions of the Supreme Court that indexing of awards serves only to preserve the real value of the principal of the claim and, therefore, does not involve any real economic loss to the defendant who is required to pay the principal. On the other hand, a refusal to index an award causes a real reduction in the value of the principal which the plaintiff receives. Therefore, a court will refrain from awarding [full] indexation only if there exist unusual circumstances which so justify.[72]

However, pursuant to this 1978 amendment, the 3% interest (which was later raised to 4%) was itself unindexed. Thus, the real rate of interest was nil during high inflationary periods. This situation was corrected, indeed perhaps overcorrected, by a 1989 amendment that provides for indexing plus 8% interest, which interest is itself linked.

This resulted in a real interest rate which usually was in excess of the market rate. As such, the plaintiff has received more than the retention of the real value of his claim and the defendant may, indeed, have been forced to pay more than the real value of his liability. Yet this may not necessarily have been unjust. Even a so-called full legal recovery by a plaintiff does not truly compensate him for his loss. For one thing, any monetary recovery has forced the plaintiff to convert the physical asset involved into money. Moreover, in order to reach this result the plaintiff has been forced to suffer the

72. *Naftalovitz v. Gideon*, Israeli Supreme Court Petition 461/1980, 6 Apr. 1981 (unreported); see also *Cohn v. Tuchli*, 31 (1) P.D. 248 (1976); *Bank Leumi L'Yisrael v. Ram Paving Co.*, 35 (1) P.D. 352 (1980).

economic and psychological costs of litigation. Even where as in Israel, the award of costs is designed to make a prevailing plaintiff whole, see paragraph 224, the costs taxed may be below those actually incurred. Moreover, they do not even purport to cover such costs as lost work days and other incidental expenses involved in the litigation. Nor do they, of course, compensate for the emotional unpleasantness involved in the process. Thus it may well be considered fair to improve somewhat the plaintiff's position by giving him a 'bonus' of extra real interest.

Moreover, such a bonus may have the desirable result of deterring defendants from refusing to pay obligations until sued or from prolonging litigation once brought and may, indeed, encourage them to settle litigation early.

Whatever may have been the justification for over compensating plaintiffs pursuant to the 1989 Amendment, this situation was ended by another Amendment in 1993, which lowered the interest rate in issue from 8% to 4% index linked. Thus, now the linked interest rate is close to the market rate.

Yet, even that is not the full picture. It will be recalled that even when the interest awarded was not linked, Landau P. admitted the possibility of unusual circumstances which would justify not awarding full indexation. When the issue involves indexation with no real interest at all, as was often the case prior to the 1989 amendment, it may be argued that there are no 'exceptional circumstances' that would justify not awarding full indexation and whatever interest is available.

From the point of view of the plaintiff any deviation from full indexation deprives him of the full, real value of his recovery. In terms of the defendant any such deviation may be viewed as providing him with an unjustified bonus. For, as long as he has retained the funds that rightfully belong to the plaintiff, he has under pure economic theory at least, enjoyed the benefits of the rising nominal value of such funds. And this is so, whether or not he has invested them. This is apparently the basis of President Landau's above quoted statement that the indexation of an award does not result in any economic loss to the defendant.

However, while full compensation for inflation is an important value, it is certainly not the exclusive one and therefore, providing less than such full compensation may, at least arguably, be used as a tool in order to achieve other desired ends, such as discouraging plaintiffs from using dilatory litigation tactics and encouraging them to accept reasonable settlement offers. Compare the discussions in paragraph 125, *supra* and paragraphs 224–227, *infra*.

And, indeed, even before the 1989 amendment, there were a few cases in which the Supreme Court approved awards of less than what then could be awarded to the plaintiff, on the grounds that the plaintiff has unjustifiably prolonged the litigation. Compare the discussion as to the reduction of costs to a prevailing plaintiff who has unduly prolonged the litigation, paragraphs 224–225.

5. Res Judicata

a. General

169. The basic principles of Israeli law governing the finality of litigation are based on the English common law rules in this field. Thus, the underlying principle is that litigation is final and a judgment entered in a civil case is not subject to reopening. Litigants before the courts have a right to a fair trial and a determination of every controversy or issue. However, the public interest requires the prevention of repeated litigation in order to ensure a more efficient use of the courts, to avoid disrespect to former judgments, and unnecessary vexation of parties to a dispute.

The main exceptions to this rule exist in cases concerning judgments entered by fraud. This exception, however, does not detract substantially from the basic principle of finality of judgments. Israel has also adopted the common law principles of res judicata both in terms of claim preclusion and issue preclusion. These two forms of preclusion are claims of defence, and may be raised only by a litigant and not by the court on its own motion.

b. Claim preclusion

170. Claim preclusion is based on the principle that a cause of action which has been tried and decided is finalized by the judgment. A judgment in favour of the plaintiff merges his cause of action in the judgment and the cause of action no longer exists. A dismissal of the cause of action creates a bar preventing the plaintiff from serving his action again. The application of this doctrine requires that action be between the same parties, or those who are held to be in privity with the original parties, and that the second action sought to be precluded be based on the same 'cause of action' as the previously determined action. Israeli case law has applied a number of different criteria for the definition of the term 'cause of action' regarding res judicata. The most generally accepted criterion, similar to that in the United States, is based on the identity of the facts: the operative facts must be the same or nearly the same in both actions. Thus, if different legal claims could have been brought based on the same facts, but the plaintiff omitted to do so, he is estopped from bringing such claims in the future. Such is also the case regarding requests for relief: if different forms of relief could have been requested based on the same facts but were not so requested, the plaintiff is precluded from requesting them in a later action.

Another condition is that the first action was determined on the merits. For purposes of this condition a judgment in favour of the plaintiff is always a determination on the merits. However, certain forms of dismissal, i.e., judgments against the plaintiff, may be deemed not to be determinations on the merits. The Israeli law in regard to dismissals which are not on the merits, i.e., which are without prejudice to the relitigation of the cause of action, are discussed above in this Part, paragraph 145.

171. Before leaving the subject of claim preclusion we should emphasize a major Israeli innovation in the area. As discussed above, the dominant view in Israeli law is that for purposes of claim preclusion, a cause of action is determined as a factual situation. Thus, changes in legal theory or in the relief sought do not produce a new cause of action so long as the basic factual situation is the same. In short, this is a rule against splitting claims; all legal theories and all possible relief based on one factual situation must be brought in one action. If not, the above-stated rules of res judicata will bar bringing them in further actions. So far, we have described the basic common law theory of cause of action preclusion as it has been accepted as part of Israeli law.

However, in addition to these principles of case law, Israel has also adopted rules against splitting claims as part of the Rules of Civil Procedure. Rule 44(a) provides that 'a complaint shall include all of the plaintiff's claim that is based on the cause of action of the complaint; but a plaintiff is entitled to waive part of his claim in order to bring the complaint within the jurisdiction of the court.' Rule 44(b) then provides that 'when a plaintiff does not include a part of his claim in his complaint, or waives a part of it, he shall not thereafter file a complaint for the part of the claim that he failed to bring or that he waived.' Finally Rule 45 provides that:

> one who is entitled to a number of forms of relief based on the same cause of action may sue for all or part of them; but if he does not sue for all of them [in the same action], he shall not thereafter sue for any relief that he did not sue for [in the first action], unless the court [in the first action] granted permission not to sue for such relief.

There is no doubt that these provisions of the Rules prohibiting the splitting of a cause of action, both in their intent and in their application overlap considerably with the case law rules of claim preclusion discussed above. Yet, the courts have not addressed well the relationship between these two sets of rules. There are many cases in which it would seem that both sets ought to apply, yet for some reason the court in a given case addresses only one set, completely ignoring the possible application of the other. Thus, one finds two parallel sets of cases, one based on the common law rules of res judicata and one based on the above quoted statutory rules against splitting, with no bridge between them.

Yet the prohibitory aspect of Rules 44 and 45 are not their major contribution. Rather this contribution is found in the last section of Rule 45 that provides for receipt of judicial permission to split a cause of action where such consists of different forms of relief. That is, with judicial permission a plaintiff may deliberately sue for one form of relief while preserving his right to sue separately for other forms of relief arising from one and the same cause of action.

This permission not only overrides any preclusion arising from Rule 45 itself, but also overrides any preclusion that would otherwise arise from the common law doctrine of claim preclusion.

Such permission could be given in a case, for example where one form of relief would be entitled to a special process, such as the expedited judgment procedure, whereas the other would not. This could be so if one cause of action gave rise both to a liquidated monetary claim suitable for the expedited judgment procedure and to other relief, e.g., injunctions which would not be suitable for that process. If the plaintiff sought both forms of relief in one action, as he would have to do under the general principles of claim preclusion, he would thereby forfeit his right to the expedited judgment procedure as to the relief suitable for such process.

Another example of a case in which it would be appropriate to allow splitting a cause of action would be that in which one form of relief, e.g., property damage was now 'ripe' for adjudication while another, e.g., damages for personal injury, should await further developments in order to determine its full value.

As far as we know, among systems of claim preclusion based on English doctrines of res judicata, the Israeli provision for advance permission to split a cause of action is unique. It is in our view a highly desirable innovation which is worthy of emulation.

Finally, in this regard, where splitting a cause of action is required by limitations imposed by subject matter jurisdiction restrictions, no claim preclusion arises under common law principles. Nor, in such a case, is it necessary to request permission to split the cause of action pursuant to Rule 45.

c. Issue preclusion

172. Issue preclusion has been defined as follows: if in the first action an issue of fact, necessary for the final decision in the action, was in controversy, and the issue was decided directly or indirectly, then the parties and their privies are barred from arguing the issue in a second trial, despite the fact that the causes of action may be different.

173. The first condition for the application of the doctrine is that the issue involved must be the same in both actions. Preclusion applies both to factual issues and to the application of the legal norm to the facts, e.g., the conclusion that the defendant's conduct constituted negligence, breach of contract, etc. It does not, however, apply to determinations of legal principles unrelated to their application to the facts of the action.

174. The issue involved must have been relevant to the determination of the first action. If in the first action, the determination in question was clearly irrelevant to the issues litigated in the case, no preclusion arises.

This is so since preclusion is only justified if the parties knew the issue was part of the case and therefore litigated accordingly, and the judge knew that his determination of the issue would have operative results and, thus gave its determination his full consideration and deliberation.

However, what of an issue that was fully litigated but turned out to be irrelevant to the final disposition of the case, since it was determined against the party who, despite that particular determination, prevailed in the action? In such a case despite the full litigation of the issue, there is doubt that the judge, who presumably was conscious of the final outcome of the action when he wrote in his opinion about this particular issue, gave this issue, which had turned out to be irrelevant, his full consideration and deliberation. Moreover, since under Israeli procedure only the losing party may appeal, the winning party cannot appeal an adverse determination which has not affected the outcome. For both of these reasons, therefore, in such a case there is no preclusion.

As distinguished from the above situation, the courts have given preclusion effect to both alternative determinations in a situation in which both determinations, independently and alternatively, support the result in the first action, even though in such a case neither determination could be said to be essential to the decision.

175. While Israeli law is not absolutely clear on this point, it would appear that no issue preclusion arises from a consent judgment unless the parties have intended that such be the result. As far as default judgments are concerned, the Israeli

Supreme Court has recently departed from the English common law approach by holding that a default judgment precludes the defendant from raising any argument in a future claim against the original plaintiff that he had raised in his answer to the first action (in cases of failure to appear at trial) or any argument that he could have and should have raised in the first action (in cases of failure to file an answer).[73] Such a defendant is considered to have had the opportunity to argue his defence and thus to have had his day in court.

176. Another limitation on issue preclusion is, as far as we know, unique to Israeli law: no issue preclusion arises from failure of proof. For example, if in a negligence action in his judgment for the defendant the judge states not that he has concluded that the defendant was not negligent, but rather that the plaintiff has failed to prove that the defendant was negligent, no preclusion arises as to the issue of the defendant's negligence.

177. The results as to issue preclusion which arise from determinations of incidental issues pursuant to ancillary jurisdiction provided for in section 76 of the Courts Law [Consolidated Version], 1984, are discussed in detail in paragraph 80.

178. There is no express legislation nor conclusive jurisprudence as to the issue preclusive effect, or lack thereof of determinations of the Small Claims Courts. However, there is dictum to the effect that their determinations could and should create issue preclusion, despite the significant differences between the procedures of the Small Claims Court and those of the regular courts. Recent Israeli case law suggests that decisions of the Small Claims Courts should be given issue preclusion effect on policy grounds, reasoning that it would be incongruous that decisions of a professional court which is an inherent part of the State's judiciary would be disregarded in future actions.[74]

179. Finally, the traditional view as to issue preclusion was conditioned on the two actions involved being between the same parties or those in privity with them.

As to the party sought to be precluded, the condition that he has been a party to the first action is one of constitutional dimensions: a necessary condition to precluding a party is that he has had his day in court on the issue in question. Precluding one who has not had his day in court would be a violation of his fundamental right to be heard.

The principle that non-parties to litigation are not bound by its results has necessitated the creation of devices, such as the joinder of defendants and third-party practice and interpleader, the object of which is to enable the joinder as parties of those whom it is desired to preclude by the results of the litigation.

As noted above, there has always been a limited exception to the rule that non-parties are not bound by issue preclusion: those who are deemed to be in privity with a party are bound even though they are not, themselves, parties. This group of

---

73. *Bank Hapoalim v. Weinstein*, Israeli Supreme Court Petition 2237/2006, 8 Mar. 2009 (unreported).

74. *Swissa v. Champion Motors Corp.*, Israeli Supreme Court Petition 1958/2006, 20 Oct. 2006 (unreported).

those in privity has been limited traditionally to transferees of property – by inheritance, voluntary transfer, or by virtue of law – as well as to specific other groups such as parents representing minors in litigation. However, in recent years, in Israel, as in other jurisdictions that have adopted English concepts of res judicata there has been a tendency to expand those who are deemed to be in privity with a party to include those who, in fact, control the litigation even though formally they are not parties, as well as those who are represented in various ways by the parties. See also Part VIII concerning representative actions.

However, it should be emphasized that despite this tendency, there are still strong restrictions on precluding non-parties, since such preclusion may involve an imposition on the constitutional norm of the right to be heard, to have one's day in court.

The other aspect of the involvement of non-parties in issue preclusion is that of the power of one who was not a party to the first litigation precluding in the second litigation one who was a party to the first litigation. In such case there is no problem of the constitutional norm of one's right to be heard: the party sought to be precluded had his day in court in the first litigation. Nevertheless the traditional view was that a party could not be precluded by a non-party unless the latter was in privity with a party to the first litigation so that he could have been precluded by it if the issue had been decided against his interests. This doctrine termed 'mutuality' was thought to be required by fairness, i.e., even-handedness.

However, in recent years, primarily under the influence of developments in the United States, the Supreme Court has apparently abandoned this doctrine and thus, if all the other necessary conditions are present, a non-party to prior litigation may invoke issue preclusion against a party to the prior litigation.

Thus far we have considered res judicata only in regard to in personam actions as, indeed, they are the overwhelming bulk of actions. We should mention, however, that Israeli jurisprudence has accepted the English concept that actions in rem are binding against everyone, whether or not they were parties. Typical in rem actions involve declaratory judgments for the determination of an existing status, such as age, parenthood, etc., as well as actions creating a new status, such as divorce or adoption.

6. Rectification and Clarification of Judgments

180. Section 81 of the Courts Law [Consolidated Version], 1984 allows a court, by reasoned decision, to rectify certain types of mistakes in its judgment or 'other decision', either at the request of the parties or on its own motion, after the date of ruling . In either case, it may, and generally does, hear the contentions of the parties on the matter.

The mistakes which can be so rectified are defined in the Law as mistakes of language, computation, a slip of the pen, an inadvertent omission or addition, and the like.

Case law has held that great care must be taken by the court in using this authority to rectify mistakes in order not to detract from the principle of the finality of the judgment. The courts have held that the right to rectify mistakes relates in principle to technical omissions of details of which the judge was aware and intended to include in his decision but unintentionally omitted. Factors to which the judge did not intend to refer or of which he was not aware, as well as material mistakes, may not be rectified by means of this procedure, but only by an appeal.[75]

Section 81 expressly provides that the court is authorized to rectify these mistakes within twenty-one days after its judgment or 'other decision' has been rendered or later with the agreement of the parties. However, the courts will allow mistakes to be rectified beyond this time limit even without the agreement of the parties so long as the amendment does not cause a miscarriage of justice for the other party and providing that the party requesting the rectification has a reasonable explanation for the delay.[76]

A decision to rectify a mistake is considered to be part of the original judgment or 'other decision'. Therefore, a party may appeal the decision to rectify in the same way as he may appeal the original decision. However, refusal by the court to rectify its decision is considered to be an 'other decision'. Therefore, a party may appeal that decision only with the permission of the court.[77]

181. In addition to this power to rectify technical mistakes in judgments, section 12 of the Execution Law, 1967 provides: if the Chief Execution Officer is of the opinion that a judgment or any part thereof requires clarification for the purpose of its execution, he may refer in writing to the court which rendered the judgment to obtain such clarification.

182. This provision is a major exception to the general principle of res judicata under which once a court has entered a final judgment in a matter it no longer has jurisdiction to deal with the matter. It should be emphasized that only the Chief Execution Officer, as distinguished from a party, may request such clarification.

II. Provisional Proceedings (Provisional Relief)

A. General and Historical Background

183. The term preliminary relief as used in Israel applies to all forms of relief linked to the main proceedings that are designed to insure that the plaintiff will receive the final relief he requests if he is successful in his claim. All legal systems have long recognized the need to provide the plaintiff with at least some forms of conservatory preliminary relief so as to insure that, during the pendency of the proceedings, the defendant does not take actions that would frustrate the possibility of the enforcing the plaintiff's judgment should one be obtained.

While recognizing the need to provide such relief, the law has, however, been faced with an opposing set of values. That is, provisional relief is, by definition, relief provided before the plaintiff has proven the defendant's liability. In other words, the coercive power of the courts is sought to be brought to bear, whether in

75. *Yosifov v. Yosifov*, 32 (1) P.D. 667 (1978).
76. *Asfur v. Huri*, 55 (3) P.D. 865 (2001).
77. *Levi v. Levi*, 44 (4) P.D. 212 (1990).

the form of sequestration of the defendant's property or by an order directed against him personally to restrain him from acting as he otherwise would, before it has been determined definitively that he is liable to the plaintiff. This is a drastic step indeed – a restraint of the defendant's property or liberty prior to a definitive adjudication of his liability.

By the nature of litigation there must be some lapse of time between the institution of an action and its completion. Thus the problem of provisional remedies necessarily arises in all jurisdictions and in all historical periods. However, it becomes exacerbated when there are extensive delays in the adjudicatory process which cause the length of time between the initiation of an action and its completion to be measured not in terms of months, but in years – indeed, four or five years in many jurisdictions.

Moreover, the situation becomes even worse when during this lengthy period of time the value of the plaintiff's claim may be reduced by inflation or when the plaintiff is a relatively poor individual who needs to have his claim satisfied in order to continue to provide sustenance for himself and his family.

In extreme cases such situations may result in the judicial system becoming worthless as a tool for the enforcement of obligations. When this occurs, as it has to some degree occurred in many jurisdictions, it becomes necessary to reform the system.

These reforms may include, *inter alia*, a reconsideration of the existing balance between a plaintiff's need for preliminary relief and a defendant's right not to be restrained in his property or person before he is definitively judged to be liable, with the tendency, therefore, being to tilt the balance more and more in favour of the plaintiff's need for preliminary relief.

Yet the recent trend in Israel as to preliminary relief is exceptional. In recent years Israel not only has not tilted the balance between the interests of plaintiffs and defendants further in favour of plaintiffs, it has done the opposite. It has actually tilted the balance further in favour of defendants.

This most interesting phenomenon may be explained by the fact that until about ten years ago in Israel the balance between the interests of plaintiffs and defendants as to preliminary relief was tilted overwhelmingly in favour of plaintiffs. This plaintiff preference in the Israeli system was manifest both in the wide range of preliminary relief available to the plaintiff and in the relative ease by which such relief could be obtained, both in terms of the legal rules on the books and of their implementation in practice.

In terms of the wide range of preliminary relief, Israel has inherited both the civil law preliminary remedy of temporary attachment (*seise conservatoire and seise revendication*) and the common law remedies of preliminary injunctions and temporary receiverships. The former is a legacy from the Ottoman Turkish law that prevailed in the territory that is now Israel until the First World War, while the latter were, of course, incorporated into what became the Israeli legal system during the period of the British mandate. Moreover, in Israel, almost uniquely there has historically been very widespread use of orders preventing the defendants in civil proceedings from leaving the country during the pendency of such proceedings. Finally, while Israel never has had a general provision for interim monetary payments such as exists in England, Israeli law does provide for interim monetary payments to road accident victims as well as for the more traditional temporary support orders.

In recent years none of these forms of preliminary relief has been abolished. Indeed, Israel has adopted two new forms that were created in England: Mareva injunctions and Anton Piller orders. Thus, in terms of the variety of preliminary relief, there has not been any pro-defendant tendency, but rather the opposite.

Yet, as to the most draconian form of preliminary relief, that of orders preventing a defendant from leaving the country, there has been a notable shift in favour of defendants by rules, both case law and rules of court, which have made it much more difficult for plaintiffs to obtain such orders.

Granting any type of preliminary relief necessarily involves a delicate balance of the plaintiff's interest in not preventing the defendant from frustrating the litigation and that of the defendant in not having his liberty or property restrained prior to the definitive adjudication of his liability. In attempting to reach a proper accommodation of these two interests in a particular case, many legal systems condition the granting of preliminary relief on two cumulative conditions:

(1) a preliminary determination that the plaintiff has a good case on the merits; and
(2) the existence of special circumstances, such as probable cause for believing that the defendant is about to remove his assets from the court's jurisdiction, such that it is necessary to grant the preliminary relief in order to prevent the defendant from frustrating either the litigation or the implementation of the judgment.

In Israel, historically the situation was different and tended towards the protection of the interests of the plaintiff at the expense of those of the defendant. Thus, while in general granting a temporary injunction has always been conditioned upon the cumulative existence of the two above-stated requirements, the same was not true as to temporary attachments and preventing a defendant from leaving the country. As to the former, the sole condition for granting the relief related to the quality of the plaintiff's case, with no consideration at all given to the necessity of granting the relief on the facts of the particular situation.

This situation was reversed as to orders preventing the defendant from leaving the country, i.e., the sole condition related to the necessity for granting the relief with no consideration being given to the probability of the plaintiff's success on the merits of his case.

Moreover, as to these two forms of preliminary relief, in practice the courts did not insist on clear proof even of the one condition that was, in theory, required for the granting of the relevant relief. Thus, temporary attachments were granted as a matter of course without any real evaluation of the plaintiff's case. Israeli courts, on a daily basis, also issued orders preventing defendants from leaving the country on the grounds that they intended to leave the country permanently or for an extended period and that their absence from the country would burden the plaintiff either in proving his case or in enforcing his judgment without insisting on proof that this extreme remedy was truly essential for this purpose.

184. As indicated above, this situation changed greatly in the last few years. In part these changes resulted from academic criticism of the existing system. Even more significant was the adoption in 1992 of the Basic Law: Human Dignity and Liberty which includes provisions protecting property and the right to leave the country.

As a formal matter of law, this 1992 basic law did not affect the constitutional status of the then rules concerning preliminary relief since it provided that none of its provisions shall affect existing legal rules, which, as defined includes the Rules of Civil Procedure. However, it did help create a new legal climate which emphasized defendant's rights more than did the previous one.

Thus, in 1996, the Rules of Civil Procedure were amended to require a plaintiff seeking a temporary injunction to prove that, in addition to his having a prima facie case on the merits of the claim, 'failure to issue the [temporary attachment] order may hinder the enforcement of the judgment'.

Even more significantly, the Supreme Court held that due to the adoption of the 1992 basic law that recognized the right of a person to leave the country, when a court is requested to exercise its authority to prevent a defendant from leaving the country it should give great weight to the right of a person to leave the country.

In a series of decisions in 1992, the Supreme Court set new conditions governing the granting of an order preventing a defendant from leaving the country. These conditions represent the application of a constitutional norm and contain the following cumulative elements. In seeking an order preventing the defendant from leaving the country the plaintiff must convince the court that there is a grave and tangible danger that the proceeding will be impeded or the execution of the judgment heavily burdened. In addition, the court can grant the order only after determining that there are no lesser measures available to accomplish the same end. The order must be granted with great caution and only in rare cases. In addition, when a court exercises its power to prevent a defendant from leaving the country, it should take into consideration the substantive character of the case. For example, the court should clearly differentiate between proceedings that can be conducted despite the defendant's absence and those that cannot.

In a later, 1999 decision, the Supreme Court expressly held that, in addition to all the other conditions mentioned above, an order preventing a defendant from leaving the country should not be granted unless the plaintiff has convinced the court that prima facie he has a good case on the merits.

B. The New Rules

185. As a culmination of this tendency to reduce the former undue plaintiff bias of preliminary relief in Israeli law, as well as to provide a more comprehensive and uniform system of preliminary relief, in 2001 the Rules of Civil Procedure were amended so as to create a new scheme regulating the granting of all forms of preliminary relief.

This new scheme is divided into two parts: a general part and a specific part. The general part is a major innovation in the Israeli law of preliminary relief as it sets forth, for the first time, general rules applicable to all forms of preliminary relief.

Both the general and specific parts are quite detailed. We will describe herein only their basic principles, starting with the general part.

C. The General Part; Rules 360–373

186. The basic principle underlying the granting of all types of preliminary relief is that in order to grant such relief the court must be persuaded, on the basis of prima facie reliable evidence, that the plaintiff has a good case on the merits and that the specific conditions of the particular preliminary relief sought, which are contained in the specific part, have been met. As the Supreme Court has clarified, it is sufficient for the plaintiff to prove at this stage that prima facie the claim raises a serious question and that it is not a false claim.[78]

In addition, in determining whether or not to grant the preliminary relief, the form of the relief, its scope and conditions, including the security which the plaintiff must post, the court is required to consider, *inter alia*, the following:

(1) The damage that will occur to the plaintiff if the preliminary relief is not granted as opposed to the damage that will occur to the defendant if it is granted, as well as damage that may occur to third parties; a reciprocal relationship exists between this consideration and the duty imposed on the plaintiff to prove that he has a good case on the merits. This means that where the 'balance of convenience' tends to the direction of the applicant, the burden of proof regarding the existence of a good case on the merits will be lessened, and vice versa.[79]

(2) If the request was made in good faith and the grant of relief is just and proper in the particular case involved, and will not cause greater injury than is necessary. If the court finds that the applicant did not act in good faith, he may reject the application on this ground, even if the other conditions for granting the preliminary relief have been met.[80] As to considerations of justice and equity, the courts have ruled that weight should be given to the specific time at which the applicant filed the application for preliminary relief. A delay in filing the application is a reason for rejecting the application in and of itself.[81] Preliminary relief may be granted before the action is filed if the court is convinced that it is justified to do so on the facts of the particular case involved. In such a case the order for preliminary relief will end automatically if the action is not filed within seven days of the granting of the order. For very special reasons the court may set a longer time than this seven day period.

No order for preliminary relief is to be granted unless the plaintiff has filed a written undertaking to compensate the person against whom the order is addressed for

---

78. See for example: *Ita v. Bank Mizrahi*, Israeli Supreme Court Petition 5841/2011, 20 Sep. 2011 (unreported).
79. *Ibid.*
80. *Rider v. L. Raphael Construction Company Ltd.* Israeli Supreme Court Petition 3071/2010, 20 May 2010 (unreported).
81. See: *Ita, supra* n. 78.

all damage that the order will cause him, if the action is withdrawn or dismissed or the order for preliminary relief is otherwise cancelled.

In addition, the plaintiff is to post security, usually in the form of a bank guarantee, in an amount determined by the court as sufficient to compensate the person against whom the preliminary relief is directed for all damage that has been caused him by the preliminary relief, if the action is dismissed or withdrawn or the order otherwise cancelled.

While the giving of the above mentioned undertaking is absolutely mandatory the court may relieve the plaintiff of the obligation to post the security if it believes that it is just and proper to do so in view of the very special circumstances involved in the given case.

However the court may increase this burden on a plaintiff by requiring the deposit of collateral, in addition to the usual bank guaranteed security bond discussed above, if it believes that it is just and proper to do so on the facts of the case involved. Moreover, the court must require the deposit of such collateral if the preliminary relief order is granted ex parte, unless it is convinced that on the facts of the case in question it is just and proper to excuse the plaintiff from the deposit of the collateral.

The sum of the collateral that is to be deposited is set by the Rules at NIS 50,000 (c. USD 13,000). However, the court may set a greater sum if it is convinced that it is just to do so in the particular circumstances of the case involved. This designated sum of NIS 50,000 is to be adjusted annually according to the consumer price index.

These very detailed provisions as to the written undertaking, the security bond and the collateral represent a new compilation of principles, some of which were formerly part of the details of the rules concerning some forms of preliminary relief, but most of which were the product of independent Israeli case law, which, in turn, was influenced by English law in this regard.

187. The request for preliminary relief must be supported by an affidavit verifying all the facts, including the facts of the plaintiff's claim, relevant to the request. In terms of the hearing on this request, the Rules provide that requests for temporary attachments, Mareva injunctions and Anton Piller orders are to be issued ex parte, unless the court is convinced that a hearing attended by all parties will not frustrate the issuance of the order. However, all other forms of preliminary relief, i.e., ordinary temporary injunctions, orders preventing the defendant from leaving the country and interim monetary payments are to be issued after a hearing attended by all parties unless the court determines by prima facie reliable evidence that there is a reasonable fear that the delay involved in a hearing attended by all the parties would frustrate the granting of the order or cause serious damage to the applicant.

The logic of these provisions is clear. The presumption concerning temporary injunctions, Mareva injunctions and Anton Piller orders is that if the defendant is warned of the impeding issuance of the order by being informed of an upcoming hearing on the request he is likely to try to dispose of his assets or otherwise place them beyond the reach of the preliminary relief before the granting of the order. Thus the norm is ex parte relief. As to the other forms of preliminary relief, the presumption is the opposite, thus a full hearing before all the parties is the norm.

In all cases of ex parte relief, except as to temporary attachments, the court granting such relief is to fix the date for the full hearing, which ordinarily should be held no longer than fourteen days after the granting of the relief ex parte. Historically in Israel temporary attachments were always granted ex parte with no date being set for the full hearing. Rather, the burden was on the defendant to request a full hearing by filing a motion to abolish the attachment order. The new rules continue this unique.

The rules contemplate that the full hearing on the granting of preliminary relief, whether before or after the initial granting, will be a relatively brief one. They provide that the hearing should normally be completed in no more than one day. The hearing is based on the affidavits that have been filed with the parties having the right to cross-examine the affiants. The parties are to summarize their positions orally following the evidentiary part of the hearing.

The non-final nature of preliminary relief under Israeli law is emphasized in the new rules by their provision that, at the request of a party, the court may reconsider and change or abolish any order for preliminary relief if it is convinced that it is just to do so for any one of the following reasons: (1) circumstances have changed since the issuance of the order; or (2) new facts have been disclosed; or even (3) the court later realizes that it was wrong to have issued the order.

D. Preliminary Injunctions and Interim Monetary Orders

188. As noted above, the general part applies to all forms of preliminary relief subject to the specific provisions that may be involved in the specific part as to particular forms of preliminary relief. However, there is no reference in the specific part either to temporary injunctions, other than to the Israeli version of Mareva injunctions, or to the limited forms of interim monetary relief contained in Israeli law. More specific rules concerning interim monetary relief are contained in the particular enactments that pertain to those forms of relief. However, as to preliminary injunctions the general part contains all the relevant provisions, thus affirming their status as the archetype of preliminary relief in Israeli law.

E. The Specific Part: Temporary Attachments; Rules 374–382

189. The specific part contains specific provisions as to temporary attachments, Mareva injunctions, preventing a defendant from leaving the country, Anton Piller orders, and temporary receiverships.

As mentioned above, the Israeli rules as to temporary attachment find their origin in the Ottoman Law of Procedure 1879, which in turn was influenced by continental European practice, particularly that of France.

It is of interest to note that as originally adopted in 1879 this Ottoman Code related only to temporary attachment as to certain types of monetary claims, with the probable intention being to limit its use to commercial matters. This, indeed, was the prevailing use of *seise conservatoire* in France until recent times. Since this time, the use of temporary attachments as to monetary claims has been expanded in

Israel to include all actions for money judgments as, indeed, it has been expanded also in France and elsewhere.

In addition, in 1913, while the territory that is now the State of Israel was still within the Ottoman Empire, a new paragraph was added to this provision of the Ottoman Code of 1879, that provided that 'the plaintiff in an action relating to any specific object may apply for provisional attachment of the property in dispute, whether it be moveable or immoveable property, in the possession of the defendant or a third party, until the conclusion of the action'. That is, *seise revendication*. Since that date, these two forms of temporary attachment have been treated alike by the Israeli rules and their predecessors.

The theory of both types of temporary attachment in Israeli law is clearly conservatory, i.e., to prevent loss, damage or destruction of the property, or its removal from the enforcement power of the courts, prior to the conclusion of the main proceedings.

And, in practice, this is also the case. The result of a temporary attachment is not the transfer of the object to the possession of the debtor, but rather its seizure for safekeeping. Indeed, it may even remain in the possession of the defendant with him being appointed 'trustee' for its safekeeping. In theory, under the rules of the Execution Law 1967, which also apply to temporary attachments, the Execution Officer could appoint the plaintiff as trustee for the object and transfer its possession to him in that capacity. Yet, this would be an extreme departure from normal practice in this regard and would only be justified under the most unusual of circumstances.

The specific rules as to temporary attachments in the specific part restate the previous rules in this regard. In particular, Rule 374(b) provides that the court may issue a temporary attachment order (both *seise conservatoire* and *seise revendication*) as to the respondent's property which is in his possession or in the possession of the applicant or in the possession of a third party. Included in the respondent's property are not only tangible assets but legal rights as well (e.g., a future debt where the date of repayment has not yet been reached). However, mere expectation or a chance to receive an asset is not subject to temporary attachment.[82] Subject to the provisions of the general part, Rule 374(b) states that the court may grant the applicant the order if it is persuaded on the basis of reliable prima facie evidence that there is a reasonable fear that not granting the order will hinder the execution of the judgment. This question will be decided in accordance with the circumstances of every case, including the amount of the claim, the financial ability of the respondent and the fear that the property will be removed from the enforcement power of the courts.[83] It should be noted that although the applicant must prove that granting the order is necessary for the execution of the judgment, the level of proof required from him is low in comparison to other temporary remedies. It is sufficient that he proves that there is a 'reasonable fear' that not issuing a temporary attachment order will hinder the execution of the judgment.[84] However, the courts have

---

82. See for example: *Eyeni v. Shifris*, Israeli Supreme Court Petition 6621/2008, 24 Aug. 2008 (unreported).
83. *Israel Discont Bank Ltd. v. ICC Industries Lnc.*, Israeli Supreme Court Petition 10076/2007, 28 Nov. 2007 (unreported).
84. *Ibid.*

also stressed that a temporary attachment order should not be given carelessly. Since the adoption of Basic Law: Human Dignity and Liberty, more weight should be attributed to the quality of the evidence that supports the application than previously.[85]

The reference to the general part in this and the other rules of the specific part clearly incorporates the provisions about the plaintiff having a good case on the merits, the factors of the relative harms and good faith, the undertaking of the plaintiff to compensate the defendant for damage caused, the posting of security for such undertaking, the form of the hearing, etc.

The specific rules then go into great detail as to challenges to the ownership of the property by the defendant brought by third-party holders of the property. A full discussion of these specific rules would be well beyond the purposes of this monograph.

More to the point herein is the duplication in the Israeli law of preliminary relief as a result of its twin sources: Ottoman and English. As stated above, along with both types of civil law temporary attachments Israel has also inherited common law temporary injunctions. This has created for the plaintiff a choice of preliminary relief as to claims concerning the recovery of specific property: *seise revendication* or temporary injunction. However, since similar rules now apply to both, this redundancy does not today create real problems in practice.

F. Mareva Injunctions; Rule 383

190. Given the existence of *seise conservatoire* in Israeli law, it would seem that there would have been no reason for Israel to have adopted Mareva injunctions. As is well known, the English courts invented Mareva injunctions because traditional English law did not contain temporary attachments or any other remedy equivalent to *seaise conservatoire.*

However, Israel has, indeed, also adopted Mareva injunctions. This was done in order to deal with a case where the defendant's property was abroad. Since temporary attachments are in rem forms of relief directly against the property, it is understood that they cannot be used in cases where the property is not within Israel. However, while Mareva injunctions do contain some aspects similar to that of in rem relief, they are clearly in personam, i.e., orders directed against defendants restricting the use of their property. Thus they may be used in cases concerning property abroad.

This use of Mareva injunctions in Israel has now been codified in Rule 383, although the term Mareva injunction is not used. Rather the rule in question refers to orders 'restricting the use of property'. According to the language of the rule, a court may, subject to the rules of the general part, 'order the respondent acting by himself or through another on his behalf, to refrain from divesting property from his control, or from the control of its holder [on his behalf], from selling it, encumbering it, or changing its condition or his rights in it, if it is convinced on the basis

85. *Signal Electronic Services Ltd. v. Danbar Ltd.*, Israeli Supreme Court Petition 5242/1995, 2 Oct. 1995 (unreported).

of prima facie reliable evidence that there is a reasonable fear that not granting such an order will substantially hinder the execution of the judgment. A Mareva injunction will be granted if two additional conditions have been met: first, the provisions of the general part have been fulfilled. Second, the person against whom the injunction is granted is subject to the Israeli court's jurisdiction.[86]

Two things are clear here. First, this is a codification of Mareva injunctions. Second the rule is not limited to property not within the State of Israel. Hence, there is another duplication between civil law type of temporary attachments and common law based temporary injunctions. This time, between *seise conservatoire* and Mareva injunctions.

However, this Mareva injunction rule makes quite clear that it can be used against property abroad by expressly defining the term 'property' as 'including property existing beyond the area of the State'.[87] This also clearly hints as to the primary expected use of this rule as distinguished from the use of ordinary temporary injunctions.

G. Preventing a Defendant from Leaving the Country; Rules 384–386

191. The provision as to preventing defendants from leaving the country follows the pattern described above as to temporary attachments; i.e., a restatement of existing law including the relatively new limiting provisions. Thus, Rule 384 provides that the court may, subject to the provisions of the first part, issue an order preventing a defendant from leaving the country, if it is convinced by prima facie reliable evidence that there is a reasonable fear that he is about to leave the country forever or for a long period of time, which situation would substantially hinder the maintenance of the action or execution of the judgment; if the defendant is a foreign resident an order preventing him from leaving the country should not be issued except in the most unusual circumstances which are to be recorded.

The violation of the right to freedom of movement involved in an order preventing the defendant from leaving the country has led the courts as well as the legislature to adopt a cautious approach towards this temporary relief. Thus, the applicant has to prove that not granting the order would **substantially** hinder the execution of the judgment; the order will be granted only if the court has been persuaded that all the conditions set out in the provision were strictly proved;[88] finally, Rule 384(c) states that, excluding alimony claims, an order preventing a defendant from leaving the country may be granted only in respect of claims that exceed NIS 50,000 (c. USD 13,000).

86. *Standard Charter Bank v. Katav*, 57 (6) P.D. 1 (2003).
87. *Ibid.*
88. *Troim v. Gaydamak*, Israeli Supreme Court Petition 9877/2008, 24 Nov. 2008 (unreported).

H. Anton Piller Orders; Rule 387A

192. Another innovation in the particular part of the rules of preliminary relief is the adoption of the English-derived Anton Piller orders concerning the preservation of evidence. As with Mareva injunctions, the English term does not appear in the rules. However, it is clear that the new Israeli form of preliminary relief termed 'seizure of property' is based on English Anton Piller order. Thus, the rule in question provides that the court may, again subject to the provisions of the general part, 'appoint a person for the purpose of executing a search, photographing, copying, or seizing property found on given premises, if it is persuaded by prima facie reliable evidence that there is a substantial fear that the defendant or another acting on his behalf is about to hide or destroy the property, which situation would substantially burden the maintenance of the action'. 'Property' is defined in Rule 387A(d) as 'property which is evidence or [otherwise] necessary for the determination of the action'.

An Anton Piller order involves a severe violation of the respondent's right to privacy and property. As a result, the conditions for granting this temporary relief are stringent. An order will be granted in the exceptional circumstances in which there is a **substantial** fear that not granting the order would **substantially** burden the maintenance of the proceedings.

I. Temporary Receiverships; Rule 387B

193. Finally, the special part includes a traditional Israeli form of preliminary relief – temporary receiverships. However, here again the requirements for the appointment of temporary receivers have been tightened and rewritten to conform to the general rules concerning the other forms of preliminary relief described above. Thus, the rule provides that the court may, subject to the provisions of the general part, order the appointment of a temporary receiver as to certain assets of the defendant, if it is convinced by prima facie reliable evidence that there is a substantial fear of significant damage to their value or that the defendant or another acting on his behalf is about to hide or destroy such assets or that the assets were produced in the course of, or used in the commission of, the act or omission which is the subject of the action and that the failure to issue such order would substantially hinder the execution of the judgment.

Among the powers of a temporary receiver is that of the management of the assets involved and, otherwise, to act with them as if he were their owner. In practice, the majority of cases in which temporary receivers have been appointed involve management of property in which several people share administrative rights.

As the Supreme Court has explained a temporary receivership is a severe remedy since in his actions the temporary receiver expropriates the defendant's control in his property and thus violates his constitutional right to property. Therefore, the court should exercise caution when making a decision whether to grant this relief. It also follows, so the Supreme Court has ruled, that temporary receivership should not be granted if it will force the defendant to stop his activity or will substantially hinder it.[89]

194. When these new rules are compared with the previous ones two points are very clear. First, they tend to tighten the requirements for obtaining preliminary relief thus tilting the balance more in favour of the defendants than under the previous rules. In our view that is a most welcome development. Second, they have created great uniformity as to the procedures for the obtaining of the various forms of preliminary relief. This is true not only in regard to the uniformity created by the applicability of the general part to all the specific forms of preliminary relief, but also by the near uniform language used in the particular part as to the requirements for the granting of the different forms of preliminary relief.

Yet there are also minor differences as to these requirements. All of the forms of preliminary relief refer to the 'fear' of an 'adverse effect' on the maintenance of the action or the execution of the judgment if the preliminary relief involved would not be granted. Yet there are differences in their language as to the extent both of the fear and the adverse effect required. At one extreme are temporary attachments, as to which there is required only a 'reasonable fear' that the failure to issue the order 'will hinder' the execution of the judgment. At the other extreme are the provisions concerning preventing the defendant from leaving the country, Anton Piller orders and temporary receiverships all of which require that there be a 'substantial fear' that the failure to issue the order 'will substantially hinder' the maintenance of the action or the execution of the judgment. In between these extremes, the issuance of Mareva injunctions requires only a 'reasonable fear', as is true with temporary attachments, but that the failure to issue the order 'will substantially hinder' the execution of the judgment, similarly to the other forms of preliminary relief except temporary attachments.

It seems that the draftsmen of the rules intended to make it somewhat easier for the plaintiff to obtain an order for a temporary attachment than orders preventing the defendant from leaving the country, Anton Piller orders and temporary receiverships, with Mareva injunctions being in the middle.

Such distinctions among the forms of preliminary relief seem to be justified. Each of the above mentioned preliminary remedies involves a different level of negative impact on the defendant's constitutional rights. Some of the remedies involve a severe violation of the defendants' rights, while others involve a less severe violation of his rights. Accordingly, the distinctions described above between the remedies is well founded.

Moreover, it should be noted that even the somewhat more relaxed rule as to temporary attachments is stricter than that which preceded the new rules. The previous rule as to temporary attachments required only that the plaintiff show that the failure to grant the order 'may hinder' the execution of the judgment; whereas the new rule requires him to show that it 'will hinder' the execution of the judgment.

89. *Talpaz Refueling and Investments Ltd. v. Paz Oil Company Ltd.*, 56 (6) P.D. 550 (2002).

§2. DEFAULT PROCEEDINGS

I. Types of Default Judgments

195. The two principle forms of default judgments at the first instance are failure to file a defence and failure to appear at trial.

A. Failure to File a Defence

196. Rule 97 of the Rules of Civil Procedure provides that where a defendant who is required to file a defence fails to do so within the period specified in the notice of suit, the judge or register *shall* enter judgment against the defendant.

Despite this apparently absolute statement in the Rule, a defendant who does not file his defence within the stated period may still avoid the entry of judgment against him. He may do so on one of two grounds.

First, he may petition and obtain an extension of time for filing his defence, according to Rule 528 that enable the court to extend a time period that has passed. As discussed in paragraph 124 such extensions of time are granted liberally since the time period here has not been established absolutely by statute or rule.

More significant, however, is the fact that a defendant generally need not avail himself of the extension provision. This is so, since the courts have held that, despite the language of Rule 97, a defendant may file his defence late, without the necessity of receiving an extension, as long as the court has not yet considered the plaintiff's motion for a default judgment.[90] This approach has received a lenient interpretation by the courts. Thus, preliminary proceedings to the hearing of the plaintiff's motion for a default judgment are not considered to be part of the hearing. Therefore, a defence filed during the preliminary proceedings will prevent the court from granting a default judgment.[91] More important, the Supreme Court has made it clear that this issue should not be ruled upon according to formal and strict criteria. The defendant's constitutional right to access the courts and present his case and the public interest in conducting a procedure in the presence of both parties justify the adoption of flexible criteria. Accordingly, the court should consider the unique circumstances of each case, including the length of the delay in filing the defence and the possibility of compensating the plaintiff for the damage he has suffered due to the delay.[92]

The lenient approach adopted by Israeli courts toward this issue is reflected in two other rulings: first, when the defendant requested an extension to file his defence and was denied, but nevertheless filed a defence (in delay) and did so before the court considered the plaintiff's motion for a default judgment, a default judgment was not granted. This approach was justified on the ground that though the defendant contravened the court's decision, it would have been artificial and

90. *Casif v. Rubin*, Israeli Supreme Court Petition 6265/2004, 10 Oct. 2004 (unreported).
91. *Ibid.*; *Ariad Constructions Ltd. v. Avi and Arik Electrical Engineering Ltd.*, 56 (4) P.D. 61 (2002).
92. *Ibid.*

undesirable to ignore the existence of a defence.[93] Second, the court will not enter a default judgment on its own motion, but will do so only at the request of the plaintiff. Moreover, the plaintiff is not obliged to file such a request immediately upon the period of time specified in the notice of suit elapsing.[94] In practice, plaintiffs do not make such requests at the earliest possible moment. It follows that often the defendant's opportunity to file a defence extends beyond the period of time specified in the notice of suit. In contrast to the English rule which distinguishes for this purpose among many types of claims, the Israeli Rule 97 has greatly simplified the process of entering judgment for default of pleading. The Rule distinguishes only between two types of claims:

(1) claims for liquidated demands;
(2) claims for unliquidated demands.

The object of the Rule, it should be emphasized, is that to the greatest extent possible judgment is to be entered without requiring any proof from the plaintiff.

As to liquidated demands, judgment is to be entered automatically on the basis of the complaint without any hearing whatsoever. Where the complaint is however, for an unliquidated demand, the court is authorized, if there exist 'special reasons', which reasons must be recorded by the court, to require from the plaintiff full or partial proof as to his claim before entering judgment in his favour.

The strong tendency of the Rule against holding hearings when there has been a default of pleading is further attested to by Rule 97(b) providing that even where the plaintiff is required to furnish proof as to his claim, the defendant is not to be invited to the hearing unless there exist further special reasons for inviting him.

Where there is more than one defendant, each defendant is treated separately for purposes of Rule 97. Thus the failure of any one defendant to file a defence entitles the plaintiff to enter judgment against him, even if other defendants have filed defences and even if the substance of their defences would apply also to the defendant who failed to file a defence.

A plaintiff against whom a counterclaim is filed is in the position of a defendant as to the counterclaim and must file a defence to it. Rule 97 applies in the case of a plaintiff who fails to file a defence to a counterclaim in the same way as it applies to a defendant's failure of defence.

B. Failure to Appear at Trial

197. Under Israeli procedure a party need not appear in person, but may be represented by an attorney who appears for him. Thus, when we speak of failure to appear at trial, we are referring to the failure of a party to appear either in person or by his attorney.

Rule 157 of the Rules of Civil Procedure divides the procedure as to the failure to appear at trial into three situations:

---

93. *Casif, supra* n. 90.
94. *Ben Tov v. Orot Hagalil Holdings Ltd.*, 59 (5) P.D. 693 (2005).

(1) failure on the part of both plaintiff and defendant to appear;
(2) failure of only the plaintiff to appear;
(3) failure of only the defendant to appear.

198. In the first situation, i.e., the failure of both parties to appear, the court is authorized, in its discretion, to choose between two alternatives. It may postpone the hearing to a later date, or it may dismiss the complaint without prejudice, i.e., the plaintiff is not barred by res judicata from re-instituting the claim.

199. When the plaintiff appears and the defendant, after having been duly notified, fails to appear, the plaintiff is entitled to proceed with the proof of his case. If he succeeds in proving it to the satisfaction of the court, he is then entitled to the relief he requested. The difference between this procedure and that involved in a failure to file a defence discussed above is quite striking. In the latter case, the tendency of the Rule was against requiring the plaintiff to prove his case. The Rule acquiesced in the plaintiff proving his case only if it were for an unliquidated demand and then only if special reasons existed and only to the extent that these special reasons necessitated proof.

Where the defendant has, however, filed a defence and then fails to appear at trial, the plaintiff, in order to have judgment entered in his favour, must, in all cases, prove his case to the full extent of the burden of proof that rests upon him.

This difference in treatment is justified by the fact that once a defendant has filed a defence, he has indicated his desire to defend and has contradicted or avoided the allegations of the complaint. From this point onward, even if the defendant fails to appear at trial, it is incumbent on the plaintiff to prove his case in order to recover.

Moreover, once the defendant has filed a defence, the court has before it the defendant's arguments against the plaintiff's claim. It could not, and should not, thereafter blindly enter judgment for the plaintiff even when the defendant has defaulted. Rather, the court requires the plaintiff to prove his case and thereby refute the defendant's defence.

200. Where the defendant appears and the plaintiff, having been duly notified, fails to appear, the complaint may be dismissed, either with or without prejudice. In such a case, if the defendant has filed a counterclaim, he is considered to be in the position of a plaintiff as to the counterclaim and thus is entitled to a judgment on the counterclaim only if, and to the extent that, he proves his counterclaim.

The Supreme Court has stressed several times that failure to appear on the part of the plaintiff does not per se justify the dismissal of the claim with prejudice, but will only do so in the most exceptional circumstances. It has also been held that in order for the court to dismiss the claim with prejudice, two cumulative conditions have to be proved: first, that prima facie the plaintiff does not have a cause of action which would entitle him to a relief so that dismissal of the claim with prejudice would not cause a miscarriage of justice. Second, the failure to appear is an expression of manifest contempt for the court, as opposed to a mistake.

The rationale for the adoption of these strict conditions is twofold. First, a dismissal of the claim with prejudice violates the plaintiff's constitutional right to access to the court and is equivalent to a denial of the plaintiff's material right. Second, a dismissal of the claim with prejudice contradicts the basic goal of the legal procedure which is to rule on the material rights of the parties.

Given the severe results of a dismissal of the claim with prejudice, the Supreme Court has ruled that the courts should consider whether less drastic measures may be used, for example, dismissing the claim without prejudice or the imposition of legal costs on the plaintiff.[95]

II. Status of Default Judgments

201. A judgment entered upon default, is an enforceable judgment in all respects. Further, the filing of an opposition, as discussed below, does not delay or otherwise affect the enforceability of the default judgment.

III. Opposition

202. There is, however, one major difference between default judgments and other judgments: the right of opposition that exists as to default judgments, pursuant to Rule 201 of the RCP.

A request to set aside a default judgment must be made by motion within thirty days from the date the judgment was served on the defaulting party. The moving party must attach an affidavit to verify the facts on which he relies. A hearing is held on the motion to which the opposing party is invited to appear. The opposing party may file counter affidavits. Both parties may be permitted to cross-examine the opposing party's affiants.

Rule 201 and the rules concerning summonses set forth the process as described above for setting aside default judgments. The Rules, however, do not prescribe the substantive criteria by which the court is to determine whether or not a default judgment should be set aside. The courts, however, have filled the gap and developed two complementary standards for setting aside default judgments.[96]

(1) where the law requires setting aside an invalid default judgment; and
(2) where a court may exercise its discretion to set aside a default judgment despite the fact that it was validly entered.

The first standard refers to cases in which the entering of judgment was contrary to applicable legal principles. The clearest example of such a case is a situation where the court lacked international jurisdiction over a foreign defendant. In such a case it is the defendant's right to have the judgment set aside and the court has no discretion in the matter. The reason for the default as well as the defaulting party's chances of eventual success are both irrelevant to the decision to set aside the invalid judgment.

---

95. *Nadav v. Central Salon for Washing Machines and Television*, 55 (5) P.D. 43 (2001).
96. *Ben Zion v. The Trustee of Ben Zion Assets*, 48 (1) P.D. 830 (1994).

The second standard, allowing a court to set aside a default judgment even if such judgment was properly entered, is another reflection of the tendency of the Israeli system to avoid terminating litigation by default, and instead striving to afford all parties, even defaulting ones, their day in court. In applying this discretionary doctrine the courts consider two issues:

(1) the reasons for the default; and
(2) the possibility that the defaulting party will succeed in the litigation if the default judgment is set aside. While a party does not have to prove that his chances of success are high, he must prove that he will benefit from the cancellation of the decision.[97]

Emphasis is given to the latter issue. Thus, even if the default is the result of an innocent mistake, the court should not, so it has been ruled, ignore the importance of complying with the deadlines set in the RCP.[98]

In the case of a defendant who has defaulted in not filing a defence, this latter criterion requires that he set forth in his petition and accompanying affidavit the essence of his defence. In other cases, the court can evaluate the defaulting party's chance of success from the pleadings already filed.

Where the court does set aside a validly entered judgment on discretionary grounds, it generally requires the defaulting party to reimburse the other party for the expenses, including counsel fees, that he incurred as a result of the default and the motion to set it aside. And this, without regard to the final result of the litigation. The court may, indeed, expressly condition setting aside the judgment on the defaulting party's paying these costs by a certain date.

IV. Appeal

203. In principal, default judgments are treated as all other judgments in terms of appeal. That is, the losing party has a right of appeal to the court of the next higher instance. In the light of the above, following the entry of a default judgment there are two avenues available to overturn it; appeal of the judgment or a motion of opposition to set it aside.

However, the Supreme Court has ruled that as a general rule the appropriate way to attack a default judgment is by way of a motion of opposition to set it aside and not by way of an appeal.[99] Moreover, the appeal option is available only as to allegations that the default judgment was entered invalidly. That is, on an appeal as of right on the judgment, an appellate court would not overturn a valid default judgment on discretionary grounds as might the court that rendered the judgment pursuant to a motion to set it aside. Thus by filing an appeal and not a motion to dismiss, the appellant would thereby waive the possibility of overturning a valid default judgment on discretionary grounds.

97. *Ibid.*
98. *Fadida v. Refaeli*, Israeli Supreme Court Petition 10152/2007, 15 Dec. 2012 (unreported).
99. *Yahalom v. Ramat Gan Municipality*, 37 (4) P.D. 357 (1983).

204. It should be noted, however, that a refusal to grant a motion to set aside a default judgment is considered not a final judgment but rather 'another decision' and this is appealable only with leave of the appellate court.

However, a party may preserve his appeal of right as to the judgment itself while availing himself of the possibility of vacating the judgment on procedural grounds by pursuing both procedures simultaneously. This possibility is facilitated by a relatively recent amendment to the RCP, Rule 398A, which provides that the period of time in which a party must file an appeal on the judgment (as distinguished from requesting leave to appeal from the denial of his motion to vacate the judgment), does not begin to run until the delivery to him of the decision denying his motion to vacate the judgment.

Chapter 2. Review Proceedings

§1. Appeal; Rules 397–471

205. The basic form of attack against first instance judgments is appeal. In Israeli law, in such an appeal the appellate court does not try the case de novo, but rather sits to correct errors of the first instance court. The appellate court reviews alleged errors, both of law and fact, but tends to defer as to factual determinations to the first instance court, particularly when they are based on the first instance court's impression of the credibility of witnesses who testified orally before it.[100] Only in very exceptional circumstances will the appellate court admit evidence that has not been presented at the first instance. Moreover, generally an appellate court will not entertain legal arguments that have not been raised at the first instance.

See paragraph 39 as to the right of appeal and the distinction between appeal of right as to 'judgments' and appeal by leave as to 'other decisions'.

206. Rules 397 and 398 hold, respectively, that an appeal as of right must be filed within forty-five days from the entry of the judgment and an application for leave to appeal within fifteen days of the entry of the decision. These dates are set absolutely in the Rules of Civil Procedure and thus their extension is subject to the strict rule requiring special reasons, see paragraph 124. And, indeed, the courts have been extremely reluctant to find the existence of special reasons to justify the extension of these time limits.

A respondent wishing to argue that the lower court decision should be changed in his favour, may file a counter-appeal; the counter-appeal must be filed within thirty days of service on him of the appellant's notice of appeal.

Where leave to appeal is required, as a rule such leave must be granted by the appropriate appellate court. The only exception to the above is a second appeal by leave to the Supreme Court, on an original judgment of the Magistrates' Court; in such a case leave to appeal may be granted either by the Supreme Court or by the District Court that has determined the first appeal.

In all cases where leave to appeal is sought from an appellate court, the applicant must request such leave in writing, setting forth his arguments and authorities concerning the reasons why leave should be granted. The decision as to granting leave to appeal is made by a single judge of the appellate court.

That judge may, on the basis of the written application alone, reject the application ex parte. However, leave cannot be granted ex parte; the respondent must be allowed to be heard, either in writing, orally, or both, depending on the discretion of the appellate judge.

Following a hearing on the application for leave to appeal, the judge who has heard the application for leave, without any further hearing, may determine the issue on the merits as if leave to appeal had been granted and the hearing on the leave to appeal was the hearing on the appeal itself. This may be done with the consent of the parties or even without their consent, as long as the judge has given the parties

---

100. See for example: *Amar v. S.A.S. Zafon & Amakim – Security and Guarding Ltd.*, Israeli Supreme Court Petition 7638/2011, 21 Nov. 2012 (unreported).

an opportunity to object to this expedited process and has determined that no right of any party will be damaged thereby. As might be expected in an era of even more crowded dockets, appellate courts use the expedited procedure quite frequently.

As set out in Rule 427 a necessary condition for the determination of an appeal is that the appellant file security, in an amount set by the registrar, for the respondent's costs if the appeal fails.

On appeal from final judgments of a lower court, the appellate court is composed of a panel of three judges. However, when leave to appeal is given as to other intermediate decisions of a trial court, the appeal is heard by a single judge.

207. The filing of an appeal from a judgment does not, by itself, delay the enforcement of the judgment. However, the Rules of Civil Procedure do authorize both the court that entered the judgment and the appeals court to delay the enforcement of a judgment pending determination of the appeal. Such delays in enforcement are granted in situations where if the judgment were enforced prior to the appeal it would be very difficult to restore the situation to the *status quo ante* in the event that the appeal is successful.[101]

208. Subject to the authority of an appellate court to order the submission of written statements in lieu of oral argument, as discussed below, appeals in Israel have traditionally been heard by oral argument, at which a party may appear in person or by his attorney, with the latter situation being almost the exclusive one in practice. However, due to the increasing number of appeals, there is increasing use of written statements in lieu of oral argument.

When an oral hearing on the appeal is to be held, a preliminary hearing may be held before a single judge. The holding of this preliminary hearing is at the discretion of the president of the appellate court. Its aim is similar to that of the pre-trial conference at the trial level: expediting the appeal process. Rule 445 of RCP concerning the preliminary hearing also states expressly that its aims include that of determining if it is possible for the parties to reach a compromise settlement.

In keeping with this settlement purpose of the preliminary hearing – and consistent also with pre-trial conferences – the judge involved may order the parties to appear personally along with their counsel.

209. Unless otherwise held by the court, the appellant must submit his 'points of argument' to the court, at least fourteen days before the date set for oral argument on the appeal. The respondent must submit his 'points of argument' seven days before the date set for the hearing.

These points of argument are to include, in summary form, the party's contention as to each point on appeal along with the legal sources upon which he relies to support these contentions.

Rule 446 (c) further provides that at the hearing of the appeal each side is entitled to rely on the arguments and sources set forth in his points of argument. In general, additional arguments or sources may be raised only with permission of the court.

---

101. See for example: *Association of the Institutions of Hazon Yeshayaou v. Registrar of Associations*, Israeli Supreme Court Petition 7907/2012, 20 Nov. 2012 (unreported).

However, if a party has filed points of argument, he may raise additional arguments and sources without the need for leave of court, if he is doing so in response to the other party's points of arguments.

210. As noted above, this oral procedure preceded by written points of argument is that generally used in appellate proceedings. However, the Rules also authorize the appellate court to require the filing of more extensive written statements of argument, if it sees fit, either in lieu of or in addition to the oral argument. The use of written statements in addition to the oral argument is usually the result of a decision taken by the court during the hearing of the oral argument where the court feels that a particular issue needs further elucidation in writing. As mentioned above, the use of written statements in lieu of oral argument is a growing phenomenon in Israel, resulting from the ever increasing number of appeals. This is especially evident in the Supreme Court, where the use of written statements in lieu of oral argument has become the norm.

211. Following the hearing of the appeal, the appellate court renders its written judgment. If a panel of three judges has heard the appeal, the judgment is according to the majority, but each judge may, and often does write his own opinion, setting forth his own reasons for the judgments. See paragraph 35 as to reasoned decisions on appeal.

As noted at the beginning of this section, the appeal is not a trial de novo but is aimed at correcting the errors, if any, of the lower court. However, if the appeal is accepted the power of the appellate court is not merely limited to correcting errors and remanding the case to the lower court for further proceedings. Rather the appellate court is authorized to, and generally does, enter the final judgment that in its view the lower court should have entered in the action. Moreover, the appellate court may enter such a judgment even if the appeal only referred to a particular issue in the lower court's judgment, and even if the judgment is to the benefit of the respondent or other parties, who may not have filed appeals or counter-appeals.

However, not every error of the trial court necessarily justifies upholding the appeal. In this regard the case law provides that a judgment of a lower court is not to be overturned unless its error is unreasonable.[102]

§2. Other Types of Attacks

212. See paragraph 74 concerning the cassation type jurisdiction of the Supreme Court sitting as the High Court of Justice over judicial tribunals that are not part of the regular judicial structure, in particular the labour courts and the religious courts.

---

102. See for example: *Agricultural Insurance Ltd. v. Sayag*, Israeli Supreme Court Petition 10842/2002, 20 Sep. 1996 (unreported).

Part V. Incidents

Chapter 1. Interlocutory Applications

213. As of 1998, Rule 240 of RCP provides that the usual manner of submitting requests to the court during the course of proceedings, unless otherwise provided in the Rules, is by filing a written application. In this written application the requesting party must state the arguments supporting the request, including relevant references. Factual information in the application must be supported by an affidavit, which, in general, should be attached to the application. An affidavit which is not attached to the application may be submitted later only with permission of the court. A copy of the written application and any accompanying documents must be served on all other parties. Such other parties may respond to the application within twenty days of the service or such other time as the court has determined. This response is also in writing, with relevant references and an affidavit as to factual assertions. In turn, the requesting party has ten days to reply to the response.

All the papers having been filed, the court may decide the matter without an oral hearing. However, if a party requests to cross-examine an adverse affiant, he must be permitted to do so. Even if there has been no such request to cross-examine an affiant, the court can decide to hold an oral hearing on the application. However, this is not the norm.

Affidavits filed in this process and cross-examination of the affiants may be used later as evidence in the course of the main proceedings on the merits.

Chapter 2. Withdrawal and Discontinuance of Actions

214. A plaintiff, or a defendant who has filed a counterclaim, who wishes to discontinue the action without prejudice must receive judicial permission to do so. The major consideration which the court has to consider is whether the discontinuation of the action will damage the defendant and whether it is in fact an abuse of process. Moreover, if the court accepts the plaintiff's application to discontinue the action it should consider the possibility of stipulating conditions that would prevent damage from being caused to the defendant.[103]

Rule 154 states that on receiving a request to permit an action to be discontinued the court may either grant the permission and allow the action to be withdrawn without prejudice, i.e., allowing the plaintiff to reinstate it at a later date, also deciding on the costs of the case, or may refuse the request. In the latter case, where the party nevertheless discontinues the action, the court may, if it so decides, dismiss the action with prejudice, i.e., precluding its reinstitution.

A 1984 amendment to Rule 156 of the RCP has created somewhat of a loophole in the above provisions. The Rule concerns dismissing an action for want of prosecution and permits the court to dismiss an action which it is unable to try or continue to try because of the inaction of a party. Prior to 1984, the above Rule permitted the court to dismiss the action, either with or without prejudice. Following the amendment, in such a case, the court may only dismiss the action without prejudice; thus the plaintiff is not barred from refiling it at a later time. It would seem, therefore, in practice, that a party wishing to discontinue an action has two alternative courses of procedure. He may submit a request of withdrawal, and thereby risk, if his request is rejected, dismissal of the action with prejudice, or he may refrain from prosecuting. In the latter case, according to Rule 156, the court only has authority to dismiss the action without prejudice.

For further discussion of the reasons for this 1984 change as to want of prosecution, see paragraph 123.

103. *The Central Pool of Car Insurances v. Kabudi*, Israeli Supreme Court Petition 3771/2012, 8 Jul. 2012 (unreported).

Chapter 3. Challenge of Judges

215. Prior to a 1992 amendment to the Courts Law [Consolidated Version], 1984, there were no statutory provisions, or even rules of civil procedure, that set forth the procedure for disqualifying a judge in civil litigation. The 1992 amendment provided for such procedure in section 77A to the above law.

This section provides that a judge may disqualify himself from sitting in a proceeding, following the request of a party or at his own initiative, 'if there exist circumstances which may create a real fear of bias in the conduct of the proceeding'. In addition to this general principle the section lists a number of circumstances where, if met, a judge must disqualify himself. First, where a party to the procedure, his attorney or a major witness is a family member of the judge or there is a real affinity between them. Second, where the judge or an immediate family member of the judge has a real financial or personal interest in the procedure or in its consequences, in a party to the procedure or in his attorney. Third, where before being appointed, the judge was involved in the subject matter of the procedure as an attorney, arbitrator, mediator, witness, professional consultant or any other similar way. Notwithstanding these rules a judge may hear a case if, due to the urgency of the case, it is impossible to transfer the case to another judge and severe damage or a miscarriage of justice would be caused if he did not hear the case. A request to disqualify a judge must be filed at the outset of the proceedings or immediately upon discovery of the basis for the request if such is not known at the outset of the proceedings.

Following such a disqualification request, the judge requested to disqualify himself must decide the matter immediately and before he makes any other decision in the proceeding. The decision must be explained.

A party may appeal as of right from a decision of the judge on the disqualification request to the Supreme Court. It should be noted that this appeal is to the Supreme Court, whether the proceeding is pending in a District Court or in a Magistrates' Court. The appeal may be heard by the President of the Supreme Court, a panel of the Court, or another individual Supreme Court judge, as the president shall decide in the particular case.

216. In determining what constitutes 'circumstances which may create a real fear of bias' and thus require a judge to disqualify himself, pursuant to these new statutory provisions, it may be expected that the courts will avail themselves, *inter alia*, of long standing jurisprudence in this matter.

The courts have long held that the prohibition of a judge acting in a matter in which he has a personal interest is part of the principles of natural justice that are binding on judges and all others who act in judicial matters.

Such disqualification is necessary not only to ensure that justice will, in fact, be done, but also to ensure that justice will be seen to be done. Thus, if a disinterested observer would have a reasonable suspicion that the judge would favour one of the sides, then the judge must disqualify himself. And, indeed, Israeli judges generally have done so.

217. Two cases have involved the question of whether a judges' expression of opinion on the merits of the litigation in the course of preliminary hearings disqualifies him from sitting as the trial judge on the merits of the action. The first, a 1988 case[104] involved a judge who, during the pre-trial conference, attempted to induce the parties to settle the action. In the course of such an attempt the judge stated:

> therefore, the court suggests that, if the background as explained by counsel for the plaintiff is correct (and it is probable that it is correct in light of the documents), it is advisable that the defendant compensate the plaintiff for all his expenses and damages for which he can show particulars to the defendant's attorney, and that they compromise on the amount that the court would have to evaluate. ...

Following this statement, the defendant's attorney moved that the judge disqualify herself from sitting on the remainder of the action on the ground that in the above statement, she had expressed an opinion in favour of the plaintiff before she had heard even one witness.

In rejecting the motion, the judge stated that she had not stated that the plaintiff's review of the facts was correct, but only that it was probable that it was correct in light of the documents that had been submitted to the court at that stage of the proceedings, and that, of course, if contrary evidence is presented and it turns out that the background is not as presented by the plaintiff's attorney, a judgment would be rendered in accordance with the evidence as presented to the court.

The judge stated expressly that she had no preconceived view as to the action and did not know any of the parties. Therefore, she saw no reason to disqualify herself from sitting on the rest of the action.

On appeal to the Supreme Court, the Deputy President affirmed refusal of the judge to disqualify herself.

In so deciding, the Deputy President emphasized that for a judge to have to disqualify himself on the grounds that he has conducted himself thus far in the litigation so that he has lost the objectivity required for a true judgment, it is not sufficient that there be 'a reasonable fear' that such is the case; rather there must be 'a real possibility' that such has occurred. Moreover, the test is not the subjective feeling of a party but rather an objective one determined by the court.

Furthermore, in this case the judge's statement was made in the course of attempting to induce the parties to settle the action. This, stated the Deputy President, is a most desirable and important function of a judge and should be encouraged. In the course of trying to produce a settlement, it is natural for the judge to express his prima facie views on the merits of the action in order to explain the reasons for a settlement proposal and indeed, so as to persuade the parties to accept it. This expression of opinion, if done cautiously, should be seen, however, only as a prima facie analysis based on the relevant stage of the proceedings and does not, thereby, disqualify the judge from sitting on the remainder of the action if a settlement is not reached. As a professional judge who knows his craft, he is presumed

104. *Manof Signal Financial and Investment Co. v. Saleima*, 44 (3) P.D. 758 (1988).

not to make final determinations as to the matter before him before the completion of the entire litigation.

The second case, decided a year later (1989),[105] involved the determinations of a judge on the motion for a preliminary remedy pursuant to which he must consider *inter alia* the plaintiff's chances of success on the merits of the case. Such a determination of the plaintiff's chances of success do not disqualify the judge from later sitting on the merits of the action.

However, in this case the judge sitting on the preliminary motion went beyond a determination that the plaintiff had a good case on the merits and stated quite clearly that in his view the plaintiff had an invincible case on the merits.

Under these circumstances, applying the same test as had the Deputy President in the previous case, another judge of the Supreme Court held that the judge should have disqualified himself from handling further proceedings in the action.[106]

105. *Koto Food Services Ltd. v. Seaside Buildings in Herzlia Ltd.*, 43 (1) P.D. 579 (1989).
106. For the rule regarding disqualification of a judge see also *Mulkendof v. weiss*, Israeli Supreme Court Petition 9391/2011, 28 Dec. 2011 (unreported).

Part VI. Legal Aid and Legal Costs

Chapter 1. Legal Aid

218. The Legal Aid Law, 1972, empowers the Minister of Justice to set up legal aid bureaus, to give 'legal services, including the expenses … involved … to persons unable to bear the expenses'. Each bureau is headed by a member of the Chamber of Advocates. Three such bureaus have been set up, in Jerusalem, Tel Aviv and Haifa.

These bureaus employ staff attorneys who provide legal aid. However, they mostly refer cases to outside, private attorneys, with a fixed fee for their services laid down in the Regulations adopted pursuant to the law.

The staff attorneys are also supplemented by law students who provide, under supervision, legal services pursuant to programs operated by the law faculties.

The legal aid provided pursuant to the 1972 law is limited to the poor with the criteria provided for in the Regulations.

However, in 1977 an amendment to the National Insurance Law provided for the provision of free legal aid, through the legal services system, to litigants bringing actions based on their rights under the National Insurance Law. Such rights, include, *inter alia*, old-age pensions and survivors insurance, work accident insurance, maternity benefits, child allowances, unemployment compensation, and various types of benefits paid to handicapped persons. It should be noted that this free legal aid is provided without a 'means test', i.e., there is no requirement that the claimant be 'unable to bear' the legal expenses. Each and every claimant, no matter what his means, is entitled to free legal aid in pursuing his claim.

Finally, it should be mentioned that certain types of non-governmentally sponsored legal aid also exist. They include these provided by such groups as labour unions, consumer organizations, civil rights groups, clinical courses in law schools and groups involved in problems of child welfare.

Chapter 2. Legal Costs

§1. Attorney's Fees

219. Attorney's fees are a matter of agreement between attorney and client and are generally not subject to judicial control. Attorney's fees are included in the costs accorded the winning party. However, this awarding of costs does not effect the actual fee paid to the attorney.

§2. Court Filing Fees

220. A significant portion of the cost of maintaining the court system is paid for by the consumers of that system, i.e., litigants, in the form of court filing fees.

The court filing fee structure is based primarily on initial filing fees imposed on the plaintiff. Generally, as to monetary claims the fee is set as 2.5% of the amount claimed. This is quite a significant percentage and may produce very high court filing fees. This effect, however, has been ameliorated by a number of other provisions.

First, this filing fee is payable in two equal instalments: the first when the complaint is filed; the second twenty days before the first evidentiary hearing, i.e., after the pre-trial conference. Moreover, the plaintiff is excused from paying the second instalment if the defendant does not file a defence or does not receive leave to defend in an expedited judgment procedure action or if the action is withdrawn, dismissed, compromised or otherwise terminated prior to the end of the third pre-trial conference (in which case the plaintiff is also entitled to a partial and modest reimbursement on the first half of the filing fee). This instalment procedure, therefore, not only eases the burden of the plaintiff, but also encourages settling actions before the first evidentiary proceeding.

Second, the filing fees for non-monetary claims are set sums, unrelated to the value of the claim; these sums can be quite small, in comparison to the fees based on the percentage of monetary claims. As of 2013, these fees were set at NIS 3,076 for claims filed in the District Courts and NIS 1,646 for claims filed in the Magistrates' Courts (c. USD 840 and USD 450 respectively). These sums are adjusted periodically for inflation, but remain constant in real terms.

In addition, there is a special class of non-monetary claims to which even lower, indeed, truly nominal, filing fees apply. They are claims which are expressly listed in the Court Rules (Filing Fees), 2007, as being '*viewed as*' not being capable of being expressed in money. Such claims include, *inter alia*, declaratory judgments, injunctive actions (both affirmative and negative), specific performance, and ejectment actions. We have emphasized the wording in the above Rules – that these claims are 'viewed as' not being capable of monetary expression – since many of them are, indeed capable of evaluation in monetary terms and in fact may be so evaluated for purposes of determining subject matter jurisdiction. However, the test is not factual, but rather the claims included in this class are those expressly listed in these Rules.

As of 2013, the fees for such claims were set at NIS 1,115 for actions filed in the District Courts and NIS 633 for those filed in the Magistrates' Courts (c. USD 320 and USD 170 respectively). Similar to the set filing fee sums for other non-monetary actions, also these sums are adjusted periodically for inflation but remain nominally small in real terms.

There is, therefore, a two-tier system of fees: one, a high fee system based on the value of monetary claims and the other, a low fee system for non-monetary claims which includes even lower fees for those claims which appear in the select list of claims which are not viewed as capable of monetary expression.

Finally, we should note that the filing fee for actions in the Small Claims Courts are set at 1% of the amount claimed, with a minimum fee of NIS 50. Under the current Small Claims Court limit the maximum fee would be NIS 332.

There are obvious results of such a system. Attorneys and litigants attempt, if at all possible to frame actions as non-monetary and, within the non-monetary group, to fit them into the select group as to which the lowest fees apply.

Thus, for example, this system has been one of the major causes for the disproportionately high use of declaratory judgments in Israel.

221. A further, special exception to the regular method of assessing court filing fees applies to bodily injury actions. As to such actions, the Rules have been changed a number of times in recent years, both in terms of the amount of the fee, and the percentage to be paid at the initiation of the proceedings and in terms of the identity of the initial payer, who from 1987 until 1992 was not the plaintiff but rather the defendant.

Since 1992, the system is composed of a number of distinct elements. The first is a most important distinction between the filing fee applicable to the action and the amount to be paid by the plaintiff at the initiation of the action. In general, the former is the usual filing fee as to monetary actions, i.e., 2.5% of the amount claimed. An exception to this 2.5% is made only for personal injury actions based on the special Road Accident Victims Compensation Law, 1975: as to these claims there is a set sum (as of July 2012, NIS 41,203 in the District Courts and NIS 6,592 in the Magistrates' Courts).

More important, however, is that neither the whole nor even half of the filing fee is payable at the initiation of the action. Rather at this stage, as to all personal injury actions, the plaintiff must pay only the same nominal sums stated above as apply to actions that are viewed as not being capable of monetary expression.

In addition, the plaintiff must attach to his complaint an undertaking to pay the remainder of the filing fee, with linkage differentials and interest, as required by the provisions to be discussed below. The defendant must attach to his answer a similar undertaking to pay the remainder of the filing fee if he is required to do so.

If the plaintiff's action is dismissed following the beginning of the evidentiary hearings, he is obligated to pay the entire remainder of the filing fee. However, if his action is dismissed prior to that stage, he has to pay only one-third of the total filing fee.

However, the defendant must pay the entire filing fee, either if he is held liable to the plaintiff or if the action is settled by compromise after the beginning of the evidentiary stage. If the action is settled prior to the evidentiary stage, the defendant must pay only one-third of the total filing fee.

As mentioned above, these provisions are the latest of a number of attempts to deal with the problem of court filing fees concerning personal injury actions. They attempt to balance the interest of the State in high filing fees as to monetary actions, without, however, deterring plaintiffs from bringing meritorious claims because of the need to pay such high fees at the initiation of the action. Moreover they provide a strong incentive to reach settlements prior to the evidentiary stage of the proceedings. While on its face this incentive applies only to the defendant, to the extent that the amount of the filing fee that the defendant will have to pay, may itself be a matter of the settlement negotiations, there is provided an incentive to both parties to settle the action before the start of the evidentiary hearings.

In 2012, a Rule was added to the Court Rules (Filing Fees), 2007, setting the particular filing fee regarding a claim for exemplary damage claims, which do not exceed a limit of 20 million NIS and result from an act of terror, as equal to the filing fee for claims viewed as not being capable of being expressed in money. Note however that exemplary damages are extremely rare in Israel on the whole and no such damages were actually awarded in terror-related claims.

222. The same provisions discussed above as to personal injury actions apply also to maintenance actions, as to which the total filing fee is the same as for traffic accident claims brought in the District Courts.

223. Concerning all actions, there are provisions for postponement and eventual exemption of the fee in favour of an indigent party who would otherwise have to pay the fee. If the indigent party who is excused from paying the fee prevails in the litigation, the losing party is required to pay the fee. This rule is consistent with the general principle that court filing fees are part of the taxable costs of the litigation which are generally awarded to the prevailing party.

§3. Taxing Costs

224. The taxing of costs has become an integral part of the sanctions on procedural irregularities; the subject thus is discussed quite extensively in paragraph 125.

As noted therein, the basic principle is that the losing party is generally required to pay the winning party's costs, including attorney's fees. The exceptions to this rule refer primarily to cases in which the prevailing party was at fault during the litigation, even though he ultimately prevailed. Thus the lowering of costs or even their complete disallowable may be a sanction for the prevailing party's improper conduct.

No recognition is taken of the converse situation: the good conduct of the losing party. While such good conduct may, in fact, play an unarticulated role in cases in which less than full actual costs are awarded, the good conduct of the losing party (e.g., his good faith pursuance of a claim or defence as to which there were issues, factual or legal, that were reasonably in doubt and thus were properly brought to the court for its determination), as distinguished from the bad conduct of the prevailing party, has not been recognized as a factor in determining the taxation of costs.

However, in a 1982 decision, Supreme Court Judge M. Elon, in a concurring judgment, suggested that such good conduct of the losing plaintiff should be taken into account in determining the amount of damages the plaintiff should be required to pay to the winning defendant in order to reimburse the latter for damage caused to him by a temporary injunction.[107] If so, it would seem that it might also be taken into account in taxing costs.

Concerning the improper conduct of the winning party serving to reduce the costs in his favour, there is some authority to the effect that the failure of a plaintiff to accept a reasonable settlement offer is not a reason to reduce the costs awarded him. However, this authority is not, itself, clear. Moreover, it would seem to be contrary to the basic principle, clearly accepted, that undue prolongation of the litigation by the prevailing party is a reason for reducing the costs awarded him. An unreasonable refusal of a settlement offer would seem to be a clear example of undue prolongation of the litigation.

225. There is, however, a specific procedure in the Rules of Civil Procedure by which a defendant can assure that under certain circumstances, a plaintiff's refusal to accept a settlement offer will be considered when costs are awarded.

In this procedure, based on the English Rules of Court, the defendant may accompany an offer of settlement by paying the amount of the settlement offered into court. The plaintiff has thirty days in which to accept the offer. If he does so he will receive the money and the court will then determine the costs until the date of the payment into court on the basis that the plaintiff has prevailed. If the plaintiff does not agree to the settlement offer the money is returned to the defendant.

In that event Rule 509 of the RCP provides specifically that when determining the costs at the conclusion of the litigation, the registrar or judge 'will take into consideration both the fact that money had been paid into the court and the amount of such payment'.

There has not been extensive use of this provision and we know of no jurisprudence that has interpreted and applied Rule 509. However, the English courts have interpreted their payment into court procedure, on which the Israeli procedure is based, as dividing the litigation into two parts for purposes of awarding costs where the plaintiff does not accept the settlement and then prevails on the merits. Such a plaintiff is entitled to his costs incurred until the payment into court. After that date, he is entitled to his costs if, and only if, he is awarded a sum greater than the settlement offer which he declined. If this is not so, not only does he not receive his costs, but the defendant is viewed as the prevailing party for this purpose, and thus he is entitled to be awarded costs.

This procedure could possibly be viewed as the exclusive way in which a plaintiff's refusal to accept a settlement offer could be considered in determining costs; thus a defendant who does not avail himself of the payment into court procedure,

107. *Erens v. Beit-El-Zichron Yaacov*, 35 (2) P.D. 645, 664.

could not later argue that an unreasonable refusal of the plaintiff to accept an out-of-court settlement offer should reduce the costs awarded to a prevailing plaintiff.

226. Related to this question of a plaintiff's failure to accept a settlement offer is that of a plaintiff's partial recovery. Is the determination of who is the prevailing party an all or nothing proposition for purposes of awarding costs or should partial recoveries result in a reduction of the costs awarded?

The Israeli case law has recognized that a prevailing plaintiff who has exaggerated his claim grossly and, thereby, caused a prolongation of the litigation may be punished by reducing the costs awarded him. However, the courts have not recognized a direct relationship between the percentage of the claim recovered and the percentage of the costs awarded, e.g., a plaintiff who recovers only half of his alleged claim should receive only half of his costs. However, such a situation of partial victory has been recognized in a case concerning the defendant's recovery for damages caused by preliminary attachment of his property where the plaintiff only recovered a portion of his alleged claim.[108]

In addition, Rule 512(b) provides: 'In taxing costs and determining their amount, the courts or registrar shall consider, *inter alia*, the value of the relief in dispute between the parties and the value of the relief awarded at the end of the proceedings, as well the manner in which the parties conducted the litigation.'

227. Finally, as to recovery of costs, the Rules of Civil Procedure provide that a court may require a plaintiff to provide security for the payment of the defendant's costs if the latter prevails in the action.

While the Rules themselves contain no criteria for the implementation of this Rule, the jurisprudence has limited it so as not to impose an undue burden on plaintiffs. Thus, in practice security for costs pursuant to the Rules of Civil Procedure is imposed on plaintiffs only in two situations.

First, where a particular plaintiff has acted in such a way, for example by giving a defective address, as to suggest that he is attempting to avoid the payment of costs if he loses.

Second, and more generally, where the plaintiff is a foreign resident with no assets in the country that could be reached in execution of an order for costs. The rationale for this is quite clear: a local defendant should not have to pursue the plaintiff abroad and bring an action in a foreign state in order to implement an award for costs.

However, this basis for security for costs is limited by the fact that Israel is a signatory to the 1905 and 1954 Hague Conventions on Civil Procedure and has implemented these conventions by appropriate Rules of Civil Procedure. The Hague Conventions provide for the creation of expedited proceedings for the recovery of costs awarded in other signatory States and, in return, prohibit a signatory State from requiring a plaintiff from another signatory State to give security for costs merely because he is a foreign plaintiff. The Rules of Civil Procedure adopted to implement the Hague conventions provide, therefore, that a plaintiff who is a citizen or domiciliary of another signatory State to either of these Conventions, will not

108. *Ben Yehuda v. Rose*, 24 (2) P.D. 537 (1970).

be required to give security for costs because of the fact that Israel is not his place of domicile or residence. These rules do not preclude the imposition of a security requirement for other reasons.

Note should be made of a special provision concerning security for costs applicable to plaintiffs who are limited liability corporations. This provision, found in section 322 of the Companies Ordinance [New Version], provides that as to such corporate plaintiffs, the court may require the posting of security for costs, if it has reason to believe, pursuant to reliable evidence, that the corporation will not be able to pay the defendant's costs if the latter prevails in the litigation.

Thus, whereas concerning individual plaintiffs, the mere fact that the plaintiff may not be able to pay the defendant's costs is not sufficient to require him to post security for costs, the opposite is true as to corporate plaintiffs.

If a plaintiff does not comply with an order to provide security for costs by the specified time, his action will be dismissed with prejudice, unless he is allowed a voluntary dismissal by the court. If the action has been so dismissed with prejudice, the court may cancel the dismissal, on the application of the plaintiff, if it believes that there was a sufficient reason for the plaintiff's failure to comply with the order by the specified time. In this last case the court may attach conditions to this cancellation, including a new order for security as well as the payment of current costs to the defendant.

Part VII. Evidence

Chapter 1. Introduction

228. The law of evidence in Israel is based primarily on Anglo-American law. Thus the principal statute in this area remains that of a mandatory ordinance, now in an official Hebrew version: The Evidence Ordinance [New Version], 1971. In addition many other principles of Anglo-American evidence have been adopted by the courts.

Due to this Anglo-American base, the law of evidence emphasizes oral testimony and cross-examination, and consists of strict rules concerning admissibility, as compared with free evaluation of all relevant evidence. However, inspired by developments in Anglo-American jurisprudence, Israeli case law has shown a growing tendency to relax some of the rules of admissibility, e.g., admitting certain kinds of hearsay evidence, thereby allowing the court discretion to consider the probative value of the evidence and decide the weight it should be given under the circumstances of the case.

The laws of evidence determine how the facts of a case may be proven in court. Only facts and not points of law require proof. An exception to the above rule is a foreign law, which must be proven, as a fact, by an expert of the foreign law.

The pleadings, as amended and as determined finally by the decisions of the pretrial conference, limit the proof, i.e., they determine what facts are relevant and, therefore, may be proved.

The three principal means of proof are testimony, documents and things or real evidence. In order for evidence to be accepted in court it must be shown, first and foremost, to be relevant to the case at hand. This principle is important not only for the opposing party but also for the court, in order not to delay proceedings with irrelevant material. Accordingly, the issue of relevance may be raised not only by the opposing party, but also by the court. In addition to being relevant, the evidence must be shown to be admissible. All evidence is admissible unless it is included in one of the exclusionary rules, for example the rule against hearsay evidence. Unlike the issue of relevance, which may be raised by the court, an objection regarding admissibility may be raised only by the opposing party, and absent an express objection, the evidence is deemed admissible.

Where evidence has been presented and the opposing party opposes the evidence, he must state his opposition immediately. If he does not so act he will be seen as submitting to the evidence being introduced. Where a party does oppose the evidence on grounds of admissibility or relevance, the court must decide the matter immediately . Such a decision may be appealed either by requesting permission to appeal at the time or, at a later time, as part of the appeal on the final judgment. See paragraph 39.

Where evidence is admitted, the court determines its credibility and the weight to be given to it. Generally, the court is free to weigh the evidence as it sees fit and to determine the issue on the evidence brought before it. There is no general requirement for corroboration, and the court may base its decision on any *single* piece of *evidence*. However, the Evidence Ordinance provides exceptions in which the court cannot base its judgment solely on the testimony of certain types of witnesses e.g., minors under 14 years of age, certain relatives of a party, unless such testimony is corroborated by other evidence or the court finds special reasons to rely on such testimony alone.

Chapter 2. Burden of Proof

229. Following the English law, the term 'burden of proof' is used in two senses. The burden of producing evidence and the burden of establishing a case, or the burden of persuasion. The former means that a party relying on specific facts for the substantiation of his allegation has the burden of producing the evidence to prove these facts. The burden of persuasion is important only at the end of the hearing, when the court decides whether this burden was met by the party bearing it, which is generally the plaintiff.

230. There are, a number of legal presumptions which cause the burden of proof to be shifted from one party to the other. There are three principle forms of presumptions – a presumption of fact (*praesumptio facti* (or *hominis*)), a presumption of law (*praesumptio legis* (or *juris*)) and a presumption of law which cannot be rebutted (*praesumptio juris et de jure*).

A presumption of fact, which is established in case law, is one based on practical experience allowing the court to reach a particular conclusion without it being necessary to prove the fact. For example, a person making use of a particular object, is presumed to be holding it lawfully. Similarly, if it was known that a person was alive on a particular date, it is presumed that he continued to live for a reasonable time after that date. Such a presumption may cause the burden of producing evidence to pass from one party to the other, but not the burden of persuasion.

A presumption of law which may be rebutted is a presumption set forth in legislation, which, if not rebutted, must be accepted as final by the court. An example of the above is the presumption stated in section 29(a) of the Bill of Exchange Ordinance: unless proved otherwise, a person signing a bill of exchange is deemed to be a party to a bill of exchange based on consideration. This presumption thus shifts both the burden of producing evidence and that of persuasion as to lack of consideration to the opposing party.

A presumption of law which may not be rebutted is, in reality, a rule of substantive law, though couched in terms of an evidentiary presumption.

231. With regards the quantum of proof necessary to prove a case, whereas in criminal cases the case must be proven beyond a reasonable doubt, in civil cases it is usually enough to prove it by a preponderance of evidence or probabilities. In certain civil matters, however, a higher level of proof is required. An example of such is a claim against the estate of a deceased person where a higher level of proof is necessary since the deceased, were he still alive, may have been able to rebut the evidence. In addition, in a civil case where a criminal issue, for example fraud, must be proven, a higher level of proof will be required.

Chapter 3. Admissibility of Evidence

§1. Privileged Evidence

232. In principle, a witness must present any evidence relevant to the issue. However, in certain cases he may claim that the evidence is privileged. For example, an advocate, is not bound to give evidence on matters connected with his professional services; similarly a clergyman concerning information given to him in his professional capacity. Physicians, social workers and psychologists have more limited privileges. Evidence need not be given where the security of the State or an important public interest is thereby likely to be impaired. Further, a person is not bound to give evidence where it is likely to incriminate him in a criminal offence. Case law has held that a journalist has a privilege as to the identity of his sources as well as any information which may lead to the disclosure of their identity. Case law has also recognized a bank-client evidentiary privilege.

It has also been held that matters discussed in settlement negotiations are privileged. For a discussion of privilege concerning material produced in anticipation of litigation, see paragraph 150.

§2. Exclusionary Rules

I. Hearsay

233. The rule against hearsay evidence in Israel is based on the traditional English rules of evidence. The rule provides that oral or written testimony of a statement made out of court is not admissible as evidence to establish the truth of what is contained in the statement, as distinguished from the fact that it was made.

The above rule is based on the theory that it is important for the judge to hear the evidence first hand. Second-hand evidence is likely to be a source of mistakes or even trickery. The person making the original statement has not been warned of the importance of telling the truth, and is not liable to legal sanctions if he does not so act. Furthermore he cannot be cross-examined.

234. There are many exceptions to the hearsay rule, most of which developed by force of circumstance where it was not possible to bring the witness who made the original statement to court. In such cases, although the court will admit the evidence, it will usually give it less weight than direct testimony. The following are a number of examples of such exceptions:

The statement of a deceased person may in certain circumstances be accepted as admissible evidence in court. A declaration of a deceased person against his pecuniary or proprietary interest is admissible. It is presumed that a person will not make a statement against his own interests if it is not true. Second, a declaration of a deceased person made in the course of duty may be admitted as evidence. Third a statement of the deceased referring to public interests is admissible, since it is assumed that a statement not concerning private interests is true. Fourth, a statement of the deceased as to the pedigree of another member of the family is admissible, providing the statement was made before the controversy broke out in the family.

Another exception to the rule against hearsay evidence is the Common Law principle of *res gesta.* According to this principle a spontaneous statement made contemporaneously with the action or the event, or so clearly associated with it that it seems part of the action or event, is admissible despite the fact that the person making the statement is not in court.

In addition, public documents such as birth certificates, death certificates, and marriage certificates are admissible as evidence, despite the fact that they are hearsay evidence.

So too are informal out-of-the-courtroom admissions of the parties to the dispute. Such admissions may be made directly, either in writing or orally, or may be made indirectly by behaviour, for example the defendant's paying interest for an extended period of time may be seen as an admission on his part that he must repay the loan, as is claimed by the plaintiff.

Where a witness in court does not remember a particular event but remembers that a document was prepared by him or under his supervision at the time of the event, the witness may make use of the document to refresh his memory. The opposing party has a right to examine the document. In some cases the document may revive the memory of the witness ('present recollection revived'). Where the document does not succeed in reviving the memory of the witness, the document itself may be served as evidence. This is termed 'past recollection recorded.'

Additionally, in this regard even if an out-of-court statement of a witness testifying at trial does not fit into any exception of the hearsay rule, it may be used in cross-examination in order to effect the credibility of the witness.

Finally, we should note that recently English law has virtually eliminated the rule barring the use of hearsay evidence. In light of this development it is not surprising that one can discern a similar trend in the Israeli law of evidence.

II. Opinion Evidence

235. The rules of evidence require that only reliable and credible sources of information be presented as evidence in court. Thus, ordinary witnesses are generally allowed to testify only concerning facts and not to express opinions. The task of drawing conclusions and forming opinions based on the facts reported by the witnesses is considered the exclusive role of the court.

An exception to this rule is made, however, for the expert witness. The expert must have specialized knowledge, skill or experience in the area of his testimony. For the most part he does not only testify concerning facts but draws inferences from them. The court, however, is free to accept or not to accept the expert's conclusions, or to prefer the evidence of another expert, whether of the opposing party or of the court itself, for further discussion on expert testimony, see paragraphs 248–250.

III. Unlawfully obtained Evidence

236. In 2006, the Israeli Supreme Court adopted a broad and general exclusionary doctrine, which accords the courts wide discretion in deciding on the admissibility of unlawfully gathered evidence in criminal proceedings. In civil proceedings, however, unlawfully obtained evidence is deemed admissible, subject to two exceptions, one enshrined in the Protection of Privacy Law, 1981, and the other in the Secret Monitoring Law, 1979.

The former law precludes the admission into evidence of any matter obtained in violation of the right of privacy protected by that Law, unless the injured party consents to the admission of the evidence, or the court, in its discretion, allows its admission for special reasons that it must specify.

The Secret Monitoring Law, 1979 goes even further. It absolutely forbids the admission in civil proceedings of evidence obtained by any form of wiretapping even if such is not in violation of the Law. In criminal proceedings, evidence obtained through lawful wiretapping is admissible.

Chapter 4. Administration of Evidence

§1. Judicial Notice

237. In certain cases the court may make a finding, not based on any evidence but on its judicial notice. Judicial notice is to be differentiated from the judge's own personal knowledge. It may be based on a number of sources. A fact known to everyone, for example the number of days in a month need not be proven. Similarly, judicial notice may be taken of information which can be clarified from sources not in controversy, for example historical facts. In addition the court is deemed to have judicial knowledge of the law. It should be emphasized, however, as mentioned above that the provisions of a foreign law must be proved in court. The Israeli case law has as yet not given a clear answer as to whether a party may attempt to bring evidence to rebut factual judicial notice.

§2. Testimony by Witness

I. Compelling Testimony

238. In principle, all evidence whether real, oral or written, must be presented to the court by means of a witness. There are a number of exceptions to the above rule, for example a physician's certificate may be presented as evidence by a person other than the physician who signed the certificate (and if necessary the physician who signed the certificate may be summoned to give evidence). In addition, public documents and institutional records (e.g., bank statements) may be presented as evidence directly.

A party wishing to bring a witness to court may request the court to summon the witness either to give evidence or to produce documents. A witness summoned by the court is obliged to appear, and if he does not appear and the party shows that his testimony is necessary, the court will postpone the hearing in order to summon the witness again. Where a witness is summoned but does not appear the court may apply the measures laid down in section 73 of the Courts Law [Consolidated Version], 1984, in order to enforce his appearance. This section provides the court with authority to order a witness to be brought to court or to impose a fine or imprisonment on a witness who does not appear. A witness appearing but refusing to give testimony may be forced to give testimony through section 5 of the Contempt of Court Ordinance, which allows the court to impose imprisonment for up to thirty days in order to compel obedience. He may also be charged with the criminal offence of refusal to testify.

In accordance with the Act for the Amendment of the Laws of Evidence (Warning Witnesses and Cancellation of the Oath), 1980, a witness no longer takes an oath prior to the giving of testimony, but he is warned instead that he must testify to the truth and only the truth, and that he will be liable for the sanctions laid down in the law if he does not so act. Where the court has special reason to believe that the taking of an oath by a particular witness will aid in discovering the truth, the court may require him to take an oath. For religious reasons or reasons of conscience the witness may also make a declaration instead of an oath.

II. Capacity

239. As a rule, all persons are competent to give evidence in all cases. The special cases of minors and mentally incompetent persons have been dealt with by case law that has fashioned tests designed to determine their ability to understand, remember and communicate, as well as their understanding of the duty to tell the truth. Nevertheless, such persons are generally deemed to have the capacity to testify and any difficulty they encounter may only affect the weight given to their testimony.

Similarly, persons who have a physical disability effecting their capacity to act as a witness, such as blind or deaf persons, are competent to give evidence, but their disability may affect the weight and credibility of their evidence.

III. Preparing a Witness for Trial

240. Case law has held that an attorney has not fulfilled his obligations if he has not properly prepared a witness for trial. He must take care, however, not to tell the witness what to say in the proceedings. He is also forbidden to arrange a meeting between the witnesses. Such a meeting does not make the witnesses incompetent but may have an effect on the credibility of their testimony. If an advocate knows that such a meeting where the contents of the evidence was discussed, has occurred, he must so inform the court.

IV. Credibility of Witnesses

241. One of the most difficult decisions before a court is deciding the credibility of a witness, especially, as often is the case, where there is conflicting evidence. Since the trial judge is the only one who has come into direct contact with the witnesses, appellate courts generally will not intervene in his determination of the credibility of the witnesses.

V. Examination of Witnesses

242. There are four forms of examination; examination in chief, cross-examination, re-examination and an examination by the court.

A. Examination in Chief (Direct Examination)

243. The examination in chief is the most simple form of examination, the witness having often been prepared in advance by the advocate. The witness is interrogated by the party who summoned him and also by other parties on the same side of the action (e.g., where there are a number of plaintiffs, a witness summoned by one of the plaintiffs may be interrogated by the other plaintiffs). An exception to the above is where there are opposing interests, for example where there are a number of defendants each trying to impose liability on the other.

Generally, during direct examination the witness must not be asked leading questions, that is questions which themselves include the answer to the question, and require a yes/no answer. Nor may an attorney impeach the credibility of a witness summoned by him.

However, in certain cases a witness may be declared a hostile witness. Such a witness is one who shows his animosity to the party who summoned him. Such animosity may be detected in a number of ways: the witness may reply in answer to many of the questions that he does not remember, and the court may form the impression that he is not merely forgetful but does not wish to give evidence; or the witness's evidence may contradict his out-of-court statements.

Where, at the request of a party, the court declares a witness hostile, the witness continues to be a witness of the party who summoned him and continues to be examined in the examination in chief. However, the advocate is no longer limited in his interrogation, and both may ask leading questions and attempt to impeach his credibility.

As discussed, *supra*, paragraph 23, there is now a growing tendency to substitute affidavits for this testimony in chief.

B. Cross-examination

244. The Israeli system, based as it is on the English, gives great prominence to cross-examination of a witness. Its purported primary purpose is to attempt to discover the true version of the events, drawing facts from the witness which he did not mention in the primary examination. Where the advocate conducting the cross-examination realizes that he will not succeed in obtaining the desired version of events from the witness, he will move to the second stage of the examination and attempt to impair the credibility of the witness. Leading questions may be asked in cross-examination. It should be noted that the judge is authorized and obliged to supervise the extent of the cross-examination in order not to harm the legitimate interests of the parties. Moreover he is obliged not to allow an examination which is irrelevant or unfair, or in which there is undue embarrassment, intimidation or trickery.

During the cross-examination a statement by the witness made out of court may be presented to the court, but only in order to raise doubt as to the veracity of the witness's testimony.

Where a party is able to but does not cross-examine a witness the court may, if it so decides, deem that party as accepting the witness's version of events in the examination in chief. Where a party is unable to conduct cross-examination, for example because the witness refuses to cooperate, the court may, if it sees fit, not take into account the witness' evidence given in the examination in chief.

C. Re-examination (Re-direct)

245. The re-examination is conducted by the party who summoned the witness. The re-examination must be confined to matters arising out of the cross-examination, and new matter may only be introduced with leave of the court. Its purpose is to clarify issues raised in the cross-examination. In the re-examination the witness will be requested to explain issues raised by the opponent in the cross-examination. As in the examination in chief, leading questions may not be asked.

D. Examination by the Court

246. The Rules of Civil Procedure authorize the court to ask any question of a witness it sees fit and, for this purpose, also to recall a witness who has completed his testimony. Moreover, the court may order any person present in the courtroom to testify or to present any document in his possession. However, the adversarial nature of the procedural system results in the fact that, in general, the court does not take a very active role in the examination. Moreover, when the court does interrogate a witness it is generally to clarify matters that have already been raised in the testimony rather than to raise new matter.

As to court appointed expert witnesses, see *infra*, this part, paragraph 249.

VI. Affidavits

247. The Rules of Civil Procedure allow the judge, at the pre-trial conference or at trial, to order that a potential witness first submit an affidavit or that a given fact be proved by affidavits. Such affidavits would then serve as the direct testimony of the affiant unless the court, for special reasons, decides otherwise. In keeping with the English emphasis on cross-examination, the affiant would still be subject to oral cross-examination even if his affidavit was used in lieu of his direct oral examination.

If the affiant does not appear when summoned for cross-examination, the affidavit may not be used as evidence except with special permission of the court.

VII. Expert Testimony

248. Provisions concerning the testimony of expert witnesses are set forth in the Evidence Ordinance [New Version], 1971, in the Rules of Civil Procedure, and, with regards actions concerning road accidents, in the Road Accident Victims Compensation Law, 1975.

Section 20 of the Evidence Ordinance states as follows:

The court may, unless it apprehends a miscarriage of justice, admit as evidence, in writing, an opinion by an expert as to a matter of science, research, art or professional knowledge (hereinafter referred to as an 'opinion') and a certificate by a physician as to the state of health of a person (hereinafter referred to as a 'medical certificate').

Unlike the situation of ordinary witnesses as to which neither their identity nor the substance of their evidence need to be disclosed before the evidentiary hearing in which they testify, the Rules of Civil Procedure require the parties to disclose and exchange copies of the opinions of expert witnesses which they expect to introduce in evidence, prior to the evidentiary hearings. Such copies are also provided to the court.

In addition, the Rules of Civil Procedure provide that a party wishing to prove a *medical matter* must attach to his pleadings a medical certificate or an opinion of an expert. Such a requirement is an exception to the general rule according to which evidence is not to be included in the pleadings. The Rules state further that a party upon whom a medical opinion has been served may within thirty days of receiving the opinion demand that the subject of the opinion be examined by a doctor or a medical expert on that party's behalf, provided that the requesting party notifies the party who filed the opinion that he will furnish him, upon demand, with a copy of the opinion.

249. In keeping with the English adversary system, expert witnesses traditionally have testified as witnesses for the parties; each side submits the expert witness or witnesses supporting his position. However, Rule 130 of the Rules of Civil Procedure permits the court, whether at the request of the parties or on its own motion, to appoint an expert to give evidence on an issue in controversy. Moreover, the appointment of such an expert is listed expressly among the issues to be determined at the pre-trial conference.

While the great majority of experts continue to testify on behalf of the parties and are not court appointed, the practice of court appointed experts has increased in recent years, especially in cases where an objective opinion is required in order to reconcile disparities between the opposing opinions of the parties' experts. Such an increase reflects a growing dissatisfaction with the 'battle of experts' produced by experts for the parties.

The fees and expenses of a court appointed expert are set by the court.

A medical expert appointed by the court has the authority to demand the examination of the person who is the subject of the medical issue; he also may hear the opinion of the doctor or medical expert who submitted an opinion on behalf of a party, and may also receive from any person or institution for inspection the medical records relating to the person.

The court has the authority to direct the medical expert to conduct, if necessary, a further examination of the person requiring examination.

Where a party does not conform with the above rules concerning medical expert testimony, that is, does not attach a medical certificate or a medical expert's opinion to his pleadings, or does not comply, without reasonable justification, with a demand, whether of the opposing party, the court, or the medical expert appointed by the court, to submit to an examination, the court will not entertain medical proof on his behalf on the matter in question.

Upon receipt of the opinion of a court appointed expert, whether a medical or other expert, a party may amend his pleadings in light of the opinion, without the need to obtain leave to do so.

The mere fact that there is a court appointed expert does not, in and of itself, prevent the parties from bringing their own experts. However, where an expert has been appointed by the court at the request of all the parties, or with their agreement, they are precluded from introducing other expert testimony on the issue, except with special judicial permission.

In any case, a party may cross-examine a court appointed expert in the same way as if he were an expert for the opposing party, unless the parties have agreed beforehand not to cross-examine the court appointed expert. Such an agreement if arrived at is binding and a party may only be relieved from it by permission of the court.

It should further be emphasized, of course, that a court which has appointed such an expert may give full weight to the professional aspect of the opinion, but will not necessarily decide in accordance with the opinion. In order not to undermine the authority of decision of the court, the opinion of the expert must be presented in a way as to allow the judge to make an independent decision. The expert must present all the facts and the process of his decision making. The final decision is, as always, in the hands of the court.

250. Particular provisions apply to the appointment of experts in actions in accordance with the Road Accident Victim Compensation Law, 1975, and the Regulations adopted thereto. A plaintiff who brings an action in accordance with this law does not attach a medical opinion to his complaint, but instead is required to attach to his complaint a request to appoint an expert, an affidavit answering questions concerned with previous illnesses and details of the accident incurred, a letter waiving medical confidentiality and details of his illness from the file of the institution in which he was hospitalized or where he received medical care. The defendant, on his part, may include in his answer a request that an expert be appointed concerning any other issue for which the plaintiff has made no such request. A defendant not filing an objection to a request to appoint an expert will be deemed to have agreed with the appointment as requested by the plaintiff.

Where there is no agreement between the parties as to the appointment of an expert, the court will make a decision concerning the appointment, after having given the parties an opportunity to be heard.

There are also provisions concerning the authority of the expert to require the victim to be examined and the serving of documents relating to the medical care afforded to the victim. The Regulations set forth the procedure concerning objections to the demands of the expert, and contain provisions authorizing the court to order that the demands of the expert be fulfilled. Where a party does not comply with the demands of the expert or with the court's order, without reasonable justification, the court may strike out his pleadings.

The parties may present the expert with questions in order to clarify his opinion, and may also interrogate the expert concerning his opinion and clarifications.

Part VIII. Representative Proceedings

Chapter 1. General

256. Traditionally, following English precedents, Israeli law has viewed civil litigation as a matter between individuals who are seeking to vindicate their private interests, and thus, generally has been wary of 'officious inter-meddlers' who seek to vindicate not their own, private interests, but rather those of others. Yet in the past decade this situation has changed greatly.

257. Since 1976, Israeli jurisprudence has recognized shareholder derivative actions, i.e., actions brought by a shareholder on behalf of the corporation in order to vindicate a right of the corporation, when the authorized organs of the corporation have refused to do so. Since 2000, shareholder derivative actions have been authorized and regulated by statute.

Both the courts and legislature have recognized that such actions may be the only effective way of preventing management or controlling directors in a corporation from abusing their power for personal gain or otherwise oppressing minority shareholders.

258. Since 2006, class actions have been regulated by a comprehensive statute which recognizes the possibility of bringing representative class actions 'American style'. In general, such class actions are designed to be brought against a common defendant on behalf of numerous claimants who are connected to a particular event or transaction or a series of events or transactions. This action is brought by one or more of the claimants as 'representative' of all of them even though they have not appointed him their representative and, indeed, generally do not even know that he intends to bring such an action on their behalf.

The class action device is aimed primarily at encouraging the bringing of claims in situations in which each injured party has himself suffered very small damage, but the total damage to the class has been great. In this way, injured parties who have suffered very small individual damages may receive compensation, whereas without this possibility of aggregating their claims it would not have been feasible to sue. Moreover, and, indeed, perhaps more important, the fear of being sued in a class action may encourage entities, such as manufacturers, distributors, and purveyors of services to take care not to endanger or injure the public. Thus, the use of class actions brought by private individuals serves as a device to enforce conformity with the law.

259. There are, therefore, strong reasons to encourage the use of representative actions, both derivative actions and class actions. However, there are also negative aspects to these actions.

In both types of actions the representative is self-appointed. Moreover, the personal economic interest of the representative in the relief requested is generally quite small as compared to that sought for the represented party or parties. In the case of shareholder derivative actions, the monetary interest of the shareholder is represented by his percentage interest in the corporation. This situation raises the possibility of abuse of representative actions, either at the expense of the defendant or the represented parties. A defendant who is faced with a large representative claim, may tend to try to 'settle' the matter with the representative even if he believes that he is not liable, since if he is finally held to be liable, he will be compelled to pay the total, large sum claimed. This situation clearly permits abuse of the process by a form of 'blackmail'.

However, if the defendant is, indeed, liable, it is possible that the plaintiff-representative will be amenable to settlement of the action by a form of 'bribery'. Since, as stated above, his own monetary claim is, generally, very small relatively, he may accept a payment of many times the value of his individual claim, as well as the expenses of the litigation including a significant fee for his attorney, in order to settle the matter – at the expense of the represented parties.

Thus conditions may be created which could encourage blackmail and bribery abuses. In order to counter these possible abuses, rules relating to representative actions must consider such matters as determining the suitability of the self-appointed representative, affording greater judicial control over the litigation than is generally the case in the adversarial system, and regulating settlements and other means by which the representative may discontinue the action.

Chapter 2. Shareholder Derivative Actions

260. As noted above, Israeli jurisprudence has recognized the possibility of bringing shareholder derivative actions since 1976. In so doing the Israeli courts followed the lead of the English courts in this regard. In the Corporations Law, 1999, which went into effect in February 2000, Israel diverted from English practice by adopting a detailed legislative scheme for such actions. The specific conditions that a shareholder must fulfil in order to receive court permission to bring such an action would go beyond the scope of this book.

We would, however, note that these conditions are aimed at allowing the shareholder to bring the action after the corporation has been given a full opportunity to do so and has refused. We should also note that the corporation must be joined as a party, thereby making the results of the action binding on the corporation and, thus, preventing further actions as to the cause of action, either by the corporation itself or other shareholders. Finally, in this regard the statute provides for extensive court supervision of the proceedings, including settlements, in order to reduce the possibility of abuse of this type of representative action as well as other aspects of the differences in incentives that may exist between the shareholder-plaintiff and the corporation.

Relating to this problem of differential incentives between the shareholder-plaintiff and the corporation, is that of creating sufficient incentives for the bringing of shareholder derivative actions. Since the recognition of such actions in Israel in 1976 and until the enactment of the Corporations Law in 1999, very few derivative actions have been in fact brought. To many observers the reason for this seemed to be the lack of incentives for a shareholder to bring an action which he would have to finance himself and from which, even if successful, he would not receive the proceeds. Rather, these proceeds would go to the corporation and would, therefore, benefit the shareholder-plaintiff only to the extent of his interest in the corporation.

To attempt to deal with this problem, the Corporations Law provides that the court may order the corporation to provide the required interim financing and also authorizes the court to pay the successful shareholder-plaintiff an individual bonus from the proceeds which would otherwise go to the corporation. Moreover, the court is authorized to require the corporation to compensate the successful shareholder-plaintiff for his costs, to the extent that they are not paid to him by the defendant pursuant to the usual Israeli rule on taxing costs. See paragraph 224, *supra*.

Conversely, an unsuccessful shareholder-plaintiff may be required to pay the costs not only of the defendants, but also of the corporation.

Chapter 3. Class Actions

261. From 1988 until 1999, Israel adopted American-style class actions for specific forms of actions in a series of individual statutes. These actions included those for violating the securities and antitrust laws, as well those involving the environment, certain forms of consumer actions, including those against insurance companies and banks, and various types of actions involving corporations.

The basic concept contained in all these provisions was that of the American Rule 23 of the Federal Rules of Civil Procedure, but a number of special provisions in them should be noted. First a number of them expressly contained a provision to the effect that a class action was not to be certified unless the court concluded, *inter alia*, 'that there exists a reasonable chance that the substantive questions of law and fact common to the class will be determined in favour of the class'.

Second, in order to encourage the bringing of class actions these laws provided for the payment of bonuses, i.e., beyond their proportionate share of the damages awarded, to victorious class plaintiffs.

Third, and most significantly, these laws diverged from the purely private American class action model by providing for not insignificant public involvement in such actions. Thus, the Attorney General was to be provided with notice of all class actions thus encouraging his appearance in these actions, see paragraph 61, *supra*, including in the all important stage of judicial approval of settlements. Similarly when an action was filed against defendants, such as corporations registered on the stock exchange, banks and insurance companies, which are regulated by public authorities, the plaintiff had to notify the relevant public authorities, which could then act pursuant to their regulatory authority.

Finally, in regard to public involvement in Israeli class actions, similar forms of interim financing, as discussed above, paragraph 260, in regard to shareholder derivative actions, were also applicable to class actions involving violations of the securities laws. Also bonuses for victorious class action plaintiffs were contained in all the class action statutes.

262. The fact that there was no comprehensive class action statute in Israel, but rather a series of specific statutes, produced two major problems. The first was the lack of uniformity among the different statutory provisions adopted at different times pursuant to ever changing political pressures. The second, and more important, was that of the *lacunae* produced by the lack of comprehensiveness of the statutory scheme. The two major types of actions not covered by the individual statutes were consumer actions not based on the very specific and limited provisions of the Consumer Protection Law, 1991, but rather on more general provisions of tort and contract law, as well actions against governmental authorities at all levels.

Following extensive legislative, judicial and academic activity, the Knesset passed a comprehensive class action statute, the Class Action Law, 2006. In the context of this monograph we cannot discuss all of the provisions of the law, which includes 45 paragraphs and three addenda, so we will limit the following discussion to its main points.

263. The Class Action Law deals with the *lacunae* problem by providing for class actions as to all consumer actions as well as for a limited form of class actions against governmental authorities. It also greatly increases the public participation in Israeli class actions. Thus while recognizing the basically private nature of class actions by providing that the primary entity having standing to bring a class action is 'an individual who has a … claim that raises substantial questions of fact or law common to a group of people who are part of a class – in the name of the class', it also extends standing to initiate class actions or to participate in existing actions, under certain conditions, to relevant public authorities and non-governmental organizations.

Similarly, the law extends the possibility of public financing of all forms of class actions by establishing a fund for that purpose.

One of the most troublesome aspects of class actions relates to settlements, since there is a fear that proposed settlements may be for the benefit of the class plaintiffs and their attorneys but to the detriment of the other class members or the greater public. Thus all class action schemes that we know provide that settlements are subject to court approval. In addition the Israeli schemes have long provided for the possibility of the Attorney General opposing proposed settlements and he has, indeed, done so. Also, even before the enactment of the Class Action Law, in actions involving securities violations, objecting class members were given standing to present their objections. The law strengthens the process of judicial approval of settlements in two ways. First, the participation of relevant public authorities, both governmental and non-governmental, in ongoing class actions includes their participation in this crucial stage. In addition, class members who object to a proposed settlement are permitted to opt-out of the class at that time even though they did not so opt-out at the time of the certification of the class action as they could have done. Not only is this to the advantage of the individual objecting class member, but the cumulative effect of a large number of class members opting out of the settlement may thwart the settlement completely.

Finally, while as indicated above, the Class Action Law continues the American derived opt-out basis for ordinary class actions, it expressly recognizes that where, as in mass tort situations, the amount of damage to each class member is so great that it would be worthwhile for each one to bring an individual action, any class action should be on the basis of opt-in, i.e., the class members must affirmatively join in the action rather than passively refusing to opt-out of it.

Part IX. Seizure for Security and Enforcement of Judgments

Chapter 1. Seizure for Security

264. Preliminary seizure of property in order to ensure its preservation for purposes of execution in the event that judgment is rendered for the plaintiff, is discussed extensively in paragraph 187. This part will concentrate, therefore, on post-judgment seizure and other forms of judgment enforcement.

Chapter 2. Enforcement of Judgments

§1. Enforcement of Domestic Judgments

I. Sources

265. In contrast to the Rules of Civil Procedure which are based almost entirely on the English Rules of the High Court, the law concerning the execution of judgments and means of enforcement available to a court is an outstanding example of the multi-source nature of Israeli law.

The law of execution of judgments in Israel is closely connected to the common law world by the fact that it includes the classic common law indirect enforcement device, contempt of court. Israel has also inherited from the British Mandate significant parts of English equity jurisprudence, including such equitable enforcement devices as the appointment of receivers.

However, Israel has also inherited from Ottoman Turkish law another enforcement device, that of pre-judgment attachment (*seise conservatoire*, and *seise arret*) which is unknown to the traditional common law. It is, however, well known in the civil law and entered Ottoman law as a result of continental European, particularly French, influence on the Ottoman legal system.

Moreover, until 1967 the primary law governing the execution of judgments was the Ottoman Execution Law of 1914, which remained in force until replaced by the Execution Law, 1967, which latter law is still heavily based on the concepts of the prior Ottoman structure.

Two points should be stressed about the resulting law as to enforcement of judgments. First, although the source of the current provisions can often be traced to Ottoman or English Law, the legal force of most of them today is a result of their incorporation into positive Israeli law enacted after the creation of the State, such as the Execution Law, 1967 and the Rules of Civil Procedure, 1984. In the course of the incorporation of such provisions into Israeli legislation or rules they naturally underwent changes and adaptations.

Moreover, even parts of current Israel law still in force due to their pre-State status, such as contempt of court, the legal source of which is the 1929 Contempt of Court Ordinance adopted by the British Mandatory authorities, may differ significantly from their original sources.

Second, the multiple source nature of Israeli law as to enforcement of judgment has resulted in a cumulative array of enforcement devices derived from different sources and at times leading both to overlapping remedies and to the availability to the plaintiff of many and varied enforcement devices.

II. General

266. The Execution Law, 1967, has created an execution authority combining both judicial and executive elements. The Offices of the Execution Authority are attached to the Magistrates' Courts. Until recently, the execution authority was part of the general system of the courts' administration. In 2008, the legislature adopted an extensive amendment to the Execution Law (hereinafter the '2008 Amendment') which included, *inter alia*, the establishment of a separate execution authority, which operates independently from the administration of the courts. Each of its offices is composed of a Registrar of the Execution Authority and of an Administrator of the Execution Office who is subject to the Registrar. The Registrar is appointed by a special appointment committee. His powers involve most of the important discretionary and judgmental powers involved in execution, including ordering fines and imprisonment. The Administrators of the Execution Offices, appointed by the Minister of Justice, are members of the executive branch and direct the daily routine work of the Execution Authority.

Notwithstanding the 2008 Amendment, there exists a two-way interaction between the Execution Authority and the court system. For example, section 12 of the Execution Law, 1967 provides that 'if the Registrar of the Execution Authority is of the opinion that the judgment or any part thereof requires clarification for the purpose of its execution, he may refer in writing to the court which rendered the judgment to obtain such clarification'. This provision is an exception to the general principle of res judicata by which once a court has entered judgment in a matter it no longer has jurisdiction to deal with the matter. It should be emphasized that only the Registrar, as distinguished from a party, may request such clarification.

Judgments and other judicial decisions of the courts and of other judicial tribunals, amongst them the religious courts, as well as mortgage foreclosures and enforcement of negotiable instruments, including checks, are generally enforced by the Offices of the Execution Authority.

No proceedings in the execution process will be undertaken by the Execution Authority unless it has been so requested by the judgment creditor, and unless the judgment debtor has first been directed to satisfy the judgment. Where a judgment creditor has requested two or more proceedings to be undertaken, the Registrar decides whether they should be taken successively or simultaneously. The Registrar is also authorized to direct that a particular proceeding requested not be undertaken if he considers that in the circumstances of the case the proceeding is ineffective 'or that the judgment can be executed by a less drastic proceeding'.

III. Procedural Rights

A. Right of Hearing

267. The procedure to be followed in the Office of the Execution Authority is set forth in the 1979 Regulations promulgated by the Minister of Justice. These Regulations provide that requests for an order from the Execution Authority should be in writing and supported by appropriate affidavits. However, they do not provide the interested parties with a right to be heard in the proceedings. There is no general provision in the Execution Law, 1967 concerning a hearing before the Execution Authority, and the Regulations expressly leave a hearing before the Registrar of the Execution Authority to the discretion of the latter.

The Execution Law, 1967 itself, however, provides that prior to the issue of two specific types of orders a hearing before the Registrar must be conducted. These orders are those involving the judgment debtor's contention that the judgment has been complied with or that he need no longer comply with it, and those that impose on three particular third parties [one who has been appointed as a trustee for the keeping of the attached moveable property, a third party in possession of attached property of the debtor, and an appointed receiver] liability to pay the judgment because of their dereliction of duty.

The hearing procedure provided for these specific orders emphasizes their judicial nature, of which there can be no doubt. However, there are many other orders which are judicial in their nature and for which no hearing as of right is guaranteed in the provisions. These include matters of such serious consequences as orders preventing debtors from leaving the country and arrest orders which, if issued by a court clearly would require a prior adversary hearing. The situation is difficult to reconcile in particular in the light of the fact that the Israeli courts have long accepted as a fundamental part of Israeli law the maxim *auditur et altera pars,* see paragraph 33, which maxim has not been limited to judicial decision making but has been employed by the courts primarily as a restraint on administrative agencies.

It should be noted that according to the Execution Law, an arrest order may not be issued unless the judgment debtor has been heard concerning his capacity to pay the judgment. The relevant provision of the law, however, does not address specifically the right of debtors to be heard, but rather relates exclusively to the specific sanction of imprisonment, as will be discussed further *infra.*

B. Right of Appeal

268. The decisions of the Administrator of the Execution Office may be appealed to the Registrar. Most of the Registrar's decisions are appealable to the Magistrates' Court only by leave given by the Magistrates' Court. However, the specific types of orders described above, as to which a party has a right to an adversary hearing before the Registrar, are also appealable by right to the Magistrates' Court. The decisions of the Magistrates' Court on appeal from the Registrar are appealable to the District Court by leave given by the District Court.

IV. Prevention of Judgment Debtors from leaving the Country

269. Where a judgment debtor is about to leave the country and thereby frustrate or burden the enforcement of the judgment, the Registrar of the Execution Authority may order him not to leave the country or condition his leaving on his posting a bond to guarantee payment of the judgment. This provision in the Execution Law, 1967 is in addition to the provision in the Rules of Civil Procedure, 1984 authorizing the courts to make such an order as a form of preliminary relief. See paragraph 186.

Leaving the country for even a short period of time is sufficient to justify a post-judgment order issued by the Registrar of the Execution Authority. However, the order is conditioned on proof that the defendant's absence will 'frustrate any proceeding' or 'render the execution of the judgment more difficult.' Thus, as held by the Supreme Court in 1983, a judgment debtor may not be prevented from leaving the country solely as a means of coercing him into complying with the judgment.[109]

Rather, he can be prevented from leaving the country if, and only if, his impending absence will itself burden the enforcement of the judgment. If thus applied in practice, this proceeding would be limited to the relative rare situations in which performance of a judgment can only be accomplished by the personal act of the judgment debtor and also perhaps, to a temporary prevention of the debtor from leaving the country in order to discover his assets.

Unfortunately, in practice these proceedings have not been so limited neither in the pre-judgment nor in the post-judgment stage. Rather they have been used extensively, despite Basic Law: Human Dignity and Freedom, which enshrines the freedom of movement as a constitutional right, and despite the case law to the contrary, both as to money and non-money judgments, as pressure on judgment debtors to comply with the judgment.

V. Execution of Money Judgments

270. A monetary judgment or equivalent, e.g., a negotiable instrument which, as mentioned above may be enforced directly by the execution authority without the necessity of obtaining a prior judgment, may be enforced by means of several alternative, or cumulative, proceedings. A number of these proceedings, such as preventing a defendant from leaving the country and an appointment of a receiver, are employed as to both money and non-money judgments. We will, however, concentrate in this section on those devices that are used exclusively, or at least primarily, as to money judgments.

A. *Discovery of Assets, Searches of Persons, Effects and Premises*

271. In order to aid in discovery of the debtor's assets, the Registrar may order the carrying out of a search upon the person of the debtor, among his effects, or of the premises occupied by him. He may also order a search amongst the effects or on the premises of a third party if this is necessary in order to discover the debtor's property. In this latter situation the Registrar may condition the search on the giving of a security by the execution creditor; and if it later appears to him that the application for the search was unreasonable, he may order the whole or part of the security to be forfeited to the third party in compensation for the damage caused to him by the search.

109. *Na'im v. The District Rabbinical Court, Jerusalem*, 37 (2) P.D. 701 (1983).

B. Attachment and Sale of Property

272. All forms of property may be attached, whether in the hands of the debtor or a third party. There are a number of exceptions to this rule, for example essential foodstuffs and clothing, articles required for devotional purposes provided their value does not exceed a sum prescribed in the Regulations, and tools, etc., necessary for the judgment debtor's work which is a source of his livelihood and the livelihood of his family. The Wage Protection Law, 1958, restricts the attachment of wages, guaranteeing the wage earner a certain minimum monthly wage that cannot be attached. In addition, maintenance due from a third party to the judgment debtor under a judgment or agreement confirmed by the court cannot be attached in the hands of the third party. However, these two last restrictions do not apply when the judgment debt as to which attachment is sought is itself one for maintenance due to the judgment creditor.

The period of the attachment will be the 'last opportunity' of the debtor to pay his debt willingly before his property is disposed of by the court to settle his debts.

During this period no new transactions involving the property can be carried out. In order to ensure this, attachment of land is noted in the Land Registry. Personality may remain where it is or be removed for safekeeping. A trustee may be appointed for the attached personality. If a third party is holding the debtor's attached asset, he must be given a copy of the order of attachment. The third party must then inform the Registrar of the Execution Authority what property of the debtor he is holding and turn it over in a manner determined by the Registrar.

After the passage of a specified period of time – fourteen days as to moveable property and thirty days as to immovable property – upon application of the judgment creditor, attached property may be sold to pay the judgment debt. However, the Execution Law, 1967, provides that attached property used by the debtor as a dwelling house may not be sold until alternative accommodations has been found. Similarly, agricultural land which is the debtor's and his family's source of livelihood may remain in his hands.

C. Investigation and Ordering Payment by Instalment

273. In many cases the debtor neither has sufficient means nor is otherwise capable of paying the judgment as rendered, which is generally for an immediate lump sum payment. In order to deal with this most common problem, the Execution Law, 1967, provides a very important process of determining the debtor's financial means, and, in the light of such determination, ordering the payment of the judgment in instalments. Such an order effectively replaces the judgment as far as the execution process is concerned. An investigation of the means of the debtor may be initiated by the creditor, the debtor, or by the Registrar of the Execution Office on his own motion. In such an investigation, which may be held in public or 'in camera', the Registrar may compel the attendance of the judgment debtor and other witnesses, the giving of evidence and the submission of documents in the same manner as a court is competent to do.

Additionally, where parties have agreed in writing on an instalment arrangement, the Registrar may base his order on such agreement without further investigation.

Two further provisions of the Execution Law 1967 concerning the above issues should be noted. First, the Registrar, in lieu of the above procedures may direct the debtor to reply by affidavit to a questionnaire as to his means and may enter a payment order based on this reply. If the debtor does not reply to the questionnaire within the prescribed time, the Registrar may enter an order even in the absence of a reply. Second, the Execution Law, 1967 was amended in 1978, providing that notwithstanding the above procedure for investigating a debtor's means as a condition for granting instalment payments, 'the Registrar may, at the request of the judgment creditor, immediately after an application for execution is submitted to him, order that the judgment debt shall be paid at such time or in such instalments as he may proscribe'.

These two provisions, it would seem, undermine the entire rationale of instalment payment orders, i.e., that they are based on a determination of the Registrar of the Execution Authority of the debtor's ability to pay. Payment orders may be made without the Registrar having any real information as to the debtor's financial ability.

D. Imprisonment

274. In the past, debtors had been regularly imprisoned without it having been determined that they were capable of paying the judgments involved. Due to the Supreme Court's criticism over this practice, and following the 2008 Amendment, the Execution Law now provides that a judgment debtor may be imprisoned only after it has been determined that he refuses to pay the judgment despite his ability to do so and that there is no other way of enforcing the judgment. .

This situation was clearly not the original intention of the Israeli legislation in this regard. As adopted in 1947, the Execution Law allowed the imprisonment of a judgment debtor in three circumstances:

(1) failure to pay an instalment payment determined as described above;
(2) judgments for maintenance of a spouse, minor, invalid child or parents; and
(3) consent judgments.

The common denominator of all three circumstances was that the debtor's immediate obligation which he had not paid was based not solely on a determination of his legal liability, but also, and more importantly, on a determination of his individual financial ability to pay the obligation. This common denominator continued to exist as to maintenance and consent judgments. The former are themselves founded, *inter alia*, on a judicial determination of the debtor's ability to pay. It would also appear that the underlying legislative assumption as to consent judgments is that a party would consent to a judgment against him only where he is financially capable of paying such a sum. As noted above, however, the 1978

Amendment as to the determination of instalment payments removed the assumption of the ability to pay as to the most common form of imprisonment: that for failure to pay an instalment payment as determined by the Registrar of the Execution Authority. Accordingly, since 1978 instalment payment determination could be, and regularly were, made without any determination whatsoever as to the judgment debtor's financial ability to pay such instalments.

Therefore, it was necessary for the Supreme Court to intervene and declare expressly that imprisonment could not be imposed unless the Registrar of the Execution Authority was convinced, after a full hearing on the matter, that the debtor is capable of paying the sum due and that there is no other way of enforcing the judgment. The 2008 Amendment brought the Execution Law in conformity with the aforementioned decision of the Supreme Court.

According to the 2008 Amendment, the judgment debtor must be summoned to the hearing. The summons itself must set forth clearly the debtor's obligation to appear at the hearing, the substance of the hearing and the consequences of his failure to appear. The decisions of the Registrar of the Execution Authority must be based on a full hearing of the issues involved, and not merely on a failure of proof. The amended law therefore provides that if the judgment debtor does not appear at the hearing voluntarily, the police should be ordered to bring him to such hearing, as if he were a witness who is compelled to appear in a court proceeding.

The 2008 Amendment further provides that an imprisonment order may be issued only if the amount of the debt exceeds NIS 2000 (c. USD 540).

Finally we should note that the 2008 Amendment limits the imprisonment of the judgment debtor to a maximum of seven days. In cases of multiple imprisonment orders based on different judgments, the total period of imprisonment is not to exceed thirty days. Moreover, with the exception of maintenance judgments, such imprisonment may not be renewed. In any case, the judgment debtor's imprisonment will be terminated the moment that he fulfils the judgment, since, even as to a debtor who has refused to pay a judgment which he is capable of paying, the purpose of imprisonment is not to punish him, but rather to coerce him into paying the judgment.

E. Expedited Execution Process

274.1. Since regular execution proceedings (in which the aforementioned enforcement devices are utilized) may take a considerable amount of time and require the extensive involvement of the creditor, the legislature saw fit to introduce (within the 2008 Amendment) a new mechanism of enforcement which is more efficient and expedited. The new execution process is characterized by minimal involvement on the part of the judgment creditor, who only needs to submit the initial execution application. All subsequent proceedings are initiated and carried out by the Execution Authority. The new process is limited to the enforcement of money judgments which do not exceed the sum of NIS 10,000 (c. USD 2,700). The legislature also limited the applicable enforcement devices to those considered the most efficient and the easiest to employ. Accordingly, the Execution Authority may only order the attachment of the debtor's vehicle or debtor's funds held in the hands of third parties. The expedited process, which should be carried out within no more than eight months, is finalized with the sale of the attached property. If the sum does not cover the debt in full, the creditor may initiate regular execution proceedings. He may also transform the expedited procedure into a regular one at any earlier stage.

VI. Execution of Non-money Judgments

275. It should be emphasized that non-monetary judgments represent a significant part of the judgments rendered in Israel. A major contribution factor to this is the fact that the Israeli contracts law is based primarily on that of continental Europe, particularly Germany. Therefore, specific performance and not damages, is the normal remedy for breach of contract.

A. *Direct Methods of Enforcement*

1. Substituted performance

276. The basic premise of the Execution Law, 1967, is that where a judgment debtor has been served with a warning to comply with a non-money judgment within a prescribed period of time, and fails to so comply, the judgment is to be executed, if possible by substituted performance, rather than by further attempts to force the judgment debtor to perform personally. Thus, for example, where the judgment requires the debtor to surrender or vacate any property, the Administrator of the Execution Office, after serving notice, is to seize the property and transfer it to the person entitled to receive it under the judgment. It should be noted that although the same rule of substituted performance applies to orders to surrender a minor, special precautions are taken to act only in the interests of the child, and where there are difficulties in executing the judgment the Registrar may apply for directions to the court which rendered the judgment.

2. Receiverships

277. The Execution Law 1967 provides that the Registrar of the Execution Authority, if he deems it necessary for carrying out the judgment, may appoint a receiver for certain, designated property of the judgment debtor. The receiver can take the property into his keeping, and administer it as ordered by the Registrar.

The Rules of Civil Procedure contain parallel but broader provisions to the above, providing that, upon request, if it appears to a court 'just and convenient' to do so, it may appoint a receiver for any or all of the debtor's property, either before or after judgment is rendered. The court may arm the receiver with any or all of the rights of the owner of the property as concerns such matters as filing and defending judicial actions, actualizations of the property, its administration, safekeeping, restoration, determining its use and signing any documents.

Note should be made of the use of these provisions regarding the enforcement of construction contracts. A common form of construction in Israel involves building contractors who undertake to erect apartment complexes where, prior to the completion of the construction the individual apartments are sold to buyers who pay most, or all, of the purchase price in advance. Unfortunately it occurs not infrequently, for various reasons including economic problems caused by inflation or the disruption of supplies due to war or other circumstances, that the constructor does not perform on schedule. In such a situation the contractor may refuse to complete the project unless the buyers agree to pay more than the contractually agreed upon price, or, alternatively, may place a very low priority on the completion of the project. In the past such construction contracts could not be enforced by the Israeli Contracts (Remedies for Breach of Contract) Law, 1970, since the law provides as an exception to the general rule of specific performance of contracts, that an injured person is not entitled to enforcement if implementation of the enforcement order requires an unreasonable amount of supervision on behalf of a court or an execution administrator. However, in 1976 a precedent setting decision of the Supreme Court *Onison Construction Co., Ltd. v. Deutch*[110] held that in circumstances such as those described above, specific performance could be ordered, with the appointment of a receiver to ameliorate the difficulties of supervising performance. The receiver would take over the assets of the defendant with all the necessary powers to complete the construction of the apartment complex. Thus the court made use of a receiver in this case to help overcome judicial reluctance to issue orders that are difficult to enforce by a court acting alone.

B. Indirect Methods of Enforcement

1. Contempt of court

278. Contempt of Court in Israel is derived from the English model and its legal source in Israeli law remains the Contempt of Court Ordinance 1929, which was adopted by the British Mandatory authorities.

Section 6 of this Ordinance provides that the court 'shall have the power to enforce by fine or imprisonment obedience to any order issued by them directing any act to be done, or prohibiting the doing of any act'.

This Israeli contempt power has been termed 'civil', in that its purpose is not to impose punishment as to past action, but is 'forward looking', i.e., its purpose is to assure future performance of the order. It can thus only be employed when the judgment or order in question can still be enforced. However, one cannot ignore the clear 'criminal' aspects of the proceeding. Fines or imprisonments are only imposed after an order has been violated; a fine, once imposed and paid, is not restored to the offender even if he conforms to the order in the future; furthermore, the courts have held that a fine imposed as a penalty for Contempt of Court is a fine within the meaning of section 71 of the Penal Law, 1977, that is, failure to pay a fine may

110. 30 (2) P.D. 398.

result in imprisonment for up to three years; the defendant is required to appear before such a fine or imprisonment is imposed; appeal from a fine or imprisonment is upon the same conditions as appeal from a similar criminal penalty.

It should also be noted that in Israel contempt of court may be used in a way similar to that of the French system of 'astreinte'. That is, following an initial failure to comply with a court order, the court may, in a contempt proceeding, order the defendant to pay a specific sum per day as a fine unless and until he complies with the order. The courts have ruled that the sum must be large enough to encourage obedience to the order in question, but not so large as to amount to punishment rather than to coerce performance.

The Supreme Court has restricted the use of contempt of court to non-money judgments. It has further held that contempt of court is not limited to the enforcement of judgments but applies to all orders of the court, including interim procedural orders. Finally, as in England, contempt of court may be employed in Israel not only against the parties to an action but also as to others who, knowing of a court order, aid or abate a party in infringing it.

2. Criminal Penalties for Violating Court Orders

279. The Penal Law, 1977, provides in section 287 thereof: 'A person who disobeys a direction duly issued by any court, officer or person who acts in an official capacity and is authorized in that behalf is liable to imprisonment for two years.'

This general provision may be viewed as the Israeli version of 'criminal contempt'. The main legal problem concerns the relationship between this provision and the other enforcement proceedings, as will be discussed in the following section of this Part.

C. The Relationship among the Various Enforcement Proceedings

280. As seen from the above discussion there is a great deal of potential overlapping among the various enforcement proceedings as to non-monetary judgments. The relationship between these proceedings and the priority of the use of one rather than another are governed by the basic purposes of the Israeli execution system. From the discussions above, and also from other sources it is clear that the primary purpose of this system is to assure, as far as possible, the enforcement of a particular judgment rather than to punish a person for prior disobedience to a judgment or court order. Thus, in general, the system attempts not to burden the debtor except as to the extent that such is necessary to achieve the enforcement of the order. From this principle of reducing the burden imposed on the debtor derives the principle of economy of enforcement proceedings: that is, where alternative execution proceeding are available, *the least drastic alternative* to the liberty of the debtor must first be availed of, and only where such an alternative is proved ineffective may another, more drastic, proceeding be employed.

As will be recalled, the Execution Law provides expressly that the Registrar of the Execution Authority may direct that a particular proceeding not be taken if he considers judgment can be executed by a less drastic proceeding. Indeed, the 2008 Amendment grants the Registrar the authority and discretion to impose various restrictions on a debtor who refuses to pay despite his ability to do so, which are less harmful than imprisonment, such as prevention from leaving the country, restrictions on the use of credit cards, and limitations on receiving, holding or renewing his driver's license.

Following the above principle, the courts have ruled that contempt of court under the Ordinance may not be availed of where there exists a less drastic alternative for enforcing the order, for example substituted performance. The latter is seen as less drastic, both because it does not involve fines and imprisonment, and also since the act of performance is performed effectively without the necessity of coercing the debtor to perform it personally against his will. In a similar vein, where, during the course of litigation, procedural rules have been violated, the courts have held that procedural sanctions rather than contempt of court should be applied. Procedural sanctions are inherently more limited; generally a recalcitrant party has no more to lose than his stake in the pending litigation. Moreover, procedural sanctions are of a quid pro quo nature which relates them to the burden that has been imposed on the opposing party by the sanctioned party's failure to obey the court order. See generally, paragraphs 123–125.

§2. Recognition and Enforcement of Foreign Judgments

281. The Enforcement of Foreign Judgments Law, 1958, provides for the enforcement and recognition of foreign judgment in Israel. A foreign judgment is defined as a judgment rendered by a court in a foreign country in a civil matter, including a judgment for the payment of compensation or damages to an injured party, even if it is not in a civil matter.

Section 3 of the law lays down four conditions which must be met before a foreign judgment may be declared enforceable by the competent court (according to the subject matter of the case). These conditions are:

(1) the court of the foreign state rendering the judgment was competent, according to the laws of that State, to enter the judgment;
(2) the judgment is no longer appealable;
(3) the obligation imposed in the judgment is enforceable according to Israeli law, and its contents are not in conflict with public policy;
(4) the judgment is executable in the State in which it was given. Thus, for example, a foreign judgment will not be declared enforceable in Israel if it has already been barred by limitation from execution in the State rendering the judgment.

Further, section 4 of the Law provides that a foreign judgment may not be declared enforceable if it was rendered in a State whose laws do not provide for the enforcement of judgments of the Israeli courts, unless the Attorney General requests the court to enforce it.

The courts in Israel will not entertain an application to enforce a foreign judgment if the application was submitted more than five years after the date the judgment was rendered. The above rule will apply unless another period of time was agreed upon between Israel and the State where the judgment was rendered, or unless the court considers there to be special reasons justifying the delay.

The law sets forth five defences, any of which, if proven by the party objecting to the enforcement, will prevent the judgment from being declared enforceable. These are:

(1) the judgment was obtained by fraud;
(2) the defendant was not given a reasonable opportunity to submit his evidence and produce evidence before the judgment was rendered;
(3) the judgment was rendered by a court that lacked international jurisdiction according to the rules of private international law as understood in Israel. For purposes of international jurisdiction a person is not deemed to have acceded to the jurisdiction of the foreign court if he merely appeared before the court in order to deny the jurisdiction of the court, to attempt to cancel or stay the proceedings in order to transfer the matter to arbitration or to a court in another country, or in order to release or defend property seized or about to be seized;
(4) the judgment is contrary to another judgment given in the same matter between the same parties which is still valid;
(5) at the time the claim was filed in the foreign country, an action on the same issue and between the same parties was pending before a court or a tribunal in Israel.

In addition, a foreign judgment shall not be declared enforceable if its enforcement is likely to prejudice the sovereignty or the security of the State.

In matters of maintenance, if the court considers it justifiable, it may enforce a temporary judgment or interim order.

Where a judgment has been declared enforceable, it is to be treated for the purposes of execution as a judgment given in Israel.

The procedure for the enforcement of foreign judgments is set out in the Rules of Civil Procedure. An application to declare a foreign judgment enforceable is served by means of a motion to the court. The application must specify, amongst other particulars, the name and place of the court which entered the judgment and the date it was rendered. The petitioner must affix to the application a copy of the judgment certified by a competent authority of the State in which it was rendered, and an affidavit attesting to the facts proving the existence of each of the conditions laid down in section 3 of the law. The court may require a certified Hebrew translation of the foreign judgment.

A respondent wishing to contest the application must serve a reply to the court within thirty days of receiving the application, or within a longer period if the court so directs. A respondent denying the existence of one of the conditions laid down in section 3 of the law must attach an affidavit to that effect to his reply. A respondent who does not file a reply will not be allowed to oppose the application.

Until a foreign judgment has been declared enforceable, the applicant may withdraw his application by written notification to the court and to the respondent.

282. Section 11 of the Enforcement of Foreign Judgments Law, 1958, provides also for the *recognition*, as distinguished from enforcement, of foreign judgments. Section 11a of the law provides that the court shall afford plenary recognition to foreign judgments (by means of a defence against a domestic suit or by means of a local declatory judgment affirming the validity of the foreign decree) in cases where there exists an agreement between Israel and the rendering state and where the judgment is enforceable under Israeli law. Section 11b of the law affords recognition of an incidental nature, and provides that any court or tribunal may, in dealing with and for the purposes of a matter within its jurisdiction, recognize a foreign judgment, if it considers it just and lawful to do so.

283. In addition to enforcing foreign judgments pursuant to the Enforcement of Foreign Judgments Law, the courts have held that the common law applicable in Israel provides an alternative enforcement mechanism.

Enforcement under English Common law rules differs from the above related enforcement process primarily in the following:

(1) the common law process applies only to money judgments for debt or a definite sum of money.
(2) according to the common law, trial court judgments may be enforced as long as they are final and create res judicata, even if still subject to appeal, and even if an appeal has in fact been submitted to a higher instance. Due to the requirement for finality, maintenance judgments, which always remain subject to change, are not enforceable under English Common law.
(3) in principle, the common law does not require that the court that rendered the judgment be competent according to the laws of its State;
(4) the common law is indifferent to whether the relevant foreign State would enforce Israeli judgments;
(5) the limitations period for enforcing under the common law is not limited to five years, but to the regular period applicable to actions (i.e., seven years).

284. Israeli law also allows the recognition of foreign judgment according to English common law rules, in addition to those of the Law. The common law rules for recognition of foreign judgments are the same as those stated above as to enforcement. However, there is Israeli case law authority to the effect that as to recognition of foreign judgments, as distinguished from their enforcement, common law rules which are more stringent than those of the Law concerning enforcement will not be applied.

Part X. Arbitration

Chapter 1. The Juridical Nature of Arbitration

285. While there are provisions in Israeli law regarding arbitration in certain specific instances, in general arbitration in Israel is regulated by the Arbitration Law, 1968.

This Law provides for a dispute resolution device which exists alongside the State's judicial structure. Concerning arbitration the parties have almost complete power to determine such fundamental aspects of the dispute resolution structure as the qualification (if any) and identity of the arbitrator, the compensation of the arbitrator, the procedures to be followed and even the substantive law to be applied.

The question arises: what is the juridical basis for allowing such a deviation from the State ordained norms that require that adjudication be conducted by an independent judiciary made up of qualified jurists appointed by a special process who operate under and pursuant to binding legal norms both of procedure and of substantive law.

The immediate answer given by positive Israeli law is quite simple: the juridical basis is the Arbitration Law, 1968. Yet that answer is not sufficient. The question must be asked: why did the legislature adopt such a positive juridical norm. It has been argued that there are two reasons for this: first, to lighten the burden on the courts; second, to improve the situation of the parties to a dispute.

As to the first reason, the explanatory notes to the legislative bill that eventually became the Arbitration Law, 1968, stated very clearly that arbitration is 'a convenient, swift and inexpensive device for dispute resolution outside the court system and will, therefore, ease the burden on the courts'.[111]

As to the parties, the Supreme Court has noted as follows:

There are many positive attributes to consensual arbitration:

(1) it is a proceeding before a person or persons whom the parties have voluntarily chosen and in whom they have confidence;
(2) the parties are able to free themselves from the shackles of stringent rules of procedure and evidence and even from positive law, and to agree upon a practical and effective arbitration process;
(3) arbitration is conducted quietly and without public disclosure;
(4) when it is properly conducted, it is efficient, swift and inexpensive;

111. H.H. No. 717 of 5727.

(5) arbitration is especially suitable for family, commercial, professional or technical matters as to which there is desired a special approach and professionalization.[112]

There is, of course, a great deal of truth in these arguments and they do, indeed, provide ideological support for the legislative arbitration provisions. Yet they are not in themselves a sufficient explanation of these provisions. This is so since if they were the only support for arbitration they would have to compel the use of arbitration, at least in those cases stated above in which arbitration is a better method of dispute resolution than is judicial adjudication.

Yet as the above quote from the Supreme Court indicates, Israeli law provides only for 'consensual' arbitration; not compulsory arbitration. The juridical basis, therefore, of the Israeli law of arbitration is legislative recognition of the right of the parties to settle their dispute as they see fit.

Throughout the dispute resolution process in Israel, the emphasis is put on resolution by the parties. Thus, it is preferred that parties resolve their disputes, as far as possible, by themselves, without resort at all to formal adjudicatory processes. And, even when judicial actions are started the parties are encouraged to resolve their differences by compromise rather than by insisting on adjudication. It is in keeping with this premise that parties are entitled also to resolve their disputes by arbitration rather than by adjudication.

It should be noted here that the above emphasis on dispute resolution by the parties has received legislative validity. A 1992 amendment to the Courts Law (Consolidated Version), 1984, authorizes a court trying a civil issue, with the agreement of the parties, to transfer the matter or part thereof to arbitration. In such a case the arbitrator is appointed by the parties with the court's approval; where there is no agreement as to the identity of the arbitrator he is appointed from a list served to the court by the parties, or if such a list has not been served, at the court's discretion. The provision, of the Arbitration Law, 1968, apply to the arbitration.

In addition, the 1992 amendment initiates a new form of proceedings intended to encourage dispute resolution by the parties – mediation. (See paragraph 20.) It is important to note, however, that both arbitration and mediation proceedings are entirely dependent on the agreement of the parties.

Thus, arbitration is provided by Israeli law not necessarily because it is a better form of dispute resolution than judicial adjudication, but rather because the parties involved have agreed to have their dispute resolved by arbitration rather than by adjudication. The basis for arbitration is, therefore, consent of the parties.

Yet this basis is completely satisfactory only if the parties who agree to arbitration as a device to settle their dispute do, indeed, comply with their agreement and settle their dispute by arbitration. Only in this case can arbitration be equated with compromise settlements or other consensual forms of dispute resolution.

This is not the case, however, when despite prior agreement to arbitration, one of the parties changes his mind and instead of proceeding with arbitration brings a judicial action as to the matter that is the subject of the arbitration agreement. At this point there arises a clear conflict between two norms of Israeli law. The first is that individuals must comply with their agreements: *pacta sunt servanda.* The second and competing norm, however, is the basic and fundamental right of every

112. *Shahav v. Shahav*, 23 (1) P.D. 16, 19 (1969).

person to resort to the judicial system when he believes that his legal rights have been violated. As stated by the Supreme Court: 'One of the pillars of every country having a proper political system is the existence of an independent judicial system, that is subject to no authority other than that of the law of the State, to which a citizen is free to resort at all times pursuant to law'.[113]

286. The Arbitration Law, 1968, compromises between these two competing principles as follows: the existence of an arbitration provision does not, in of itself, prevent a party from initiating and pursuing an action in court; nor will a court specifically enforce an arbitration agreement, i.e., a court will not issue an order compelling a party to proceed to arbitration.

The existence of an arbitration agreement does, however, serve as a basis for a court to stay its proceedings. In the words of paragraph 5(a) of the Arbitration Law:

> Where an action is brought in court in a dispute which it had been agreed to refer to arbitration, and a party to the action who is a party to the arbitration agreement applies for a stay of proceedings in the action, the court shall stay the proceedings between the parties to the agreement, provided that the applicant has been and still is prepared to do everything required for the institution and continuation of the arbitration.

Yet even this stay of proceedings is not automatic; subparagraph (c) of the same paragraph 5 provides expressly that 'the court may refrain from staying proceedings *if it sees a special reason why the dispute should not be dealt with by arbitration*' (emphasis added). We will discuss shortly the Israeli jurisprudence concerning such 'special reasons', but before we do so, we should point out two other statutory provisions in this regard.

First, this exercise of judicial discretion not to stay the proceedings when there are such special reasons why the dispute should not be dealt with by arbitration, cannot be contracted away by the parties. Section 7(b) of the Arbitration Law expressly provides that 'where the court decides ... that a dispute shall not be dealt with by arbitration, any stipulation in the agreement between the parties making the commencement or termination of arbitration a pre-condition of the realization of a right between them shall be void'.

Moreover, the Israeli legislature requires that a defendant who relies on an arbitration agreement as a basis for an application to stay judicial proceedings must raise this issue 'not later than the day on which the applicant first pleads to the substance of the action'. This procedural restriction requiring the defendant to raise the arbitration agreement at the beginning of the action rather than later is identical to that required of defendants who wish to raise the defence of lack of international jurisdiction.

In the jurisprudence concerning arbitration, the courts have found such special reasons justifying not staying their proceedings:

(1) when the arbitration agreement is unclear as to its application;

113. *Ilani v. The Jewish Agency*, 10 P.D. 1693, 1698 (1956).

(2) when the matter is of great importance to the general public and an arbitration proceeding, as distinguished from a judicial proceeding, would deprive the public of access to the proceeding;
(3) when the party requesting the stay has himself engaged in delaying tactics as to the commencement of the arbitration proceedings or their progress if they have already started.

287. Interesting questions have arisen as to whether the existence of multiple parties or claims serves as a special reason for the court not to stay its proceedings. For example, the plaintiff brings an action against the defendant in which he unites two separate causes of action he has against the defendant, as to only one of which there exists an arbitration agreement. Or two plaintiffs join together in one action against the same defendant; in relation to only one of them is there an arbitration agreement between him and the defendant. Or, a single plaintiff joins in one action two defendants, and again as to only one of them is the plaintiff party to an arbitration agreement. And there are other instances as we shall shortly discuss.

In all the above cases, Israeli procedure generally encourages joinder so as to avoid multiplicity of actions. Should this desire prevail over the arbitration agreement involved, which if enforced so as to stay the proceedings will prevent the joinder and thereby cause a multiplicity of actions?

While the jurisprudence is not uniform on this issue, the prevailing view – and in our opinion the correct view – is that a plaintiff who is bound by an arbitration agreement should not be able to avoid the effects of this agreement merely by joining in one complaint a claim against the defendant as to which there is no arbitration agreement or by joining in the same action other defendants as to whom there is no arbitration agreement.

However, the result may be different when the joined claims of the plaintiff, or plaintiffs, against the same defendant, arise from the same circumstances and are very closely connected both factually and legally, at least so long as the arbitration agreement has not freed the arbitrator from adherence to the substantive law.

Furthermore, the case may be different when the joinder of parties is not merely a matter of convenience and efficiency, but is necessary in order to bind all of the parties by res judicata so as to avoid one of the parties being unfairly prejudiced by inconsistent judgments. This is the case, for example, when it is absolutely clear that one of the two persons are liable to the plaintiff but it is not clear which one. In this case, he may sue them alternatively in one action, in order to prevent the possibility of inconsistent judgments in two separate actions unjustly freeing both defendants from liability. This is also the case where, for example, a defendant claims that if he is held liable to the plaintiff, a third party is liable to indemnify him. In such a case the defendant may join such third party to the original action by use of third-party practice so as to bind him by the results of such action and thus avoid the possibility that the third party may be freed from his obligation of indemnification by inconsistent judgments if the indemnification action is brought in a separate proceeding.

In these latter cases there may be a problem if one of the alternate defendants in the first case or the third-party indemnitor in the second seeks to stay the proceedings because of an arbitration agreement as to the claim involved. In such a case the court may refuse to stay the proceedings on the ground that avoiding the possibility of injustice caused by inconsistent judgments is a 'special reason' that justifies not staying the action pursuant to paragraph 5(c) of the Arbitration Law.

Chapter 2. The Arbitration Agreement

288. As has been emphasized above, Israeli arbitration law is based on the agreement of the parties. Thus a pre-condition is a valid arbitration agreement to refer to arbitration a dispute which has arisen between the parties or which may arise in the future. Such an agreement must comply with all the general rules of contract law such as the parties having contractual capacity, *consensus ad idem*, etc.

In addition, the Arbitration Law requires that an arbitration agreement be *in writing*. As to the terms of the agreement, there are two specific statements in the Law:

(1) the identity of the arbitrator need not be stated in the agreement; and
(2) 'an arbitration agreement in a matter which cannot be the subject of an agreement between the parties is invalid'.

The latter provision emphasizes once again the basic fact that under Israeli law arbitration is viewed as a form of dispute resolution agreed upon by the parties. If the parties are not legally capable of deciding on the substance of a matter, they are not legally capable of referring it to arbitration in lieu of a judicial determination.

In terms of other provisions of the arbitration agreement, the Arbitration Law has no specific restrictions and leaves them to the agreement of the parties. However, as an aid to the parties, paragraph 2 of the Arbitration Law provides that 'unless a contrary intention appears therefrom, an arbitration agreement shall be deemed to include the provisions set out in the Schedule in so far as they are relevant'. It should be emphasized that these provisions are not mandatory, but rather apply only if no contrary intention is found in the agreement.

These provisions lay down, *inter alia*, the number of arbitrators in the arbitration and their status, the method by which decisions shall be adopted by the arbitrators, the rules of procedure regulating the proceedings, the date the award shall be made, the authority of the arbitrator to award interim relief and other reliefs necessary to the proceedings, and the payment of expenses and the remuneration of the arbitrators.

Chapter 3. The Arbitral Award

289. The arbitral award must be in writing, and, subject to the contrary intention of the parties expressed in the arbitration agreement and to the provisions discussed below as to setting aside arbitral awards by the courts, the Arbitration Law provides specifically that an 'arbitral award binds the parties and their successors as res judicata'.

As a general proposition it is expected that the parties will comply with the arbitral award without the need for governmental intervention. Moreover, as the parties were free to agree on arbitration as the device for resolving their dispute, they are still free to agree on the way the award will be enforced.

However, if the losing party refuses to comply with the arbitral award, the winning party cannot have it enforced by the State Execution Offices unless and until the arbitral award has been 'confirmed' by a District Court. When an arbitral award has been so confirmed it may then be enforced as if it were a court judgment.

A court must confirm automatically an arbitral award if requested to do so by a party, unless the other party opposes such confirmation by filing an application to set aside the arbitral award. Such an application to set aside the award may be filed either in opposition to an existing application to confirm the award, or independently, before an application to confirm has been filed. In this latter case, if the application to set aside the award is dismissed, the court must automatically confirm the award even though no application for such confirmation has been filed.

The result is that either party to an arbitral award may initiate judicial review of the award: the winner by filing an application for confirmation; the loser by filing an application to set the award aside. In either case, the court will decide the same questions and will confirm the award unless it sets it aside.

It is necessary, however, to be more specific at this point. While setting aside the award has been discussed above, and, indeed, the Statute speaks of an application to 'set aside' an award, this term is a broad one and includes setting the award aside, in whole or in part, supplementing or amending it, or remitting it to the arbitrator.

And, indeed, the Arbitration Law specifically provides that 'the court shall not set aside the whole of the award if it is capable of being set aside in part, supplemented, amended or remitted to the arbitrator'. To return, however, to the central point, the court must confirm the award unless there exists one of ten specific grounds for 'setting it aside' in the broad meaning of that term. These grounds are set forth in paragraph 24 of the Arbitration Law as follows:

(1) the arbitration agreement was not valid;
(2) the award was made by an arbitrator not properly appointed;
(3) the arbitrator acted without authority or exceeded the authority vested in him by the arbitration agreement;
(4) a party was not given a suitable opportunity to state his case or to produce his evidence;
(5) the arbitrator did not determine one of the matters referred to him for determination;
(6) the arbitrator did not assign reasons for the award though the arbitration agreement required him to do so;

(7) the arbitrator did not make the award in accordance with the law though the arbitration agreement required him to do so;
(8) the award was made after the period for making it had expired;
(9) the contents of the award are contrary to public policy;
(10) a ground exists on which a court would have set aside a final, non-appealable judgment.

It should be emphasized, however, that even when one or more of these bases for setting aside an award exist, the award will not necessarily be set aside. This is so since paragraph 26(a) of the Arbitration Law provides that 'the court may dismiss an application to set aside notwithstanding the existence of one of the grounds set out in section 24 if it is of the opinion that no miscarriage of justice has been caused'. Moreover the courts have interpreted the word 'may' here as 'shall'. That is the court should set aside the award only if there has been a miscarriage of justice as a result of the existence of one of the ten grounds set forth above.

289.1. Until recently, the Arbitration Law did not require arbitrators to reason their decisions, subject to the parties' specific request. The law was amended in 2008 (hereinafter the '2008 Amendment') and the default rule was reversed, i.e., the arbitral award should always be reasoned, unless the parties expressed a contrary intention in the arbitration agreement.

More importantly, the 2008 Amendment introduced a new appeals mechanism. Until 2008, arbitration awards were not appealable to the courts, and the option of appealing to another arbitrator was not regulated by the Arbitration Law. The parties were only allowed to request the arbitrator to correct technical errors or to petition the court to set aside the arbitral award. As mentioned above, the latter option was limited to the grounds set forth in paragraph 24 of the Arbitration Law, and was subject to the requirement for miscarriage of justice. Consequently, very few arbitral awards had in fact been set aside. The lack of an appeals option, coupled with the inability to bring about the correction of material mistakes in the arbitral award, have deterred the public from resorting to arbitration. The 2008 Amendment intended to remedy this flaw by providing for an appeals mechanism which would allow for the correction of material mistakes, thereby alleviating some of the public's concerns regarding the arbitration process. According to the Amendment, parties may agree that the arbitral award would be appealable in one of the following manners:

(1) The parties may agree that the arbitral award would be appealable to another arbitrator (new paragraph 21A of the Arbitration Law). The parties would still be allowed to petition the court to set aside the arbitral award (given on appeal). However, such a petition would be limited to one of the two latter grounds set forth in paragraph 24.
(2) Alternatively, the parties may agree that the arbitral award would be appealable to the District Court, if leave to appeal is allowed. This option, however, is limited to cases in which there has been 'a fundamental error in implementing the law, which could cause a miscarriage of justice' (new paragraph 29B of the Arbitration Law). Parties who opt for this option may not petition the court to

set aside the arbitral award, but may base their appeal on any of the grounds set forth in paragraph 24. If the court dismisses the appeal, it must confirm the arbitral award.

If the parties did not expressly include one of the abovementioned options in the arbitration agreement, the arbitral award would not be appealable.

Chapter 4. Foreign Arbitration Agreements and Awards

290. Concerning foreign arbitration clauses, where the proper law of the contract, as opposed to the law applying to the arbitration, is Israeli Law, the court may stay proceedings in the light of a foreign arbitration clause. Further, section 6 of the Arbitration Law, 1968, authorizes the court to stay proceedings in a dispute where the parties have agreed to arbitration if an international treaty applies to the arbitration and the treaty includes provisions concerning the staying of proceedings. Two international treaties including such provisions and to which Israel is a party should be mentioned: The Geneva Protocol concerning arbitration clauses,[114] and the New York Treaty concerning the recognition and execution of foreign arbitral awards.[115]

Concerning foreign arbitral awards, the law provides that a request to confirm such an award where the arbitration was governed by an international treaty to which Israel is a party shall be filed and judged in accordance with that treaty. It should be noted that specific regulations have been enacted for the execution of the New York Treaty, which for this purpose supersedes the Geneva Treaty.

114. Signed in Geneva, 1923; in force, 1924; confirmed by Israel, 1951; entered into force in Israel, 1952.

115. Signed in N.Y., 1958; confirmed and entered into force in Israel, 1959.

Selected Bibliography

Baum, I. 'Public Considerations in *Forum Non Conveniens*'. *Mishpatim* 42, (2012): 353 (Hebrew).

Baum, I. 'Requests for Leave to Appeal on Interim Decisions of the Corporations Court'. *Mishpatim Online* 3 (2011) (Hebrew).

Baum, I. 'On the Proper Place of Venue in Israeli Civil Procedure'. *Aley Mishpat* 9 (2011): 275 (with Assaf Tabeka) (Hebrew).

Goldstein, S. 'Jurisdiction over Foreign Manufacturers Concerning Damage that Occurs in Israel'. *Israel Law Review* 14 (1979): 504–514.

Goldstein, S. 'Class Actions: What and Why'. *Mishpatim* 9 (1979): 409–438 (Hebrew).

Goldstein, S. 'International Jurisdiction Based Solely on Service of Process – Now an Actuality' in 10 *Mishpatim* (1980), pp. 409–438 (Hebrew).

Goldstein, S. 'Class Actions – A Surprising Development in England'. 11 *Mishpatim* (1981): 412–438 (Hebrew).

Goldstein, S. 'Default and Opposition (Reopening)'. *Israel Reports to the Eleventh International Congress of Comparative Law* (The Harry Sacher Institute for Legislative Research and Comparative Law, The Hebrew University of Jerusalem, 1982): 64–87.

Goldstein, S. 'The Influences of Constitutional Principles on Civil Procedure in Israel'. *Israel Law Review* 17 (1982): 467–510.

Goldstein, S. 'On Unifying the Israel Trial Court Structure'. *Israel Law Review* 18 (1983): 76–98.

Goldstein, S. 'Protection of Diffused Interests in Israeli Civil Procedure'. *Rivista Trimestrale Civile* 38 (1984): 1220–1250 (Italian).

Goldstein, S. 'Derivative Action: The Procedure of their Initiation and Prosecution'. *Mishpatim* 14 (1984): 48–82 (Hebrew).

Goldstein, S. 'Preventing a Civil Defendant from Leaving the Country as a Form of Preliminary Relief'. *Israel Law Review* 20 (1985): 18–38.

Goldstein, S. 'The Protection of the Value of Claims in a Period of High Inflation: An Analysis Based on the Israeli Experience'. *Rivista Trimestrale Civile* 39 (1985): 733–745 (Italian).

Goldstein, S. 'Execution of Judgments and Means of Enforcement Available to a Court' in *Israeli Reports to the Twelfth International Congress of Comparative Law* (The Harry Sacher Institute for Legislative Research and Comparative Law, The Hebrew University of Jerusalem, 1986): 150–229.

Selected Bibliography

Goldstein, S. 'Reflections on the Possibilities and Problems of the Acceleration of the Civil Litigation Process'. *Tel Aviv Studies in Law* 7 (1985–1986): 50–76.

Goldstein, S. 'The Reciprocal Relationships among the Means of Enforcing Non-monetary Court Orders: The Least Harsh Alternative'. *Mishpatim* 16 (1986): 142–164 (Hebrew).

Goldstein, S. 'Compelling Medical Examinations of Litigants: A Comparative Analysis'. *Israel Law Review* 21 (1986): 142–164.

Goldstein, S. 'Judicial Protection of Human Rights Without a Written Constitution'. in II *The International Congress on Procedural Law for the Ninth Centenary of the University of Bologna* (Bologna 1988): 75–100.

Goldstein, S. 'Class Actions in Israel'. In *Israeli Reports to the Thirteenth International Congress of Comparative Law*, edited by C. Fasberg. Jerusalem 1990, pp. 34–55.

Goldstein, S. 'Summary Judgment Proceedings in Israeli Law: A Critical and Comparative Analysis'. In *International Perspectives on Civil Justice*, edited by I.R. Scott. London 1990, pp. 11–26.

Goldstein, S. 'Israel Law – Forty Years: Civil Procedure'. *Israel Law Review* 24 (1990): 789–806.

Goldstein, S. 'Recent Developments and Problems in the Granting of Preliminary Relief: A Comparative Analysis' in 40 and 41'. *Revue Hellenique de Droit International* (1990): 13–24.

Goldstein, S. 'Punishment Civil Style – A Comment'. *Israel Law Review* 25 (1991): 779–791.

Goldstein, S. 'Arbitration: Israel Report'. In *The Arbitration* edited by W. Levi. 1991, 165–180, Vol. 10, in the *Series Inchieste di Dioritto Coparato* (M. Rofondi, gen. Ed.).

Goldstein, S. 'Contrasting Views of Adjudication: an Israeli-American Comparison'. In *Gedachtnisschrift für Peter Arens*, edited by D. Leopold, W. Luke, S. Yoshino. München 1993, 169–186.

Goldstein, S. 'The Problematic Nature of Preliminary Relief: A comparative Analysis Based on the Israeli Experience'. in VI *Studi in Onore di Vittorio Denti* (Pavia 1994), pp. 181–230.

Goldstein, S. 'Israel: Rules for Declining to Exercise Jurisdiction in Civil and Commercial Matters, Form non Coveniens, Lis Pendens'. In *Declining Jurisdiction in Private International Law*, edited by J.J. Fawcett. Oxford 1995, 259–278.

Goldstein, S. 'Towards a New Israeli Civil Procedure: Away from the Worst of Both Worlds'. In *Essays on European Law and Israel*, edited by A.M. Rabello. Jerusalem 1996, 719–731.

Goldstein, S. 'Provisional Relief and International Jurisdiction: Israel, The European Union and the Relations between Them'. In *Essays on European Law and Israel*, edited by A.M. Rabello. Jerusalem 1996, 733–768.

Goldstein, S. 'Israel: Creating a New Legal System from Different Sources by Jurists of Different Backgrounds'. on *Studies in Legal Systems: Mixed and Mixing*, edited by E. Orucu, E. Attwoll & S. Coyle. The Hague 1996, 147–164.

Goldstein, S. 'Equity in Civil Procedure'. In *Aequitas and Equity: Equity in Civil and Mixed Jurisdictions* edited by A.M. Rabello. Jerusalem 1997, 738–748.

Goldstein, S. 'The Structure of the Israeli Supreme Court: Prospects and Problems'. In *Towards a New European Ius Commune*, edited by C.A. Gambano & A.M. Rabello 1999, 333–348.
Goldstein, S. 'Summary Judgment Proceedings in Israeli Law'. In *Israeli Reports to the XV International Congress of Comparative Law* edited by A.M. Rabello. Jerusalem 1999, 183–222.
Goldstein, S. 'The Development of Class Actions in Israel'. *Alei Mishpat* 1 (1999): 27–48 (Hebrew).
Goldstein, S. 'Reform of the Israeli Judicial Structure and Civil Litigation System'. In *Comparative Law Review, The Institute of Comparative Law in Japan* 33, no. 3 (1999): 41–80.
Goldstein, S. 'Class and Derivative Actions in the New Company Law'. *Mishpatim* 32 (2002): 461–491 (Hebrew).
Goldstein, S. 'The Depreciation in the Status of Jurisdictional Questions in the General Court System'. *Alei Mishpat* 3 (2003): 279–315 (Hebrew).
Goldstein, S. 'Remnants of Private Law Categorization in Israeli Procedural Law'. In *Classification of Private Law: Bases of Liability and Remedies*, edited by C. Fassberg & I. Gilead, Jerusalem 2003, 219–231.
Goldstein, S. 'Las Acciones Colectivas en Israel'. In *Procesos Colectivos* edited by A. Gidi & E.F. Mac-Gregor. Mexico City 2003, 201–225.
Goldstein, S. 'The Civil Litigation Process in Japan and Israel (Dialogue with Prof. Takeshi Kojima)'. In *Civil Procedure and ADR in Japan*, edited by T. Kojima. Tokyo 2004, 109–159.
Goldstein, S. 'The Reciprocal Relationship between Mass Lawsuits and Class Actions'. In *Mishpatim* 34 (2004): 21–37 (Hebrew).
Goren, U. *Issues in Civil Procedure*. 10th ed., (2009) (Hebrew).
Levin, S. *The Theory of Civil Procedure: Introduction and Basic Principles.* 2nd ed., (2008).
Schwartz, D. *Civil Procedure* (2006) (Hebrew).
Sussman, Y. *The Law of Civil Procedure.* 7th ed., (1995) (Hebrew).

Selected Bibliography

Index

Index

Index

www.ingramcontent.com/pod-product-compliance
Lightning Source LLC
Chambersburg PA
CBHW071439230926
51846CB00001B/281
* 9 7 8 9 0 4 1 1 5 1 6 3 6 *